FORGET-ME-NOT

FORGET-ME-NOT

Memories Of Germany (1939-46)

Ruth S. Ozan

Library of Congress Number: 2003093708
ISBN :   Hardcover   1-4134-1366-8
                Softcover   1-4134-1365-X

To order additional copies of this book, contact:
Xlibris Corporation
1-888-795-4274
www.Xlibris.com
Orders@Xlibris.com
18719

CONTENTS

To My Family:
Mahmut, husband, most loyal friend and mentor, journalist,
linguist, poet, teacher, political analyst, an over-all practical genius,
who has supported and encouraged me in every undertaking;
to our children Deniz, Julide, and Kerim, who listened patiently
to many renditions of this story; to my sisters Lori and Shirley;
and in memory of all the others no longer with us: Mama, Papa,
Oma, our brother Herbert, Tante Toni and Onkel Berthold,
Tante Lene, Marie, Sofie, Onkel Adolf, cousin Hildi,
and also our sister Rose Marie.

My gratitude goes to friends who encouraged me along the way,
German and American, and to all who were part of this story:
God and his angels, loving relatives, guardians, teachers,
friends, especially Erika, whom I owe a book.

This is the story of a girl born into the American Depression, who grew up during the Second World War in Hitler's Germany. It is the story of my family and other quite ordinary people living in a war-torn land, seen and experienced by me as a child, remembered and recorded as an adult. Every person and every event in this story is true though a few names have been changed.

R.S.Ozan

FOREWORD

The events in this book happened more than half a century ago. It's about people who do not make headline news, but just do their best to survive. Yet, they are the ones most affected by the disasters of war. I found myself in a war between the two countries I loved, the United States and Germany. Memories of the country of my birth pitted against the rather unique experiences and circumstances I encountered in the country of my heritage enabled me to view a world at war through a child's unbiased eyes.

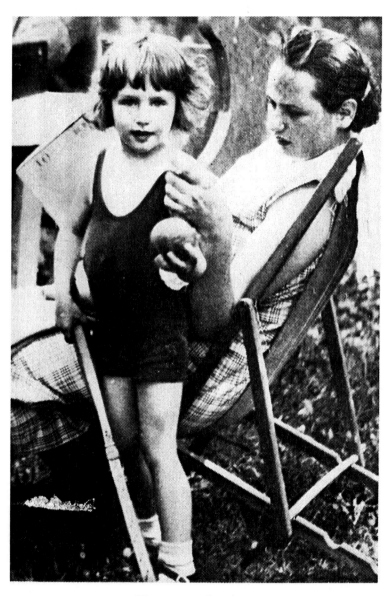

When we were American.

1

When We Were American

Once more I sit on Papa's old squeaky rocker on the porch, shaded by a huge maple that he had planted, and look at Locust Hill Cemetery across the street. I wonder how many people would think of a cemetery as a focal point when they think about home. But that has always been a problem for us. Where is home? When they ask where I'm from, I never know what to say because I've been to so many places. None of them stuck long enough to be home. Yet, this unlikely place, a cemetery in a southern Indiana town, has become the place where our family has set its roots.

The most impressive stone, from this vantage point, is that of my grandfather's aunt, Anna. She raised Papa's father after his mother died. When he was grown, she left with her second husband to the United States. That was before World War I. She brought our Uncle Adolf over to America right after that war.

Others of our family are in that cemetery now, too, Onkel Adolf, our brother Herbert, Papa, Mama, Herbie's wife Georgia, their son, Herb, and Shirley's son, Joseph.

There is a kind of dark fascination I feel for this place. It's really quite beautiful, draped across a bumpy hill, shaded by huge trees, full of all kinds of old and new gravestones, angels, small stone benches. In the dips between the little hills and walkways a few ponds have formed. You can hear the frogs at night. I used to take Shirley, when she was a little kid, for walks on Locust Hill. I never tired of reading the tombstones. Some of them were more than a hundred years old. So many marked the graves of children.

And this place reminds me always of the day when my life changed. That morning I was so excited that I was taking off to be more than a dependent, obedient daughter. I remember hearing the lawnmower, the smell of the freshly cut grass, and the song from Oklahoma, "Oh, What a Beautiful Morning," going through my mind, and how that feeling was wiped out of my life just two doors down from this house at Minnie's when I opened the paper and saw the headline: **Ex-Nazi Youth Leader to Join Navy Today.**

My name is Ruth. I am the first-born of Rosa and Kurt Schwabe, German immigrants.

They both arrived in Milwaukee, Wisconsin in 1929. My mother was seventeen and came to live with her sister Toni. My father was nineteen. His older brother Adolf brought him over. They met at Tante Toni and Onkel Berthold's house where they played cards together.

Mama and Tante Toni had grown up in southern Germany, Papa and Onkel Adolf came from the northern, big industrial city of Essen. Onkel Berthold was from some place in Bohemia. He had been a soldier in the First World War and was seventeen during the last year of fighting on the Eastern front, was taken prisoner by the Russians, and spent six years on a farm in Siberia. During the revolution he left the farm and traveled on trains, sometimes with the White armies, and sometimes with the Red armies for another year, and finally got to Sweden. Everyone at home had given him up for dead. Two years later he and his young wife, Antonie, came to the United States and then brought Mama over, too. Now they were all in a new world, starting a new life.

My parents married in 1930. I was born in 1932. The Depression was so bad that no new coins were minted that year. Roosevelt would be president of the United States the next year, and in Germany, Hitler would get into power, too.

Mama told me that Onkel Adolf hopped a freight train to go out West to become a cowboy because there was no work for him in Milwaukee.

She mused, "I could never understand what he was thinking. A city boy like that, who never even touched a cow or a horse before in his life, to be a cowboy."

Wisconsin has a lot of towns with Indian names. Kaukauna, the town in which I was born, is known more for cheese than anything else. My father had a job there for a couple of years. Then the foundry closed. I remember the long ride in the car as we moved to Milwaukee. I was about two years old according to my mother. It was evening, sunset. I was standing on the seat of the car next to her. The setting sun was shining into my face, and Mama remarked, "You know, Kurt, Ruthie's eyes are not really blue, she has some brown spots in there." This is my first memory, and I know that it was a happy one.

The next thing I remember was when I was three. We lived in an apartment upstairs from an older couple. The man was dying of TB. This worried my father very much, and he made it a point to always tell me that I am not to get near these people because I could catch a very bad disease and die. But, I was only three and didn't know how to say "no" to the lady when she insisted that I come in and have some cookies and milk. So, there I was at the table, eating cookies, drinking milk, and looking at a very thin old man in a hospital bed, who wanted to say something to me, but he kept on coughing into a towel. When I got upstairs, Papa asked if I had been in the apartment. Remembering that the lady had promised not to tell, I lied and said "no." He went downstairs and talked to her, and came back very angry. Mama pushed me into the bedroom and stood in front of the door and said, "Don't blame the child."

Papa yelled, "She lied."

I felt very sad for a long time because I had wanted to be good and please everyone.

While we lived there, Papa's cousin Bernhard visited us. He didn't eat meat and made food we never had before, like squash and sweet potatoes. He taught me to stand on my head, and one day, at the park, he walked up the reservoir steps on his hands. He was very strong and athletic. He said we should go to California, too. Papa and he could work together because he was a tool-and-dye maker and Papa was an iron-and-steel molder. But we didn't move. Onkel Bernhard went to California alone, and we got another baby, my sister Rose Marie, who was born in a hospital.

The next spring, in 1936, we moved to 33rd Street. Once again we lived upstairs. This time, however, there was a younger family downstairs. The Mayers had five daughters, the youngest being about four years older than I was. I remember being happy in this home. The sun seemed to shine every day. The windows looked out on trees and lawn and flowers. Mama put pretty, frilly curtains on all the windows. They danced when there was a breeze.

We always used the backstairs, never the front ones. All of our living seemed to be in the kitchen. I learned about right and left standing by the windows. I liked those windows because the windowsills were low enough for me to look out. You had to be careful, though, not to move the stick that held up the window, or it would come down and cut off your hands or even your head.

Sundays we ate in the dining room. There was always classical music on the radio for Sunday dinner. Before that, I looked at the comics in the Sunday paper and cut out paper dolls and dresses, a special feature in those days. In the dining room was also the door to the front stairs nobody ever used. A large mirror hung on the door. My secret friend lived in that mirror. She never spoke to me. She just looked very serious and seemed to know how I felt. If I could get inside that mirror, how would it be? What was around the corner that I couldn't see?

Inside the radio, if you looked through the little holes in the back, you could see the lights the little people used when they were playing the music, but you couldn't see them. Sometimes, at night, I didn't like the radio. A boy used to sing, "Call for Philip Morris." He didn't sound happy, and the music was spooky, too.

Beyond the dining room was the living room, which was only for company, and for Christmas. The tree would be there, and I used to sneak in when no one was around to look at my distorted face in the shiny ornaments.

The summer before I started kindergarten, I had my tonsils out on the kitchen table. Dr. Barnett and an old surgeon with a white beard and big glasses came to the house. Tante Toni was there, too, and so was Papa. Mama had to go outside because the chloroform wouldn't be good for her. I locked myself in the bathroom.

Tante Toni demanded, "You come out right now! These doctors don't have time to play games with you."

Because I was a "good girl" I came out and let her put on the new pajamas, and I went with her to the kitchen where a large lamp had been set up; a thick rubber mat was on the table with sheets to lie on and to cover me. Papa was making the floor and the walls wet with a mop.

The chloroform took my breath away. I had a dream about being in Smith Park and going around and around on a carousel. It was going very fast and I couldn't hang on anymore.

I cried, "Mama, Mama, Mama . . ." and I heard her softly say, "I'm here, Ruth, don't be afraid. I'm here."

Eventually the spinning stopped. I opened my eyes and saw my parents' bedroom curtains above my head. I was in their bed. They were both there and told me how good and brave I was. Papa went to get me a Diady Doll, which was something very new. She could drink a bottle of water and wet her diaper. She cost a whole dollar.

On the radio, Kate Smith was singing, "When it's springtime in the Rockies, I'll be coming back to you." And the apple tree outside the window was covered with blossoms.

I spent a short time in kindergarten. We sat at beautiful, polished tables that were our height. The sun shone on them, and I loved to watch the shadows of the tree branches and leaves move across the shiny surface. We were making paper lanterns for Halloween, and then I was put into the first grade because I knew how to read.

Herbie was born at home in the evening of Columbus Day. We knew that we were getting a baby. Papa made a bed for Rose Marie and me on the living room couch. We heard Dr. Barnett talking to Papa. He had brought a big black bag with him. I wondered if the baby was in the bag. We two fell asleep, but Papa woke us up and showed us our little brother, Herbie. I loved him immediately. He was sweet and cuddly and funny. I looked forward to seeing him after school. It was a happy time for me. I wasn't aware of or concerned about anything outside of my own little world.

At Easter time the next year, in 1938, Nancy, a girl who lived next door and was in my class, was skipping down the middle of the street, singing, "Look at my new coat. It's bought from a store. My Grandma bought it at a big store."

I knew it was true, because Welfare clothes didn't look like that. It was peach colored. My clothes were mostly navy blue.

A girl at school always had money for candy. Across the street from our school was a small store where she used to buy penny licorice candy ribbons. They had little shapes that you could push out. Some were cars, stars, houses, and many other shapes. She used to stand in line after lunch break and eat only the little shapes and say, "Oh, I just like the things. Does anyone want the scraps?"

Of course most of the ribbon was scraps, and everyone wanted them. She'd look around for a while, holding the ragged licorice ribbon up in the air and then smile at one of us and hand her leftovers to the lucky one. I never caught her eye, but once the girl in front of me did, she gave me some.

That year I also received Valentines from other children in the class, but I didn't have any to give and hoped no one noticed. And on St. Patrick's Day, Papa wouldn't let me wear green. He said that we're not Irish.

In the spring I started to come down with some of the typical childhood diseases. The public health nurse came when one had communicable diseases. She put a sign up for us. Quarantine: Chicken Pox. She came to take Chicken Pox down and put up Whooping Cough. After whooping cough I got mumps. Mama didn't let the two others near me. Good thing, because I also got scarlet fever that year. While I was sick with a high fever, I dreamt that I was walking down a street where there were only old brick buildings and the stones started to come loose; the buildings started to sway and tip over, and the stones were falling on my head. I cried and finally was able to scream. Papa came to lie down on my bed with me, and I went to sleep.

One night, during the summer of 1938, we joined a lot of people who went to the beach of Lake Michigan to sleep because it was very hot. But nobody could sleep there, either. There were too many people, and the ground was not comfortable at all. The next day they said on the radio that we shouldn't go to the beach because we might get polio being so close to so many people, and also the police couldn't be responsible for the behavior of everyone who might decide to be there. I heard the adults talking about kidnapping. I didn't really understand what happened to kids that were napped, but it sounded really bad. I went into the movie theater one evening, about that time, to sit with my mother at one of the lady's night shows, and I saw some men grabbing a little girl, and then a lot of movement under a blanket.

Shortly after that, one night, I thought I saw two shapes, like men, standing by Rose Marie's bed. I was terrified and had a hard time to make a sound, but finally I managed to scream. Papa came into the room, turned on the light, and there was nothing but just the curtains waving in the breeze. He looked out the window, in the closet, under the beds, and finally explained to me that I had only seen the shadow of the curtains. I wasn't totally convinced and kept my eyes on the spot where THEY had been until I fell asleep.

That summer, we were also told to boil all of the water we were going to use for drinking or cooking, and there was nearly a restraint order against children in public places, such as swimming pools, the movies, and even department stores for fear of catching polio. For me, however, the summer was full of fun. I spent some of the most enjoyable days at Tante Toni's house. Something was always happening there. We were allowed to have other kids over, and we could play at the neighbors' house, too. My cousins were older than I was, except for Hildi, who was a year younger.

Tante Toni had all kinds of wonderful things—a wind-up Victrola and really old, funny sounding records, big feather fans from a rich lady she had worked for as a cook, lots of books and games, too.

Next door, the kids used to climb in and out of their living-room window, and we did, too. They had a roller piano. It played music without anyone touching the keys. We used to sit on the couch in a heap, maybe six or seven kids, and watch the keys move, and listen to the piano music. I don't think their parents were home during the day. No grown-up ever came into the room.

At 5 P.M., Hildi and I met Onkel Schubert at the streetcar stop and walked him home. He would give us a penny. We got a Bazooka Bubble Gum and split it. I could read the comics, too. Onkel Schubert had a room at Tante Toni's house. He only ate dinner on Sunday with the family. He played the violin. It was nice to hear him practice. He never made a mistake. Sometimes he played in a concert, but during the day he worked at a hotel as a waiter.

Mrs. Smith was my first and second grade teacher. She treated me somewhat differently than others, I think. She spoke to me in a regular voice, not a little kid teacher voice. We were painting with water paints one day, and I had painted a blue sky on top of the paper, left an "air space" and then put down the green grass. She took me to the window and had me look out. She pointed at the trees, "Do you see any 'air space' out there?"

To my amazement the blue sky and the ground seemed to meet.

She put me into a spelling bee with second and third graders when I still was in first grade. I managed for quite a while, but had no idea of how to spell QUEEN. I felt really awful that I had let her down, but she and the other teachers told me that I had done very well.

Mama had knit several jackets and other clothing that I wore, and Mrs. Smith asked Mama to knit a coat and a two-piece dress for her. She paid her, of course. Mama was happy to earn some money.

At school there was a large chart on the wall above Mrs. Smith's desk. All of our names were on it. For every good thing you did, she put a gold star on it. We were supposed to get library cards. They cost ten cents. Mama said we didn't have that much money to waste. I could use her card. Mrs. Smith put a star up on the chart after my name that was different than the others. It was more orange than gold. It really stood out and didn't fit. I didn't like the way it looked. I cried. She told me to stay after school.

When all of the other kids were gone, she pulled a box out from her desk in which she had an assortment of hair clips, crayons, jacks, and a tennis ball. She said that she couldn't give me a regular star for my mother's library card and that it was hard sometimes to be different, but it was good for your character, and she said I could have anything from the box that I liked. I took the ball, but every time I glanced at the chart, I saw that orange star. It was the only one. All around it were really shiny golden ones. It looked so wrong.

I didn't know about the Dust Bowl, or how terribly other people were suffering from the Depression. I wasn't even really consciously aware of our own poverty, but I knew that Papa, although he was a skilled iron-and-steel molder, had a difficult time getting steady work. He would get a job for a few days, and when that particular order was done, he would be laid off again. There was no money in our house. The telephone was disconnected. I don't remember going to a grocery store. In those days one got goods from the "county." That's what they called the welfare agency.

Papa and I went to get the supplies from the county one day. There was a long line and people were getting restless and angry. Somebody said, looking at Papa, "If these damn foreigners would get the hell back to where they came from, there'd be enough for the people who belong here."

Some of the other men said, "Yea, yea, right," but some others looked ashamed. Papa didn't say anything, and everybody just turned back to stare ahead of themselves.

One Saturday, Papa came home from work at 9 A.M. Mama was yelling at him, "Where have you been, I've been sick worrying about you."

Papa said in a quiet voice, "I was in jail."

Mama sat down with the dish towel in her hand, and the plate she was drying, too.

"What do you mean, you were in jail?" She asked that in a worried way.

Papa explained that he had walked home from the factory because he had plenty of time since they were laid off again, and he could save the streetcar fare. But it was pretty far and it got boring just to walk, so he decided to alternate running one block, walking fast on the next one, and just walking on the third. During one of his running blocks, two policemen started after him. They arrested him on "suspicion" and kept him in jail all night. When nobody reported anything, they let him go.

"They put me into jail for nothing only because I was a foreigner. I know that." Papa always said that when he told someone about what happened to him.

Papa used to say that he didn't like the people at the German Club, but after his night in jail, we started to go there. He sat with the men and talked and played cards, and the ladies and children sat someplace else. The ladies talked about how hard life was, and how good it is now at home in Germany, and how foreigners are treated everywhere. They talked one time about some people who were kicked out of Germany; they were Jewish, and the ship came to the United States, and they couldn't come to America, either.

One of the ladies said, "It's best to be in your own country where you belong. I'm sorry that I didn't stay at home. God knows what will happen to us here if things get worse."

For us kids it wasn't very much fun to be at the club because the men smoked cigars, and the benches were very hard and there wasn't much to do for kids . . . just sit and be nice and quiet.

On my seventh birthday, we had company. The people came up the front stairs, and Mama took them to the living room. The lady was dressed in a gray suit. She spoke German to me, and gave me a quarter. Mama took me to the kitchen and said, "Ruthie, please be a very good, big girl and take that quarter and buy a package of vanilla ice cream at the drug store."

"From my birthday quarter?" I whined.

"Please. I don't have anything to offer them. I promise you that you'll have all the candy and ice cream you want very soon if you'll be good and do this," she pleaded.

I went, feeling like a martyr. I didn't know it then, but our visitors were representatives of the Krupp works in Essen. Papa had done his apprenticeship and had worked there as a young man before he came to the United States. Krupp needed skilled iron-and-steel molders, especially those trained by them.

It must have been a few weeks before school ended that June in 1939. I came home, and only Papa was there. The others were visiting Tante Toni. Papa had a large map on the dining room table. He told me then that we were going to live in Germany, that we were "going home." He showed me the map,

"See the boot, that's Italy, and here is Germany."

I wasn't looking or listening. I didn't want to hear what he was saying. This was home. I liked it here. I didn't want to go away. I turned around, and there was the girl in the mirror. Her eyes said that she didn't want me to leave, either.

But, day-by-day preparations for our journey were being made.

One day, my parents went to Chicago on the train. I had a sandwich for lunch and spent an eternity alone in the schoolyard. The cement court was hot. The walls of the school building were made of bricks; its shining, blank windows were reflecting the summer heat. I was the only living creature on earth. I sat on the step, against the locked door, watching the waves of heat over the courtyard. Finally, others started to return from lunch, and we were allowed to go into the building.

Mama and Papa had gotten our family passport at the German Consulate in Chicago.

Piece by piece our furniture was bought and carried away by neighbors. They used the front stairs. Those went straight down, and were wider than the backstairs. We moved in with Tante Toni until it was time to go by train to New York and by ship from there.

One day, Mama took me to the streetcar, and I went by myself to the end of the line in front of the drug store. I said "hello" to the Mayer girl who worked there and walked the two blocks to our home. Papa was there, painting the wood floors. I went through the kitchen and bedrooms and came back to the kitchen windows. There were no curtains, but the sun still danced on the floor. I looked out of my parents' bedroom window towards the back yard and the apple tree that was blooming when I had my tonsils out. Then I went down the backstairs to say "good-bye" to that tree and the bush behind which I played as a little girl, and the basement window, where I had seen my doll buggy half-painted for the next Christmas, across to Nancy's house. But she wasn't home, so I went down the street to Smith Park, where I had done some crazy acrobatics on the tall swings, and which we had crossed every day going and coming home from school, and finally I walked back and up the front stairs.

Papa had just gotten to the door with his painting, and I couldn't see the girl in the mirror. I knew she was a reflection of me, yet she looked so different from what I felt I looked like. She really seemed to have her own spirit and life, and lived in that world on the other side, into which I could not go. It upset me that I couldn't communicate with her any more.

The dining room floor looked lighter than it was before. The sun made it look golden, copper-colored. It was getting late. There was a strange feeling in my stomach, but it wasn't hunger. We said "good-bye" to the Mayers. They wished us a good trip and said they would miss us. Mr. Mayer and Papa shook hands for a long time, like friends who don't really want to part, and all the girls and Mrs. Mayer hugged me.

The sun was glowing on the horizon as Papa and I walked hand in hand to the streetcar stop. Our shadows were long, pulling back home. We didn't talk, not even in the streetcar. My spirit was still wandering through our home. Papa was somewhere else, too.

* * *

2

GOING HOME TO GERMANY

The train ride to New York seemed to take days. Railroad yards are ugly . . . tracks, wires, brick-colored old box cars, lines and lines of them, ugly, dirty brick buildings and a gray sky. I had left my doll, my baby doll, which Mama had saved and disinfected with alcohol instead of getting rid of her when I had scarlet fever. She was lying on the big trunk in the hall at Tante Toni's. We were going so far away, and I didn't want to go.

Mama and we three children were in a car that had velvet-covered seats. There were only women and children there. The men were in another part of the train. Somewhere along the line, the train stopped, and Papa came to us.

He said to Mama, "They have us in a cattle car, with straw on the floor. All of those guys are some kind of crooks or criminals."

Mama answered, "Well, of course. How many people, do you think, would ask to be voluntarily deported?"

"Repatriated," Papa corrected her.

"Are they dangerous?" Mama asked, alarmed.

"No, they are mostly money crooks, or like this one guy I was talking to. He was a smuggler between America and Canada. They're not hand-cuffed or anything like that." Then Papa said he had to go back, but he just wanted to let Mama know that he was OK.

I heard and remembered but didn't understand until much later that Papa had asked to be sent back home by the Immigration Department because we didn't have enough money for all of the tickets. He said he would stay if they could find him a full-time job, but he didn't want to live on U.S. Welfare anymore, and that's why he wanted to go home.

That the other men were some kind of criminals I did understand, however. It made me curious to look at the other women and children in the car, and try to imagine what kind of criminals their husbands and fathers were. One woman, in the last seat, caught my eye, especially. She was Oriental and never spoke or smiled. Every time I looked back, she was looking at me with dark eyes. I wanted to go and talk to her because she was all alone, but her exotic looks and that darkness in her eyes frightened me off.

When we got to New York we were taken with others in a small launch to Ellis Island, which was still the entrance and exit point for "special" or "problem" foreigners. Papa's status, I guess, was "special."

It was a frightening and sad place. The center of the building was a large hall with wooden benches along the walls and in double rows through the room. The ceiling was as high as the building. Women and children had bedrooms upstairs. There was a railing along the walkway to the different rooms where one could look down to the large hall. I don't know where the men stayed. Somehow, everything about the place looked very dark, including the wood benches.

We were there one or two nights and shared the room with a family whose language we didn't understand. At night one of the children cried. The mother got up and turned on the light. A very bright bulb hung down from the ceiling. The beds were hospital beds. The floor was white stone tile. Swarms of black water bugs scurried towards the drain in front of our bed.

Some of us kids went outside during the day. The island was very small. There was a high fence near the edge, and where the water lapped up at the island, garbage bobbed up and down—oranges, paper, broken fruit crates, bottles . . . Beyond that somewhere was the Statue of Liberty. I don't know if I saw her from the island or from the ship,

but I know that I looked at her with a heavy heart. As we were pulling out to sea, Bing Crosby was singing over the loudspeakers,
"When my Dreamboat comes home . . ."

The weather was beautiful every single day. The sea was smooth. We saw an iceberg and some whales. Mama was ill and spent the entire trip in her bunk. I had a great time, though. There were some children who were going to Ireland. They all had red hair and lots of freckles. From them I learned, "I see London, I see France, I see someone's underpants."

We went exploring together, up some stairs, down some corridors . . . Sailors yelled, "Will you kids get out of here?" We also got an itchy fungus on our feet because we ran around barefoot. The doctor gave Papa some powder to put into my socks, which helped a lot.

Rose Marie's birthday was on the fourth of August. The captain gave her a five-pound box of chocolates in the dining room that evening. Papa passed it around to everybody. Mama was right, we did have all the candy and sweets we could want.

The ocean crossing took ten days. Outside of Ireland, a launch came to pick up the red-headed family. But the ship stopped in a harbor for those going to England. People were talking about something political, which I didn't really listen to. I did get to see "the smuggler" though, with whom Papa talked from time to time. The day before we were to land in Germany, Customs officials came aboard and looked at the things everyone was bringing. One of the men kind of laughed at Mama for bringing black pepper and vanilla and cinnamon along.

The next day we landed in Hamburg. I'm sure that none of the people leaving the ship on that Sunday in the middle of August 1939 knew that we would be in a war at the end of the month.

*   *   *

3

GRIM DAYS UNDER GRAY SKIES

S tepping onto solid ground again gave me the unexpected feeling that the earth was moving up and down. Rose Marie and I both noticed it and thought it was funny. The dock was noisy and busy with people and carts loaded with baggage going by, and there was also a brass band playing. Two men in suits were there to meet Papa. They took off their hats and bowed to Mama. A lady came up and took Herbie from Mama's arms and carried him over to one of the tables of a small café on the dock. She was talking in German with Mama. Rose Marie and I followed. We sat down. The lady ordered something from the waiter, and we got silver goblets with four different flavors of sherbet.

Papa was sitting at another table with the men. They were drinking beer and smoking cigars. The men had papers for Papa to read, and they talked. One of the men gave him an envelope and train tickets. They were from the Krupp factories in Essen. They seemed glad to have him back. Papa looked happy, too. At our table, the lady was explaining to Mama about Krupp insurance and doctors and medicine.

We traveled by train to Essen that afternoon. It took a few hours. From the train station, we rode in a taxi. The street in which our grandmother lived was bathed in red evening sunlight. Two rows of buildings of gray stone lined the street, which was made of gray cobblestones. There was no tree, no grass, no flower, no living creature anywhere, just gray stone and shiny dead windows that reflected the red light.

The taxi stopped. We got out. From one of the hundreds of windows came a woman's voice. Then we were climbing the stairs, and at the landing stood our grandmother. She didn't look like a grandmother to me. I expected a small, old woman with white hair in a bun, a shawl over her shoulders, granny glasses on a black ribbon. But there stood a tall, strong woman in high heels with dark hair in a beauty-parlor permanent. Her eyes were gray-blue, and she really looked right into my eyes when she spoke to me. I understood her German very well. It seemed very clear. She reminded me of how teachers act and talk. I liked her.

The apartment was very small, too small for so many people. There was just one bedroom, and some of us were sleeping on couches. Grandmother, or as we called her, Oma, slept on a couch in the kitchen. Many people came to visit. They were relatives or old friends of my father's. I understood what they were saying to me, but it was soon apparent that I had spoken only English at home. My grammar, as I attempted to speak German, was everyone's amusement. Luckily, I was young enough to learn quickly and I wasn't inhibited.

Papa went to work right away. I had two weeks of vacation left before school would begin. Mama called some of the neighborhood girls together, and we spent the day outside, playing hopscotch and marbles and ball. Rose Marie played along, and sometimes Herbie got to come out with us, too.

One day, just before school was to start, I woke up early. Oma, Papa, Mama, and Onkel Gustav, Papa's older brother, were in the kitchen. They were listening to the radio and were talking loud and nervously. The word that was repeated again and again was KRIEG. I didn't know what the word meant, but I knew it was something bad. Even if it had been translated for me into its English word WAR, I wouldn't have really understood its meaning.

Germany had invaded Poland. Shortly thereafter, Germany was at war with England and France, too. There was much discussion and heated argument among Papa's friends, who often came by and spent evening hours in the kitchen, keeping us awake. There was no TV, so we didn't see the action there. I believe that there were a lot of newsreels at the movie theaters, but small children didn't go very often, only when they had special children's shows. I also didn't read the newspapers, so all of the war news was just what I passively heard on the radio, or from the adults' conversations.

Papa was working at Krupp, and was twenty-nine years old, and had a "bad leg" from an accident at a foundry in America, where a large iron casting dropped from a crane and landed on his leg. He wasn't worried about having to go into the army. Actually, at that point in time, the only thing that made me realize that this war was something serious was the black paper that Papa brought home one day. They put it on the inside of the windows. When the windows had to be closed, because it was too cold outside, it got really completely dark inside, and Oma had to turn on the lights. The black paper was so that the enemy, THEY, wouldn't be able to see us at night when the lights were on.

I wondered what THEY looked like, and what THEY would do to us if THEY saw us.

My father enrolled me in the same school he had attended as a boy. I was placed into first grade. I felt very unhappy about that, and did a lot of daydreaming and reminiscing about my happy days in my American school, where I had skipped kindergarten and had finished second grade with really good marks. But, I was told that it was necessary for me to be in first grade because I had to learn German as well as the old German script.

My teacher was a man in his late 50s who had been my father's teacher for a few years.

He was strict, and the children always paid attention and were very good. We wrote on a slate, not on paper. We did not have time out for art. We never moved from our chairs except to stand when we gave an answer, or for recess, when we went outside into the school yard.

Across the street from the school was a large church. Some of the older children from the neighborhood, with whom I went to and from school, took me there a few times after school when the organist was practicing. I loved the sound of the music and the grandeur of the building. Papa had been an altar boy at this church. But now he said, "Religion is just another big business that we end up paying for, but that does nothing in return." That's why we didn't go to church on Sundays. But I secretly wanted to go and see what God really looked like. I talked to Oma about church. She said that Papa was still angry with God for letting Opa die even though he begged Him not to. Our grandfather had been the paymaster at a mine. He died as a result of a union bombing of the mine's office. That was in 1920, when Germany was going through great turmoil, the result of World War I and its reparation imposed by the Allies who had defeated Germany.

Papa was ten years old when his father died. Oma had a portrait of Opa in the bedroom. He was a handsome man with light eyes, sandy colored hair and a very refined mustache and beard. I learned that he also played the violin like Onkel Schubert in America.

It seemed that our teacher was still occupied with the bad years after World War I. Sometimes he would stand in front of the class, look out above our heads and give a speech about the country, enemies of the country, and the importance of being right and good and proud. One day he was especially agitated, saying,

"You children are lucky to be German, not like that trash, the gypsies, for instance. They are lazy, they steal, they are unreliable to say the least. And the Jews, they suck the lifeblood out of the honest, poor man and take away the home of a poor family without a blink of an eye. They are the real devils of this world." When he said these things, I didn't know whom he was talking to, because we were just little kids. All of the others in class looked scared, too, and I was really glad that we weren't those people he was so mad at.

October came. It was gray and wet and cold. Mama took us children on the train to Erfurt to visit her sister, Johanna. I fell in love with my cousin, Heinz. He was eighteen, had dark hair and brown eyes, and was very sun-tanned. He was a student at the Gymnasium, and was allowed to drive his father's car. He took me along on some errands, and let me walk in front of him inside his raincoat. I also got to watch him practice pole vaulting. He was very good.

Tante Johanna and Onkel Ernst had a stationery store. Their apartment was next to the store on the same floor. We stayed with them for a few days, but Onkel Ernst couldn't stand so many little children, and Tante Johanna talked to Mama. It was early in the morning. Mama had us all get dressed in our coats as soon as we had had our breakfast.

We went for a walk along the river. The air was cold and misty. Leaves that had fallen from the trees were wet and rotting. Bushes with reddish-brown, maroon leaves grew along the walkway. The river was muddy and rushing furiously along. Large rocks stuck out of the water. Mama stood looking down at the river. Something about the way she stood there in the wet, gray mist alarmed me.

"Come on, Mama, let's go," I urged. She turned her head, and her eyes were very dark and so sad.

"Go along with the little ones. I'll come soon." Her voice sounded very tired.

I didn't want to leave my mother there. We walked just a short distance and let Herbie run around a bit. But both Rose Marie and I kept looking at Mama, who stood with her back to us, looking at the rushing water. We turned back. Herbie laughed as he ran to her. She turned and swept him up into her arms. She looked at Rose Marie and me for a while, and then said, "Follow me, we're going somewhere."

We walked along a tall gray wall to a big iron gate. Mother rang the bell, and a nun came to open the gate. They talked together away from us. The building inside the gate was large, built of a light gray stone. The garden surrounding it was pretty with white roses and many pastel-colored asters. Ivy covered the stone walls. There were gravel walks between the beds of flowers and grass. Large trees, even though the remaining leaves were shriveled and brown, made everything soft and peaceful.

The nun and Mama walked towards the building. We followed and entered a large hall with a shiny, waxed floor and a huge carpet. Women, who seemed to be either nuns or nurses, went silently along. Mama and Herbie went into an office with the nun. Rose Marie and I sat down on a bench in the hallway.

After a while, a young woman in a white uniform came from the room and told us to follow her. We went along a corridor with many doors on each side, through another door into a hall, up some stairs, down another corridor. At the end of it was a foyer from which I saw a chapel. We continued along and went up a narrow flight of stairs to a large open area with a wall of windows that overlooked a playground and other buildings. This seemed to be some sort of school.

The area to which we were taken looked like a nursery school. The place was crawling with toddlers and pre-schoolers, all busy playing with a great assortment of toys. Rose Marie felt at home and found herself some entertainment. It seemed like a pleasant enough place.

We had been there for some time. We ate lunch. The little children took naps, and I stretched out on the carpeted floor, too. Time went on. It was getting dark outside. I began to get anxious about Mama. But then the girls in white uniforms brought food on carts, and they set the tables. Rose Marie and I sat down to our second meal. We even had one of my favorites, rice pudding, for dessert.

The truth hit me as I was lying in a bed with very stiff sheets and pillowcases.

Rose Marie was in a crib next to me. We were surrounded by a sea of cribs. Children were fussing, crying. Women in white were feeding babies their bottles. Somewhere, far away in the great hall, was a big bed and a nightlight.

"This is an orphanage! Mama left us at an orphanage. She didn't even say 'good-bye.' When you're in an orphanage it's because nobody wants you. We'll never see her, or Herbie, or Papa again!"

More babies were crying. The whole room seemed to be crying, and I was crying, too. Rosie looked at me through the bars of the crib and asked, "Why are you crying?"

I tried to tell her between sobs that I was crying because we were alone.

She touched my hair and said, "You're not alone. I'm here."

That made me cry even more. A little four-year-old kid was comforting me. I cried an endless stream of tears. The tears ran into my ears. My hair was wet. The tears flowed on and on. I closed my eyes and remembered my parents' bed and the curtains with little purple flowers. Why couldn't it be the way it used to be? I cried all night. A few times someone in white came to soothe my eyes with a cold cloth and to give me a drink of water. None of them told me to stop crying.

By morning I was out of tears, but I was still sobbing. One of the ladies in white was talking to a nun.

"She should really be with the older children. These babies upset her."

"Yes, but I thought it would be better for them to be together for a while."

"Well, try to let her know that she'll enjoy being with the older girls and that she's here just to help the little one get adjusted. You know it's especially difficult for them because they've just come from America."

I was sitting near the row of windows, looking down to the playground. There was a small carousel down there. The lady in white asked if I'd like to go out. Yes, I would. Rose Marie and two other children accompanied me. I gave them a ride on the carousel. It went as fast as I could get it to go. The children were squealing. I hung on, my eyes closed. Everything was spinning. It was just like my dream when I had my tonsils removed.

I called, "Mama, Mama, Mama."

A voice said sharply, "Stop that thing immediately." I braked with my foot, and we came to a stop.

"What are you doing? You don't act wild like that here! This is not America! If you don't know how to behave yourself, upstairs with you."

The nun was very pretty even though she was angry. Her headdress bounced up and down to emphasize her words. The crucifix at her waist swung closer and closer before my face. What could I say? I hadn't thought about the children. I hadn't thought . . . I just felt that I had almost reached another place and time . . .

When we got back upstairs, I was exhausted. A woman in a plaid dress came and said she was a teacher and she showed me the building where I would be staying.

"But you'll be able to see your sister any time you want to. All of our children here are very close to each other."

I didn't feel anything. I would have been worried about Rose Marie, normally, but nothing seemed to matter. She appeared to be very comfortable and happy, and I was too tired to care about myself.

Before lunch the pre-schoolers and I were allowed to go to the chapel. I was excited. Finally I would get to see God. I saw him at the altar. I whispered to the nun next to me, "God really does look great."

"God? That's not God, that's a priest. You can't see God. He's invisible."

"But I have to talk to God!"

"You can talk to Him in your heart. He knows everything you think, sees everything you do. We come to a church because here we can just be with Him and leave all other thoughts outside the door."

"But we can see Him. We have pictures of Him. I know what He looks like. He wears a white dress just like that one, but usually he has long hair and a beard, too."

"Sssh, you're not supposed to talk in church, just pray."

The priest really did look like Him. I stared at the back of his head.

"God, if you can hear this, take care of Herbie, and tell Mama that I cried a lot, and tell Papa that we're here, so he can find us."

He turned, looked up at us and blessed us with the sign of the cross, a customary thing during Mass, but to me it was a sign. I knew that He had heard me.

The rest of the day was not so bad. I could sit and do nothing, or draw pictures or look at the baby books, or build towers with their blocks. I thought about Smith Park and the big swings on which we played acrobats by swinging ourselves up pretty high and then twisting our legs around the chains, and letting go with our hands, just swinging like acrobats. And once I did that where there wasn't enough room between the swing seat and the gravel ground below, I scraped my back raw. Mama felt really sorry for me because I "had fallen off the swing" and was putting salve on my back. before Papa came home. Mama told him of my accident.

He said, "I hope it hurts a lot." He always knew everything.

In the afternoon I still had an occasional involuntary sob, but by evening I had resigned myself to my fate. You can live without your parents. Just don't think about them.

We had finished dinner when a nun came in and talked to the lady in white. She went to another room and returned with our coats.

"Come with me," she said. Rose Marie and I followed her down the hall, the stairs, past the chapel, the next hall, and finally we stopped in front of one of many doors. She knocked, and opened the door to a small bedroom. Mama was putting Herbie's snowsuit on him. I was confused. Had they been here all the time? Why didn't anyone tell me?

"Mama, I thought you were gone. Were you here, or did you come back? They told me that we were going to live here. The teacher even showed me where I was supposed to stay."

Mama didn't answer. It was as if she didn't hear me.

She just said, "We have to hurry to catch the train. We're going back to Essen. Papa will meet us at the station."

It was very late when we arrived in Essen. The air was heavy with smoke and soot. Papa got us into a taxi. I remembered that the bed in which I had cried all night had really been comfortable, and this night I would have slept without crying. I don't know if Mama had intended to leave Rose Marie and me at the orphanage or not. We never ever talked about it.

That weekend, Onkel Gustav came and took me to stay with his family. My cousin, Tanja, was younger than I, but she was going to the first grade, too. Horst was ten years old. He was nice, but pretty bossy. We went to school the short way—through the dump. We looked at piles of broken dishes and other junk. Sometimes we retrieved a pretty shard. Rats scurried around, but you didn't have to worry because they had plenty to eat . . . Just don't step on any of them. The sewer flowed through the dump. You could jump across it, but just in case, you'd better take off your shoes and socks, so that if you slipped, they wouldn't get wet. I dropped a sock, so I threw in the other one, too. Our teacher was a young woman with a very sweet, little voice. The students weren't well behaved at all. I felt sorry for her.

It was mid-November when the first slushy snow fell. It snowed the day on which Onkel Gustav took me to see the surprise my mother had for me. I was happy to go. I had missed my family, although I was gone such a short time. As we came around the corner to Oma's street, we saw an ambulance at the door of her apartment building. I ran to the building and up the stairs. The kitchen door was open and several people in coats and uniforms were talking all at the same time. The lights were very bright in the bedroom, and as I made my way through, two men came towards me with a stretcher, and Herbie was on it with a nurse holding the blanket near his face. Some other people were in the bedroom. Someone was spraying white powder all over the crib in which Herbie had been sleeping. Mama was lying in bed, and in her arms was . . . a baby! Around me were voices—"diphtheria"—"quarantine"—"three weeks"—"isolation." Where did this baby come from? Why didn't I know? I knew we were going to have a baby when Herbie was born. Herb! Herbie is going to the hospital! He has Diphtheria!

This baby, our little German sister, Hannelore, was born in the evening before Armistice Day. But that year, 1939, Germany did not remember Armistice Day with shame or sorrow. The news broadcasts on the radio listed only success, victories, and pride, and the inevitable surrender of Poland. But this little one came into a family under stress.

One day I came home from school and found the rooms quite dark. My father was lying on the couch in the alcove of the bedroom. Oma was sitting next to him, and Onkel Gustav was sitting in a chair. My father was crying! I had never seen my father, nor any man, cry before.

Oma was saying, "Stop blaming yourself. It's not your fault. That's life. If we knew ahead of time what will happen, we would be God."

Then Papa had shingles on his face across his left eye. It hurt a lot, but every day he went to Krupp to see what the men in his section were doing, then to the Krupp clinic, and from there he went to the hospital to the isolation ward, where he could see Herbie, but Herbie couldn't see him. Papa was so worried about him.

"He's so little and so thin. If only they would let me in to hold him," he kept saying.

At school we were getting ready for the pre-Christmas season. Our teacher drew stars on the board.

"Practice at home. The ones who can draw all five corners even, get a prize."

I went home and practiced. Papa watched a while as I struggled to get five even corners on a star, and then he said, "I'm going to show you how your teacher taught us to make the Christmas star. It's very easy. You make one triangle like this and another one like that. You see, how easy? This is the real Christmas star. It's called the Star of David. You see, Jesus was born into the Jewish family of the House of David, and Christmas is His birthday."

"But, Papa" I said, "he doesn't like Jewish. He said that they are devils." I told him about the day the teacher was saying all those things about gypsies and Jews.

Papa was surprised.

"That doesn't sound like him at all. He used to tell us all these things about Jesus being Jewish, and he, himself, was really very religious. He told us what INRI at the top of the cross meant. The I was for Jesus, the N for Nazareth, where Jesus had lived, the R was for Rex, which meant King in Latin, and the last I was for Judiorum. The whole thing meant Jesus of Nazareth, King of the Jews. What happened to him?"

Oma said, "Maybe he's afraid that someone will remember what you just told us, and so he is deliberately denying what he believed."

Papa turned back to me and said, "This is what you do. You tell him that you know how to make the Christmas star, and you draw the Star of David. And when he asks you where you learned that, you tell him that your Papa told you that he taught that to him when your Papa was a boy."

Oma was knitting. She said, "Do you think that's wise, Kurt? The child will get into trouble."

"Why? How? Do you think he's going to report it?" Papa answered her.

"I just want him to remember that he once was a kind and decent person, and that he should stop poisoning these children's minds because he's afraid he might be found out that he doesn't believe that stinking propaganda, himself."

The next day at school, I did not volunteer immediately. Several kids went up to the board, drew something and the teacher said, "Not bad, but not quite right," and similar statements. The rest of the class was busy practicing on their slates. He asked, looking around the class, "Anybody else?"

I was not yet as brave in the German school as I might have been in America, but he did notice a willingness in me to at least try. So he called me to the board. I drew the Star of David, not very big. He looked at it, and then said, "Who told you to do that?"

I said, "My Papa, he said that you taught him that."

He took the sponge and wiped it off the board, and said very nicely, "Go back to your seat." Then he announced to the class that no one was able to get five perfect points, so no one got a prize.

On Saturday, Oma took Rose Marie and me to a very large department store. It had eight floors. Rose Marie and I went up and down the escalators. The store looked all ready for Christmas with lots of shiny, sparkling decorations, and people buying gifts. We ate strange salads with mayonnaise that Oma bought at the delicatessen department.

Oma ate a lot of things that seemed strange to us, like mussels that cried in the cooking pot, and Tartar, which was raw meat. She also ate mushrooms and pickled pumpkin rind. I tasted everything but the Tartar. Mama said you could get tape worm from raw meat.

Oma snapped, "Maybe in America, but not here." Just the same, I didn't want to take a chance.

Our grandmother also had interesting friends. She knew them from long ago, when Opa played the violin. They were singers and actors and musicians. They used to come in the afternoon for coffee, and we listened to classical music records. They talked about plays and movies that I didn't know anything about, but I liked to hear them talk about those things. And, Oma could knit and read at the same time. She made us all ski sweaters with designs of snowflakes and deer. She taught me how to knit and how to crochet and how to darn socks. She knew lots of things and told us anything we wanted to know. Mama was busy with the baby, or sometimes she was just too tired to talk to anybody, so Rose Marie and I spent more time with Oma during that time.

A few days before Christmas, Papa brought Herbie back from the hospital. They still didn't want to release him, but Papa said that he'll die if he stays there any longer. Rose Marie and I were playing out on the sidewalk as they came. I was shocked to see what had happened to our sweet, smiling, chubby little brother. He was so thin and so weak, he couldn't stand. There were dark circles under his eyes, but worse than that, there was a faraway, sad look in his eyes. When we rushed up to him, he just put his head against Papa's shoulder and gave a weary wave of his hand. Everyone believed that he really would have died if Papa hadn't insisted that he come home.

Christmas was generous. We received a lot of toys and candy. Some of the candies were so sweet we didn't like it.

Oma said, "Someday, you'll wish you'd have some of it."

One of her old friends brought me her china dolls and dishes. The dolls wore old-fashioned lacy clothes. They had real hair; their eyes opened and closed and they had jointed arms and legs. They were all so delicate and beautiful. She also gave me her album of Valentines, called *Philipchen*. All of those things were more than fifty years old. I was very happy that she had chosen me to give them to.

A few weeks after the holidays, Papa found an available flat for us. It was in his boyhood neighborhood where quite a few Jewish families lived. The flat was on the fifth floor, an attic apartment. The roof leaked, the wind blew through it from hidden places. It was damp, cold, and dark. There was no electric light, just gaslight, but it had two bedrooms, a kitchen, sort of a living room, and a bathroom on the same floor.

After the furniture was delivered and our belongings had gone from Oma's to the apartment, Mama put Hanni, our baby sister, into the baby carriage, and sat Herbie in the front of the carriage. Rose Marie and I walked with her from Oma's place to our new home. It started to snow, and Mama was worried about the little ones, especially Herbie, who was more exposed.

I remembered our Milwaukee school cloakroom. Mrs. Smith was helping us with our snow suits and mittens and galoshes and we were singing, "Three little Fishies and a Mama Fishie, too . . . swim little Fishies, swim if you can, and they swam and they swam right over the dam."

Our landlady was Jewish. She lived right downstairs from us. She gave me a red velvet marble bag full of marbles that had belonged to her son when he was a boy, and she gave Rose Marie a peacock blue top, which she called a *Drehdl*. Papa explained to us how to play marbles. He divided them between us, and we played on the living room floor. He also made a little whip with a stick and string to wind around the top so that you could make it spin.

And then Herbie got very sick. Our landlady knew a pediatrician who had studied in the United States. The doctor came in the evening. Herbie was on the kitchen table. The doctor sighed, "Double pneumonia, and maybe worse. I have to do a spinal tap. If it has gone to the brain, there is no hope." He made some marks on Herb's back. Then I had to get up on the table and sit on his legs. Mama and Papa were holding down his shoulders. Herbie let out a terrible, shrill scream.

We took turns sitting by his bed and watched him breathe. The landlady brought oranges. We didn't know where she got them because we couldn't find any, anywhere. One day, I was sitting by Herbie's bed, and he woke up from his sleep. He opened his eyes and smiled at me. The crisis was over.

Luckily, it was a mild winter. As the weather improved, I explored the neighborhood. We were a block away from a big busy street. There were many stores on that street, and also many people, mostly older men, who often stood in small groups talking to each other. Many of them had beards, and they wore black coats and had on black hats. On the other side of the street were several big buildings with bushes and trees, wrought iron fences or hedges. There also was a cemetery. The big gates were just across from our block. I crossed that street and walked through the cemetery with some girls who lived on the block. I went to the same school, but now I lived closer to it.

One day, after school, Mama and I went to the butcher on the corner. The butcher was talking to a man at the other end of a long counter. Near the door where we came in, stood an old lady. After we entered, other people also came in. The butcher came down to where we were, and asked Mama what she would like.

Mama said, "I believe this lady was here before me."

The butcher answered, "She can wait, she's a Jew."

Mama was about to say something when the old lady whispered to her, "Please, don't cause trouble. I can wait."

It was very quiet in the store. Everyone was looking at Mama. Her hands were shaking, and when she gave her order, her voice sounded like an echo. I knew that Mama was really upset because she was always very polite to older people and she didn't like what happened. I remembered what our teacher had said about Jews, but when I looked at this lady, she didn't look like a devil. She looked sad and afraid. Then, I noticed that she had a yellow-cloth star sewn on the collar of her coat. It was the Star of David. It didn't look pretty, though. There was something wrong. It reminded me of my orange star on Mrs. Smith's chart. It said that she was "different," and I couldn't understand why she would wear that mark for everyone to see. I didn't want to see my star, and I certainly wouldn't have worn it.

On the way home I asked Mama why that lady had that star on her coat.

"If she didn't wear it, then the butcher wouldn't have known, and then he wouldn't have been so mean," I reasoned.

Mama shook her head and sighed, "You ask me questions to which I don't know the answers."

I wished Oma had moved with us, she would have known the answer.

On my eighth birthday, March 11, 1940, my father gave me a whole mark to buy any kind of candy I wanted. I immediately went along the busy street to the store that had my favorite—licorice. They also had candy beads on paper, and rice paper candy that melted as soon as it got wet in your mouth. I spent the entire mark, and left with a paper bag full of candy. People in the store wished me a happy birthday, and the old man, who had sold me the candy, said something that sounded like "Maseltof," and I started on my way home.

Somewhat up the street, a crowd of people had gathered. They were looking across the street. As I reached the crowd, I walked into the street to see what they were looking at, and also to get around the people. Some men in brown uniforms were coming out of one of those pretty buildings, and they were throwing chairs out into the street. A smaller, old man was following them and shouting,

"But, why throw the chairs in the street?"

One of the men in uniform grabbed him by the arm and dragged him to a car. The old man was still talking and looking back, and he didn't want to go, but the man in the uniform was stronger than he was. The people around me were totally silent. They didn't even move. They just stood, frozen, and looked. They were afraid. I could feel their fear. I got scared, too. I felt like running, but somehow I knew that that would not be right. I didn't want anyone to notice me. I walked very slowly back to the sidewalk. My back felt like something prickly was touching it. I went to the back, behind the tall people. As soon as I got around the corner, I ran. I ran all the way to our building and up the stairs.

I told my parents what I had seen.

Mama said, "My God, the synagogue. Oh, Kurt, we've got to move away from here. I can't stand to see this happening."

Papa put his hand over his eyes and rubbed his forehead. Then he sighed and turned to me, "Child, you can not go to any of these stores alone, anymore. This is not a punishment. You didn't do anything wrong. It is something that you have to obey without questions, do you understand?"

I did understand, not like the time when I was three and he told me not to go into the apartment of the TB patient. This danger I had felt before he told me. I knew that there was something that you had to be afraid of and it was something that you couldn't talk about.

Less than a week later, we had company in the evening. It was the smuggler from the ship. Another man was with him. We children were sent to bed, but it was early, and I wasn't tired. I lay in bed and heard parts of what they were saying in the kitchen: " . . . Only over the

mountains to Switzerland . . . Impossible with all of these children . . .
Think positive, this can't go on much longer . . ."

I knew they were talking about leaving Germany, and the smuggler
was helping people to get away.

By spring 1940, Poland had already been conquered and occupied
by German forces. On the western front, Germany invaded Norway
and Denmark, then Holland, Belgium, and Luxembourg. German troops
were stationed there, closing those routes of escape. That's why the
smuggler said that the only way out would be through Switzerland.

*   *   *

4

BLUE SKIES—HAPPY DAYS

Just days after that evening visit we started our Easter vacation
at school, and Mama began packing bags ready to take us
children on another trip. We traveled by train again, but this time we
went south to Ellwangen where Mama was born. We were going to
stay with her sister, Frida, whose husband was drafted into the army.
She had a house and no children.

The train ride was enjoyable, even exciting. We traveled along the
Rhine for quite a while. In the late afternoon we saw terraced hills and
vineyards on the other side of the river. The farther south we got, the
prettier it was—trees, fields, small towns, a blue sky, and a spectacular
golden, copper, peach-colored sunset. We traveled a long time, all
through the night, too. In the morning we changed trains once. From
there it wasn't far to Ellwangen.

The station was very busy with many people, all speaking strangely.
I had not heard their dialect before, and asked Mama if we were in
Switzerland. She laughed. It was a light and happy laugh like when we
were at home, a long time ago.

She said, "No, this is not Switzerland, this is Schwabenland
(Swabia)."

Tante Frida came running up to us. She was dressed like the other
women there, in dark, plain clothes. She wore no make-up, and her

hair was in a bun. Mama looked so different in her American dress with flowers all over it, and beauty-parlored wavy hair and lipstick. Her shoes were also prettier, and she wore silk stockings. The two sisters were hugging each other, Mama speaking regular German, and Tante Frida speaking Schwaebisch. They had not seen each other since my mother was a teenager, and now she was the mother of four children.

While the two women were talking, our whole group managed to get out of the station and board our transportation to the suburban village in which Tante Frida lived.

We were going in a farmer's wagon, pulled by two cows, real milk cows. The farmer had been a classmate of Tante Frida's, and he remembered Mama as a little girl. The three adults sat together up front on a board. They talked and laughed. We children were allowed to lie down on the sacks of grain in the wagon.

I looked up at the green roof of leaves. Huge trees lined both sides of the road. Birds were flitting back and forth or chirping in the branches. The blue sky peeked through here and there, and flashes of sunlight were reflected by the dew on the leaves. The road was not paved, and every so often the wagon went over a loose rock, and it creaked and shook and bounced. It was a nice feeling, like being carried in someone's arms.

Mama sighed, "It's so nice to be home again."

We spent several weeks at Tante Frida's. I went to the village school and got somewhat accustomed to the dialect, enough to understand most of what was being said.

But I couldn't manage speaking their way, so I was considered an outsider by the village children and really had no friends. I think it didn't seem very important to me, though, because I knew this was a temporary stay, nothing more than a visit.

So many things were happening in the countries around us during April and May of that year of which I was totally oblivious. In April, the occupation of Norway and Denmark took place; by the end of May,

Germans had simply taken, without warning, the other Lowland countries of Holland and Belgium, too.

Mama and Tante Frida never talked politics. I don't even remember hearing the radio in that house. They sewed or worked in the garden, did other housework together, and talked about long ago, when they were children and lived in a big old house that had belonged to their father's grandparents. Once, they talked about the apple orchard and the apples, which were to go to the market. Grandmother gave them one by one to the children to put very carefully into baskets, but Mama, who was the youngest, let them roll down the hill instead of carrying them. Then they laughed about the kettles full of applesauce that was made from those apples.

When school ended for summer vacation, our family walked to another village where Tante Sofie lived. Our baggage got there with the milk truck. Mama set Hanni and Herbie into the stroller, which also held a bag or two of immediately needed things, including sandwiches and something to drink for us all. We were going to Hohenberg, which means "high hill or mountain." The road went up and up, sometimes steeply, other times we hit a bit of a plateau. On the first leg of this hike, we passed the house in which Mama and all of her thirteen siblings were born, and the orchard and the oil mill that had once belonged to Grandfather before he lost it all during the bad years after the First World War. He had taken a small loan against the title when grandmother was diagnosed of having cancer. The bank took everything—the house, the land, the mill. It had to do with inflation.

We stood and looked at the house for a while.

Mama reminisced, "I was nine years old then, and my poor mother was sick with cancer, and she had to be carried out of the house to live with her sister-in-law until she died. And all of us, even I, had to live with other people and work for my keep. I was on a farm and took care of children right after school, and brought water and firewood, fed the chickens, and that woman treated me like an animal. Nobody loved me, or smiled at me, or even said a nice word . . . Oh, well, that was a long time ago. I just feel so bad for my parents. My father was just a broken man after my mother died. He died a year later. Frida found him dead in his sister's garden. He died all alone."

Mama was quiet for quite a while. The road was really steep, and she was pushing the stroller with two children in it. I was dragging Rosie along, who by that time was complaining about being tired. After we reached a plateau, we stopped and had a small picnic. We could see the whole town of Ellwangen from there.

Running the conversation back in my mind. I returned to Mama's words, "the bank took everything . . ." and I remembered our teacher's statement, "they take a poor man's house . . ."

I asked Mama, "Was it a Jewish bank that took your father's house and land?"

Mama looked at me in an annoyed and disgusted way.

"What do you mean 'Jewish bank'? It was a German bank right there in Ellwangen. Where do you get these stupid ideas, anyway? What is going on in your head? Why don't you think about things that other girls think about, like clothes, your hair, flowers . . . pretty things? What's the matter with you?"

That was the end of that conversation. It was very difficult for me to say the right things to my mother, and worse than that, I always seemed to ask the wrong questions. It was an important question to me, but it remained unanswered.

We arrived at Tante Sofie's in the afternoon, hungry and tired. Sofie was Mama's oldest sister, twenty years older than she. Of the fourteen children grandmother bore, she was the oldest and Mama was the youngest. Sofie took care of Mama after their father died. But when Sofie married Franz, who was a widower with three children, and she had her own babies, Mama worked for a while as a mother's helper, and then was sent to America to live with Tante Toni.

I loved Tante Sofie. She was like another grandmother to me. Oma, in Essen, was very smart. She was like a teacher grandmother, but Tante Sofie was a smiling and loving grandmother. She was kind and gentle and good. Her eyes were dark brown. She had dark curly hair that she kept in a bun, but little wisps of hair would form curls near her face. When she smiled at you, you felt like you were being hugged. I was very happy during the time we spent with her.

Jakob, her youngest son, was four years older than I. We explored the fields and forest together. He showed me the family's secret blueberry patch in the forest. You could lie down on the ground and see the berries under the leaves. We picked buckets full of them, which Mama and Tante Sofie turned into jam.

The forest was enchanted. Jakob showed me a spring. The water came from under a rock. There was soft, green moss all over the rock. The water was very cold and clear. We always went very quietly because little animals came to drink. We saw squirrels, of course, and rabbits and once even a doe and her fawn.

Sometimes I came alone. I sat on another large rock, away from the spring, and waited to see if the dwarves and fairies would come, too. The wind sighed through the tips of the tall pine trees. Birds sang. Somewhere a cuckoo called. The earth smelled sweet and moist, like strawberries and pine. Shafts of sunlight filtered down through the trees, touching the moss and soft pine needle carpet. I thought, *This is probably how heaven is.*

One day we were all out in the fields. It was a bright, hot, sunny day. Mama, Tante Sofie, and my cousin Maria, were loading fresh hay onto the wagon. Jakob was on top, stacking the hay so it wouldn't tip off on the way home. I held on to the bridle of the team of cows, brushing the flies off them with a branch from a nearby tree. Rose Marie was baby-sitting Herbie and Hanni on a blanket under the tree. There were a lot of people out in the surrounding fields, doing about the same thing. Suddenly the church bells started ringing the way they do on holidays. All over the fields people stopped and listened. When the wagon was loaded we returned to the village.

We were in the dining room for lunch. Tante Sofie had everyone kneel and pray, "Thank You, Father that the war in France is also at an end. Please protect our sons and husbands in other parts of the world. Our Father, who art in Heaven . . . Hail Mary, full of grace . . . and a special prayer for Josef, who is on the Eastern front . . . and for my dear boy, Alois, on a ship somewhere . . . and for all the boys who don't have anyone to pray for them . . . and for all of the poor, suffering people in the world, we pray . . ." We said very many prayers. I was not accustomed to kneeling on a wooden floor. Perhaps my knees were bonier than everyone else's, but I was really in pain. I said a special short prayer, "Dear God, please let me get up soon." But I didn't dare move until the prayers had come to an end.

Remembering that day, I feel it must have been a Sunday. It really seemed like a holiday. No one in the village acted silly or loud or boisterous, though. They all just seemed relieved and hopeful that the whole thing would be over soon. That another part of the war was over was reassuring, and since we only heard of victories and glory, I had no doubt that Germany would win, and then everything would be nice and peaceful.

For lunch we had soup with thinly sliced crepes, like noodles. Grandmother's family had come from Strasbourg. Her name had been Grenier before she got married. She cooked some things like French people did, and so did her daughters. On her wedding picture you could see that she looked very French with dark brown eyes and long, straight, dark hair gathered in a knot at the top of her head. She was pretty in her dark dress, with the little crown of white flowers around the knot of hair. Grandfather was tall and blond. He had curly hair and very light blue eyes. He stood with one hand in his jacket front and the other one on the arm rest of a chair. Grandmother stood next to him, her one hand on Grandfather's arm, the other hand held a prayer book.

Tante Sofie had many old pictures including one of Mama when she first got to America. She had short wavy hair, and she was wearing a V-necked dress with a diagonal stripe of a contrasting material. She also had on pointy shoes with bows on them. Tante Sofie's wedding picture was there, too. She looked very much like her mother, but she didn't look so serious. Her eyes were smiling, not so melancholy as Grandmother's, and Onkel Franz had on his forester's uniform and he had a very big mustache.

The summer went on. We all worked together, whether in the garden, the fields, or picking berries. The children had special tasks as well, except for Hanni, who was just lots of fun to have around. Rose Marie had some problems with the geese, who seemed to have it in for her. Herbie slipped in the cow stall, and got dung all over his clothes. I often helped Maria to feed the pigs, rabbits, chickens, and geese. We took the bed sheets up into the orchard to bleach under the sun after they were washed.

One afternoon, Maria and I went to visit a cousin, Frieda, who was staying with the teacher and his wife. Frieda showed me the schoolroom, and Maria and she said, "If you are brave, you'll drink some ink. It will poison your blood and you might die, but if you don't, you're a coward."

I had to prove to my older cousins that I was brave, so I drank a little ink. I waited for a sign that I was dying, but nothing happened.

There was a special apple tree, a Jakobi apple tree. The apples were very tasty already. We could eat any that fell from the tree, but we weren't allowed to pick them. They would be picked, wrapped, and sold at the market.

Before we went to bed, Jakob whispered to me, "When everybody's asleep, I'll go out and throw a couple of pebbles up against your window. Come down, but remember not to step on the third step because it squeaks."

I was afraid that I would fall asleep before everyone else, but eventually everything was still, and after a bit, I heard something that might have been pebbles against the window. I slipped out of bed and tiptoed down the stairs in my night gown and came out into the moonlit night. We ran up the hill in the cool, wet grass and came to the Jakobi tree. He picked two perfect apples and said, "Don't let your night gown get wet when you sit down."

So I picked it up and sat down onto the cool, wet grass with my bare bottom. A very warm feeling surged up to my tummy. It was a surprising sensation. I wondered if Jakob also felt the grass, but he was sitting cross-legged, munching on his apple and talking about bicycles.

Maria woke up when I crawled back into bed.

She said, "You're going to get a stomachache from eating green apples." How did she know?

The next morning as we got up, I saw a spot of blood on the sheet. My first thought was that I was dying from drinking the ink.

Maria said, "No, it's not from that. That ink wasn't poisonous. It's not from you. It's from me. And I'm not hurt. It's very natural. When you're old enough to have a baby, you'll bleed, too."

Maria was going to have a baby!? She was only fifteen, and she didn't have a husband either!

I told my mother, "Maria is going to have a baby."

"What? How do you know that?" Mama demanded.

I told her about the blood.

Mama explained, "No, no, you've got that wrong. When there's blood, there's no baby."

I didn't understand, but I didn't dare pursue the subject.

The summer was filled with ordinary and normal activities of country life. The war was a part of some other world. I had never met the cousins who were away, so I didn't miss them. I didn't know how life was supposed to be. Pictures in newspapers always showed handsome German soldiers and tanks or airplanes. It meant nothing to me, personally.

Up on the hill to the church were many Linden trees. On our last afternoon, Jakob, Maria, and I climbed the trees along the road and picked blossoms for tea. And then the wonderful summer came to an end. We had to leave and return to Essen to start school. Mama also said that Papa and Oma needed us. We were all tanned and healthy. Herbie had gained back his strength and had put on some weight. Hanni, who always was a happy, healthy baby, was more lovable than ever. She was very blond, and had blue eyes just like Papa's. I was a tomboy, but Rose Marie was still sweet, quiet, demure.

Many events had taken place on the Western front during the months we were in Southern Germany. The war had become real. People were dying. There were now air and sea battles. The Luftwaffe was bombing England, U-Boot attacks were sinking English ships. History books tell us that many German planes were lost in the air raids, though I didn't hear that on the German news. I remember that Italy joined Germany, and that Russia invaded and took over Estonia, Latvia, and Lithuania, and that there were Germans who came as refugees from those countries. And there was some news about Rumania and Greece. None of these events made any impact on our lives out in the country, but when we got back to Essen, there was a different tempo to life than what it had been before. Everyone seemed to be working long hours, and they were tired and irritable.

I noticed these things, but there were happier surprises and events that occupied my mind.

*   *   *

5

ERIKA'S BOOK

O ur first surprise was that Papa and Oma greeted us in a new apartment in a neighborhood with trees along the street, grass and flowers in the yards and in the windows. Our apartment was in a Krupp-owned building. The apartments were *Beamtenwohnungen*, which roughly translated would mean "white collar," rather than "blue collar" housing. This was really somewhat above my father's station, but he considered it a kind of bonus for coming back home. The apartment was big. We had the whole third floor of the building to ourselves. Oma had her own room, and we had bedrooms for parents, for Rose Marie and me, and for the babies, Herbie and Hanni. I couldn't believe what beautiful furniture we had in our room, and I loved the windowsills, which were wide and made of marble. The windows were really big and made more beautiful with flowing lace curtains. Out the window I could see trees, the yard across the street with grass and more trees and flowers. It was almost like 33rd Street, except that in America the houses were farther apart. Here they were right next to each other, and in our building there were five families, two on each of the other two floors. One of the families on the ground floor was from Lithuania. They had a lot of little children. Mama talked to the mother and helped her to get settled.

She told Papa, "I know how she feels. She thought she was coming home, but she's treated like an outsider. People are so rude and unkind."

One evening my parents and Oma were talking about the old neighborhood, and Mama asked if Papa had seen our former landlady lately, and how things were around there.

He told her, "I went by there two weeks ago to invite them for a visit. They weren't there. Completely new people live there now. I looked at the names by the front door. I didn't have the courage to ask anyone. I actually felt like I was being watched. It was eerie. I got on the first streetcar that came along. I didn't care where it was going; I just wanted to get away from there."

I was thinking that maybe the smuggler helped them to leave. But then Mama said, "They had a lot of connections. I hope they left on their own." And then no one said anything more. I don't remember anyone telling me, but I knew from the two experiences I had in the old neighborhood that Jewish people were picked on by tough guys like the butcher and those men in brown uniforms, and even other people, like my teacher. Even if Papa said he wasn't like that when he was young, and Oma said that he just said bad things because he was afraid, I wished that I could ask why he would be afraid. But that question, like the one about why Jewish people wore that yellow-cloth star on their coats, and if the bankers who took our grandfather's property were Jewish, and what Mama meant with "if there's blood, there is no baby," all remained questions in my mind.

But when you're eight years old, the world you live in, what happens today, takes precedence.

In this wonderful new neighborhood was a Krupp-owned grocery store on the corner of our block. It was called a *Konsum*. I was allowed to go there, and one day I bought a can of *Ruebenkraut*, which was a delicious honey-like bread spread made from sugar beets. That was something we did not have in America.

Four blocks up a slight hill was the market. It was shaded by big trees, and around the market were all kinds of stores, as well as a very large Catholic church. In the little side street across from the church was a stationery and bookstore. They had a great selection of Philipchen from which I chose new treasures for the old album from Oma's friend. The greatest attraction of the market place was a man dressed in billowing silk pants, an embroidered red vest, one big hoop earring, and a completely bald head. He was very big, and he carried a wooden tray attached to a strap around his neck. On the tray was something we called *Turkischer Honig* (Turkish Honey). We gave him whatever kind of coins we had, and with a cleaver he would cut a piece of the 'honey' off the block and hand it to us on a piece of wax paper, which he pulled off a string that was attached to the tray.

I went to a different school, of course. My teacher was a young, blond lady. The class was very large, and my seat was towards the back, behind a boy who was taller than I was. He often blocked my view. The class was also noisy, and the teacher's voice was not very strong. I didn't always see or hear what was going on. Once she did say that we should tell our mother to cook potatoes with the peeling so that nothing would go to waste, but if she did peel them first, we should bring the peelings to school and they would be collected to feed pigs. I don't remember anyone bringing potato peelings to school.

There were at least a dozen children from our block and the next one who all went to the same school. After school we often played out on the street. The girls generally played a game with a ball, which included a rather complicated series of skills. The ball was bounced against the wall of a building. Ten times with one hand, nine times with the backside of the hand, so many times with the knee, the head, the chest, and so on. Unfortunately, our favorite wall, because of its smooth surface, was located underneath the bedroom window of a man who worked at night. He would open the window and call us unkind names. We ran away. A few days later, we would try again with the same result. Finally we settled on a less desirable, but uncontested wall.

Among the girls in this group was Erika, who was so blond, her hair looked like a halo in the sunlight. Her eyes were the color of forget-me-nots. But, what made her stand out most of all was her very gentle and sweet manner. She was the first person to whom I could speak freely about anything. She listened. She told me about vacations on the North Sea islands and about drinking tea with Kandis sugar that crackles when the tea is poured over it. I told her about my American school with shining tables, and the Fourth of July and fire works, and ice cream on sticks with chocolate around them. Sometimes

I had the feeling that my mirror friend had turned into a live girl in this world, but better, because she talked to me. Erika was my first best friend. She was eight years old, too, but she was in third grade, I was only in second. In America I would have been in fourth. Every time I thought about that I was angry.

One day I was given Erika's autograph book. Everyone else had really written beautifully, and decorated the opposite page as well. I was very nervous, afraid to mess it up, but Oma helped me by giving me a very pretty verse and an extra sheet of paper to rest my hand on while I was writing. Then she helped me decorate the opposite page with watercolors brushed over a tea strainer to create a delicate picture.

I returned the album as soon as it was dry. Erika's grandmother opened the door for me, and I saw Erika with her two little brothers, as blond as she was. They were sitting together on a bench under a window. The sun shone on their heads, and they looked like three little angels. Erika was reading them a fairy tale. She was soon done and came to talk with me. And somehow, while I was admiring all the books on the shelves in that room, her grandmother gave me one of them to read at home. I had never seen such a book. It had a white quilted leather cover and gilded edges, and a buckle. On the cover was a spray of forget-me-nots. I couldn't wait to get home to read it.

I went to my bedroom, saying that I was going to do homework. I didn't want anyone to see, to keep me from this book. I sat in the chair near the window and began to read. I read until Mama called me to come to eat. Then I returned again to read. The weather was very mild. The windows were left open. A big full moon was hanging in the sky. I sat on the windowsill and finished reading by moonlight.

The story of Erika's book took place in a very small village in the Black Forest during the early 1900s. The main character was a man who made dolls' heads from papier-mâché. During the week he molded the heads. His wife carefully placed them on the picket fence around the house to dry. Then he painted them, and again they were put out to dry. Each Saturday he strapped the big basket on his back into which the doll heads had been packed carefully, and walked to the small town to deliver his week's work at the doll factory. The family was poor. He received only five marks for a whole basket full of doll heads, yet they and their two children managed.

One afternoon, a young nurse, pushing a baby carriage, came to their house. She told the father that the baby was a distant cousin of his, and that he was the only relative the little boy had. His parents were killed in an accident.

She told him, "There is formula in the bottles that should last over the weekend. The baby's papers, prescription for the formula, as well as the will and the insurance policy are under the mattress in an envelope."

Then she said she had to hurry off to catch the train to the city. And so she left the baby.

The man felt very sad for the little one who was all alone in the world. Neither he nor his wife had paid much attention to the young woman's talk. They were too concerned about what to do with this unexpected baby. The wife was not happy at all to have a baby in the house. She had been glad that their own two had survived the worst years. But, she was a good woman and cared for this one, too. Every once in a while the father came to look at the child. He didn't even know his name. He was actually a very pretty baby—blond, blue-eyed, with long eyelashes, pale and delicate. He was quiet and seemed to be no trouble. The wife, however, was concerned. The milk in the bottles would soon be gone. There was no one in the village nursing a baby at the time. No one had a cow, either. Only the old widow in the valley had a goat. Maybe she would give some milk for the little one.

Getting the milk was a hard battle. The old woman demanded vegetables. Her own children would have to go without good food. The baby drank the milk, but before he finished, he stopped to suck and started to cry. Even petting and patting didn't seem to quiet him. Finally, he fell asleep from exhaustion. Early in the morning he began to cry again. The wife got up and took the bottle with yesterday's milk. It was a bit thicker than yesterday. She added some water and shook it up and fed the baby. He drank eagerly, then released the nipple and started to cry again. The father came and asked what was wrong.

The wife said, "He doesn't like the milk. I guess he'll be happy to have it when he gets hungry enough."

It was Saturday, the day on which the father went to town. He was gone all day. When he came home, he went first to see how the baby was doing. He seemed to be sleeping. He had red cheeks. The father felt that the baby was getting used to being out in the country.

The next morning, Sunday, the wife said that she had to go to the old woman to get more milk. She packed potatoes and a cabbage into her bag and hoped it would satisfy the old witch. She also wondered how much longer she could afford to make these payments for a bottle of milk.

The father, working nearby, was surprised that the baby wasn't yelling for food. He picked him up out of the buggy. The baby's eyes seemed to shine more than before. He felt very warm, too. Maybe he had caught a cold.

The child drank very little of the goat's milk, and soon began to pull up his legs and cry. He was sick. The wife and the father carried him in their arms. The wife made a tea for the baby, but he wouldn't get better. The father thought of fetching the doctor, but how would he pay him. He hoped that the little one would soon get well again. And so they watched helplessly over him, as he got quieter. He fell asleep. He was very warm, but the wife said, "He'll sleep it off."

His wife went to bed, but the father sat by the buggy and rocked it gently. Some time later, he suddenly jumped. He had fallen asleep. He looked at the baby for a while. The child was too still. He touched the little cheek. It was not warm anymore. The baby wasn't moving, wasn't breathing. Why? Horrified, he realized the child was dead. He felt a heavy sadness enveloping him.

"Poor little child. You weren't loved enough. So beautiful, all alone without a mother or father and without even a name. I should have wrapped you in a blanket and taken you to the doctor, or taken you to the sisters at the convent. I would have done that for my own, I must confess now. It is my neglect that has caused you to die. Your death is on my head."

The priest came to the village for the funeral. He blessed the baby and called him Martin after his favorite saint. The father made a little wooden cross from a loose board of the fence. He painted "Martin" on it with doll head paint. The wife went to the creek and dug up some wild forget-me-nots and planted them into the formula bottles, which she set into the earth around the grave. The flowers were like the baby's eyes.

If only someone had been nursing, he could have grown up to be a fine young man, she thought.

The child had been with them no more than ten days, yet his absence was felt in the house that had gotten dark and sad and quiet. Even the children whispered, and both husband and wife worked in silence. Outside the late autumn weather had gotten cold and gray.

In December, the family closed doors and windows and stayed inside. It was very cold outside. The earth was frozen hard. No one went to the little grave. Soon it would be Christmas, and the parents were sad that they could not give presents to their children.

One evening, late, the father got up from his bed. He could not sleep. He went to the room that served as kitchen and workroom. He sat down by the fire, which had not quite gone out yet, and put some wood on it to revive the flames. He glanced to the side, where the baby carriage stood, and got up to look at it again. It was empty. The little pillow and the blanket were put into the coffin for the child. But the mattress was still in the buggy. The father picked it up. On the floor of the carriage lay a large envelope. He opened it. There were very fine papers in it. Surely they contained linen. Some elegantly written words were painted on them. There was a seal on one of them, and stamps and signatures. He tried to read what they said, but some of the words weren't even German, he thought they were probably Latin, and he didn't know the meaning of some of them that might have been in German.

"Anyhow, these things belonged to the baby, and he's gone. They are not my business. But, how very sad, this little one is dead, and all there is left to remember him by are these pieces of paper."

Staring at the ground, he once more saw the beautiful child's face, and he knew what he had to do. He tore up the papers and prepared them to use as papier-mâché. Through the night he worked by the light of the fire. His heart held the picture of the child before his eyes. His hands molded the papier-mâché. By daybreak the head was done. It was perfect. This would be a special doll's head. The texture was fine, and the face was not that of a pouting little girl, but that of a real baby.

He made sure that it dried well, and when he packed the basket with all of his week's work, he put the special one on top.

The factory owner picked up the baby doll head, went to the window and looked at it a long time. Then he turned to the father and asked, "Did you make this?" The father got nervous. Had he done something wrong? "Yes, I did, Sir."

"What made you do it?" the man wanted to know. The father told him about the baby who died, who looked so much like the little Christ child and now that it was nearly Christmas . . .

The factory owner said, "That's fine. I like it. You did it very well. And to show you that I also know that Christmas is nearly here, I'm going to give you another five marks for this one. And if you make more of them in the future, I will give you two more marks each week. That means that you will have seven marks each week. That is more than any one else is getting. But you know how it is. We have to keep this a secret. No one else should know that you are making baby doll heads. No one else could make them like this.

The father felt that he was walking in a dream. He had ten marks in his pocket, and would get seven each week from then on. He told his wife, "That little one has brought such good fortune to our home, may he sleep with the angels."

The factory owner said to his wife, "I received a treasure today. It will bring us a fortune, and at the same time make children happy all over the world."

A year after little Martin died, the first shipment of baby dolls arrived at the toy stores. The forget-me-nots on his little grave had gone to weed, and the name had washed off the rotting wooden cross.

As I was reading, I sometimes had to blink the tears out of my eyes. Even after I had finished reading, I couldn't fall asleep. I imagined how it would have been, had the father listened to the nurse, or even after the baby was dead, if he had waited for someone else to read the papers and he would have realized that he had inherited a lot of money from the insurance alone. I agonized over the needless death of the child, and the loss of the money. I wondered if we would have baby dolls if he hadn't died, and I also felt that the father was to blame in a way, even if he didn't mean any harm. When you don't do something you should do, it's almost as bad as doing something you shouldn't do.

In the morning I knew I was not ready to part with Erika's book. Not yet. I put it into the big sea chest that held linens and blankets we had gotten from friends and relatives, but didn't need. The chest was never opened by anyone else. On the way to school, Erika was waiting outside her building. She asked me how I liked the book. I didn't tell her that I had finished reading it last night. I said that I would bring it tomorrow. She smiled.

After school, I got the book out of the trunk and looked at it again. The cover was a very soft leather. The flowers had been burned in and painted on. I reread some sections and cried again. For the night, I put the book back into the trunk.

The weather was still mild and comfortable. The windows were open. The moon was shining. Into my dreams came a terrifying sound. A siren!

Mama, Papa, Oma scurried around in the moonlight.

"Don't turn on the lights, they'll see us. Come, children, we have to go to the basement, it's an air raid." The little ones cried. Rose Marie couldn't find her other shoe. Finally, already hearing the droning of the approaching planes, and the Flack, we stumbled down the stairs to the basement. The other families were already there. Then the noise started. It was like a terrible thunderstorm. The house vibrated. Plaster drizzled from the ceiling. The one light bulb flickered on and off. Planes, heavy ones, then fighters that came down in a whining scream . . . thunder and more thunder. How long it took I don't know. The all-clear siren finally sounded. As we went back upstairs, I saw out of the hall window that the sky was red. There were many, many fires.

Nearby there were ambulance sirens and people shouting.

Papa said, "Now it's begun here, too." He helped put the little ones to bed and said he had to go out to see if his help was needed.

The next morning I heard the news. The only building in the whole neighborhood that was hit was the one Erika lived in. She and her two brothers were still alive under the rubble. Papa was there to help clear it away. I had to go to school. As I walked by the giant mound of rubble that had been a building, I thought, *When I get back from school, you'll be out of there.*

My mind was on her, and I prayed to God to help her all day. But when I got back, she was still down there. The men were trying to get a tube through the rubble, so that the children could get some fresh air.

Papa didn't get back until we were already in bed. He told Mama and Oma, "We kept telling them not to cry, to be quiet, but they were so scared. When we finally got to them, oh, God, they were sitting on a bench. There was no rubble on them. They sat there, the girl in the middle. Their eyes were wide open, their hair was . . . so terrible. They had suffocated. I wouldn't let their mother see them. She beat against me, but I just held her. No mother should see and remember her children like that. I'm never going to forget those children's eyes."

In the darkness of my room, Erika's eyes came zooming down at me. They stayed there and stared at me. They were frightening. They had never looked like that before. And then, somewhere in the corner of my mind I knew the reason. It was the book! I should have given it back yesterday. If I had given it back, she wouldn't be dead now. It's just like in the book. It's my fault she died because I didn't do what I was supposed to do, and now all that is left is paper . . . her book.

"Erika, I can't let you be dead. I want you to be alive. I didn't know you were going to die. I just wanted to have the book a little longer. What is it that's so special about this book? It must be magic. I felt that right away." My heart started to beat loudly.

"What if they find out that I have the book and that you died because I had the book? But, nobody knows . . . Your grandmother knows . . . Will she remember? I could say that I gave it back. The whole house collapsed. They could think that it got lost in the rubble. And it's safe in the trunk. No one will look in there. But, what if it is bad magic? What if THEY kill people who have the book? Maybe THEY didn't know that I had it, and THEY could think that it still was at your house? And then THEY can't find it . . . and now THEY are going to keep on looking for it until THEY find it. Should I get rid of it? No, I can't, it's my only real thing from you. As long as I have it, you'll be near. I don't know what to do. But, I know that I'm not going to tear it up like the man in the story did. I'm going to keep it safe, and maybe it will be really great magic and you'll come alive again."

I didn't tell anyone. No one was even aware of the special friendship I had had with Erika. Oma might have known, but I don't think she connected the dead children with the girl whose album I had brought home. I wasn't allowed to bring anyone over, so they didn't know her. I just carried my grief and guilt around alone.

We had air raids at least once a night. More and more houses were hit. We children started a new fad, collecting bomb fragments. The more jagged they were, the better. We traded them. That was all very secret, not even our parents knew about it. Only Oma knew. She would examine them and tell me which ones were worth more than others. At school we were told never to touch anything that came from the planes because it was booby-trapped and would explode in our hands. But that was dumb. They had already exploded.

The strain of too little sleep and the constant fear of THEM being after me were getting me down. I was tired, but I didn't dare sleep. I would sit in the basement with my back against the wall and keep my eyes on the shadows in the hallway. Back there somewhere, Death was standing and watching me. He didn't move while I was watching, but if I didn't, he would come along the wall and get behind me, and if he touched me, I'd be dead. I kept track of the planes, too. They were circling. They were searching for the book. "Oh, God, don't let THEM find me. I promise I'll be very good. I'll do everything that I'm supposed to do."

But I wasn't good. I bought ice cream for Rosie and me from the change I had after running an errand for Papa. I said I dropped the money down a grating. Papa said I didn't have to lie; it was okay to have ice cream.

"You could have just told the truth. Why do you want to be bad?" I wished that he'd be mad, but he was sad, and that hurt more.

Herbie and I were at the market. I was buying plums. The bag, I knew, would be carefully folded, and I couldn't take one to eat on the way home. There were lots of plums on the market table. I took one. When the saleswoman gave me the bag, she noticed I had something in my hand.

"What have you got there? Show me!" she snarled. I opened my hand.

"Well, a little thief! Look at that. You should be ashamed of yourself. You're bad."

I put the plum back. She screamed, "No, you take it! You wanted it. You can have it. I don't want a stolen plum."

I took it and dropped it on the ground and stepped on it. It felt like a big, juicy bug. Its blood squirted everywhere.

"Oh," went the crowd, "Did you ever . . . look at that . . . how bad . . . at least she could have given it to the little one!"

It felt good to shock people. I liked being bad. It hurt and felt good at the same time.

The weather was getting colder. There were lines at the market. Sometimes they were very long. Mama and Oma and I took turns standing in line. The worst part of it was that sometimes there would be an air raid alert and we had to get to shelter and when we got back in line, it was a push and a scramble, and usually I got knocked out of my place and had to start all over again at the end of the line.

Some nights we would have two raids and get hardly any sleep at all. Papa started having night duty at Krupp, to be there in case of damage. I was even more scared on those nights when he was gone. Oma got tired of climbing the stairs up and down. She said, "I'm going to sleep in my bed. If they want to kill me, that's where I'm going to die." But when the planes were close, she came downstairs, too.

Oma generally knit down in the basement. The other ladies would play cards, sometimes.

They also told stories, "These people were all sitting in the basement like we are now. There was a lot of bombing, the house shook, and a tub that one of the women had used to bathe the baby was hanging on a hook by the stairs. It came loose and went bouncing down the stairs and somebody shouted, 'A bomb, a bomb,' and they all broke through the escape exit to the next house, and then they saw just a tub spinning around on the floor." The stories seemed very funny then.

One night I was dreaming that I had lost an earring under the bed, even though I didn't wear earrings then. I must have gotten out of bed and crawled under it. Mama and Papa were both trying to get me out, but I had to find my earring.

They said, "You can't hide there, come out." They kept on pleading with me to come out from under the bed, which I finally did do. Mama got all worried about me, and she was almost in tears.

"It's all right. There's no air raid now."

I said, "I know, but I lost my earring, and I have to find it." As I moved, I felt something on the floor. I suppose it was a toy. I knew it wasn't a bomb, but something made me pick up my feet, and I heard my voice scream.

"A bomb, there's a bomb!" It was as if that screaming person was someone else. And when I tried to stop, I seemed to have no control over my voice. It went on and on, screeching. My mind seemed to be outside of my body. I watched myself being held and soothed. I didn't feel anything. The noise went on.

I don't remember at all seeing a doctor, but in that or another afternoon I woke up. Mama was telling someone in the kitchen that the doctor said I was getting ill and I had to get away from here, out into the country.

Mama took Rose Marie and me to the big department store and bought both of us new winter coats. It was December 1940. The store was selling gifts for Christmas. At home, Mama baked lots of Christmas cookies and put them into a little suitcase. We got Mutter und Kind, a kind of Red Cross, tags to wear around our necks, giving our destination, and we were put on the train. We were going to spend some time with Tante Frida. We had cookies. Our baggage was in the back of the train.

I hadn't opened the trunk in our room since Erika died. The book remained behind. As the train left the station, Rosie said, "I hope you're not going to cry again like you did in the orphanage."

I told her, "I'm never going to cry again in my whole life, ever."

It was very cold as we got to Ellwangen. It was also very dark in the station. Tante Frida called "Rose Marie," and we found each other.

That same evening I already realized that she was afraid of me. What had Mama told her? She got terribly upset when I walked into the room and she didn't hear me, "Don't sneak around behind my back like that." She didn't say my name. She just said "you." She talked to me as if I didn't understand anything.

Luckily it didn't last long. Four days later, on a snowy Sunday afternoon, she packed me onto the train to Neresheim in the Schwaebischen Alb, an area rich in folklore and history, like the mountains like the American Appalachian country. I was being sent to Tante Marie and her husband, Josef. She stuck my train ticket, food card and I.D., a little money, and a new handkerchief into a little lizard-skin purse. That was her present to me.

Rosie was holding her hand, standing on the platform. She was smiling and waving to me as the train began to move. She didn't seem to need me.

*   *   *

6

EXILE IN A DIFFERENT WORLD

I started out on my journey working very hard to keep from crying, not only because I had to leave my little sister behind, but I felt unlovable and unwanted, different like the orange star.

The train ride to Aalen from Ellwangen was short and uneventful. There, I had to transfer. I had never done that without help, and did have to ask a grumpy conductor how to get to the platform for the next train, which came along shortly after that, huffing and puffing. The locomotive was small. A big bell, which the engineer rang when the train went around curves or when it entered wooded areas, was mounted on top of the cab. This, then, was the legendary *schwaebische Eisenbahn*, about which a folk song was written.

Most of the ride was uphill. We went so slowly that some of the young soldiers, going home on furlough, would jump off and run along the side and get back on. Although I ached with self-pity, it was a cheerful and amusing ride. The boys were nice and teasing at the same time.

"Look at the young lady. Where do you think she's going with that elegant handbag?"

"Oh, don't you know, she's the princess going home to her castle in the mountains."

"Oh, lovely lady, may I kiss your hand?"

"Come on, look, she's embarrassed. Leave the kid alone," said the nicest one.

I looked out of the open window. It was very cold, but I didn't know how to close it, but I was wearing my winter coat, a cap, and gloves. The snow was sparkling, blindingly white. The train cut through forests of trees heavy with snow. There was an incredibly fresh, cold quality to the air. Then I remembered Erika. She didn't have enough air . . . I saw her smiling face once more, and I then realized that I didn't even know if there was a funeral, or where she is buried. I told myself, "She's dead, but I know she's not gone, it's just that I can't see her."

The sun was low on the horizon as we pulled into Neresheim. I got off the train, wondering how I would know Tante Marie and Onkel Josef. It wasn't difficult. They found me. They stood in the snow, quiet and almost shy. There was an aura of simple goodness and gentleness about them. Perhaps it was the background of the sparkling snow and the long rays of rose-colored light that surrounded them, but I sensed the hand of my guardian angel on my head. And I felt very small and tired, and was so grateful to the very soft-spoken gentleman, who smiled and told me that they had brought a sled because Ohmenheim was four kilometers from Neresheim, "too far for a child to walk."

I was bundled into a heavy wool blanket and tucked in like a baby. Tante Marie fussed over me, brushing my hair back into the wool cap, stroking my cheek. They didn't seem to know about me. They treated me like a nice little girl. Onkel Josef pulled the sled, and Tante Marie hovered around me, smiling, patting my head.

With this sled ride I began the richest phase of my childhood in a world far removed from war, a time and place to which memories draw me for a sense of stability, tranquility, and strength.

Ohmenheim was up another hill along a road that was well traveled because it led to Noerdlingen. There were about four hundred inhabitants in the village. At the top of the hill stood the Catholic church with its cemetery and the rectory, surrounded by a beautiful flower garden, now covered in snow. The school was across the street. It would soon be shaded by huge chestnut trees. Down the street I could see several large farmhouses. On a very small side street, down an unpaved, steep hill, sat Onkel Josef's house. It was the oldest house in the village, more than two hundred years old, and really very small. On the ground floor, at the end of a dark corridor, was a very, very tiny kitchen. To the right of the front door was the entrance to the dining-living room. Straight ahead of the door were the stairs to the bedroom, which was built under the eves, a lot like an attic. Inside the basic room, where I spent all of my time when I was in the house, stood a beautiful, blue, tiled hearth, in which we baked apples with cinnamon and cloves that gave the house a very pleasant aroma, and it tasted good, too. The eating corner was very typical of southern Germany, a wooden bench along both walls in the corner, and before it, the table. The two windows facing the road were small, set into a thick wall. The other furniture in the room was completely out of place in this house: a very elegant red velvet sofa with tightly stuffed cushions that made you slide off if you didn't sit back, and against the back wall of the room stood an exquisite, ornate china closet filled with porcelain cups and a variety of lovely china objects. They had been Onkel Josef's mother's trousseau, surely never ever used in this house.

Onkel Josef also had an old Bible with many names of people in his family recorded in it . . . when they were born, were baptized, got married, died . . . The Bible had some really frightening pictures I looked at with fascination when I was alone. Once, when I was looking at it, Tante Marie caught me and took it away, saying, "That's not anything for children."

They had an absolutely wild cat who resented me. She would lay in wait for me. Once she sat on the stairs, and as I went by, she swiped at my face. Another time, she literally stalked me. Luckily, I had a big spoon in my hand and I was able to give her a good whack on the head, so she backed off.

I had arrived at the beginning of Christmas vacation, and spent most of it visiting Onkel Josef's relatives around the area. Everywhere we went, we were served a kind of pizza-like pie with lots of onions on top.

On Christmas Eve we went to the old church on the hill. It was not ornately decorated, but had a fine organ. As we entered, we were given a lit candle, which was wound into a snail house-shape container and could be unwound as the wax melted. The candles were made of bees' wax and gave off a nice, sweet fragrance. The only light in the church was candle light, which, to me, created a dreamy, peaceful world. The community sang an old Gregorian chant in Latin, and Christmas songs one from the Middle Ages, "*Es ist ein Ros entsprungen.*" My experience with religious ceremonies had been very limited, and that may be the reason why I was so impressed by it all. I felt that I was a part of a great concert and God was listening to us.

We walked home in crunching snow, the sound of the organ and the minor key melodies still echoing in my thoughts. As we approached the house, Onkel Josef went ahead of Tante Marie and me to turn on the lights. We entered the house, the living room, or *Stube*, as it's called in that part of the world, and there, on the table was a very big box. It was my Christmas box from home. Among many nice things, including mittens and a cap and a sweater, knit by Oma, was a beautiful doll, exactly the way I would like her to be. She had dark, curly hair, blue eyes, said "Mama," had a nice soft body, and pretty clothes. She sat on the sofa during the day to be admired by visitors and slept with me on that same sofa at night. The cat slept on the floor under the sofa. I felt a little uneasy about that, but since the spoon episode she didn't really bother me any more.

I can't recall thinking very deeply about anything during those days. Everything about me seemed to be resting—body, mind, and emotions.

School began, and I entered a new world. There was one teacher for all of the children in the village. He divided the classes between two classrooms. The first graders were in one room and the rest of us, grades two to eight, were in the other. Herr Eisenbart (Ironbeard) was a very strict man. He wore riding pants, boots, and a jacket with leather on the elbows every day. He also carried the pointer under his arm, as if it were a riding crop. He used it to whack lazy or inattentive students, as well as for pointing out things on the board or map. He marched up and down the aisles, giving commands, asking questions, pausing to see what we had written on our little slates.

We had arithmetic first, every morning, because that was when your mind was sharp. Each level had their own work, but I could learn what the older students were doing, too, because he explained it at the board. He dictated problems for addition, subtraction, multiplication, and then went to the next group and let them read, or whatever. He said it was good training for us to have to concentrate on our work while other things were going on around us because that was the real world.

He would give each group an assignment and choose one of the students, not always the oldest, but the one who was best at whatever subject we were working on, to be in charge while he went to be with the first graders. And when he was with us, he would send three of us to be with the little ones. If our work had to do with reading, I was always sent as one of the three, because he knew that I could read. School was really fun.

Every day was exciting and different. Herr Eisenbart always knew what he was doing and was so well organized. He remembered where each class had stopped the day before and went on. Sometimes his little five-year-old son would come down from upstairs. Mr. Eisenbart let him sit with me.

As in all German schools, even in Hitler's time, we had regular instruction in religion. In the cities, one would choose either Catholic or Lutheran. Villages were almost always either Catholic or Lutheran. This village was Catholic. Since my grade was getting ready for First Communion, we had special lessons. These classes were held in the priest's home, the rectory. We heard some of the more pleasant Bible stories, and learned the Ten Commandments and about sins.

Although I thought it had been a cold winter, the natives didn't. They said it was mild and knew that we would have an early spring. One Sunday during that early spring, Onkel Josef, Tante Marie, and I took a walk. We went to some wooded area in the direction of Neresheim. When we got to a clearing, we stopped by a huge, old tree. It had a bee's nest in it, a big one! Onkel Josef told me that this oak tree was hundreds of years old and had seen a lot of history. We walked ahead towards a rocky area, which was a heath. There were sheep grazing. I noticed many soft indentations in the field. Onkel Josef said that people believe that those indentations were made by cannonballs exploding during the Thirty Years War, which was fought here. However, they are more likely sinkholes, as we've learned through geological studies.

In the distance I saw a very big yellow building. "You see that? That's the abbey. Monks live there. I work for them. I have a span of horses and plow and do many other things. Tante Marie also works for them. She works in the fields. Someday she will take you over there and you will go into the chapel and look at the painting done by a very famous man named Martin Knoller. It shows Jesus when he was a boy and he was preaching in the temple. You can see that the people around him didn't quite know what they should think about this boy."

There was a special reason for this tour. Onkel Josef explained many things to me because he was drafted into the army and had to leave. He was forty-seven years old and completely deaf in one ear. He was being sent to the East. Mountain people could stand the cold more than the city folk, and he knew how to take care of horses.

The morning he left, I watched him walk slowly up the hill to the main street. Everything looked gray as if the color had been washed out of the world, and I knew that I would never see him again. I didn't know anything about the progress of the war. No one in that house listened to a radio or read a newspaper, and even if they had done so, I wouldn't have been interested. Battles had nothing to do with me. But I had learned about death, and I knew that this gentle man would die.

Soon after I was left alone with my Tante Marie, I realized that she was not capable of taking care of me. She was sweet and loving, but I knew more about what we needed than she did. I didn't realize it, of course, but others in the village were also concerned about my welfare.

It was a warm day. Tante Marie was working in the fields, and I had picked some raspberries. I was sitting on the bench in the little garden in front of the house. I felt lonely and remembered the previous year and the summer at Tante Sofie's. I had a bowl in my lap and began to squeeze the berries through my fingers to make raspberry syrup. My hands were red with the juice of the berries. While I was occupied with my production, the priest came walking down the hill. He nodded to me, then stopped dead in his track. He crossed himself and came running up to me.

"Oh, dear child, don't worry. It's not so bad. We'll fix it."

I didn't know what to say to him. I didn't know what he was talking about. Then I realized that he thought I had blood on my hands. I was embarrassed for him. He was a proud man, but I had to tell him that it was only raspberry juice.

He was noticeably annoyed with me. "These things wouldn't happen if you were properly supervised," he growled.

On the next school day, Herr Eisenbart told me that the priest had talked to him, and had said that I could stay at the rectory. His sister was his housekeeper, and they had plenty of room. At first I was seriously tempted. The priest's house was beautiful with white starched tablecloths and long lace curtains at the windows, roses in the garden, and lots and lots of books in the library. But some of my schoolmates said, "Are you crazy to live in a priest's house? You'd have to go to every single Mass every day. You couldn't laugh or ever have any fun . . . just pray all the time."

When I was asked, I hedged around, saying that I would hurt my aunt's feelings and I'd rather stay with her.

The priest was offended, and I was soon sorry I had turned down his offer because I was just not up to taking care of myself. I couldn't even get the stove lit, much less know how to cook anything. There was nothing to eat, anyway. The mother of some of my classmates asked me to have lunch with them almost on a regular basis. Tante Marie was always at work. I accepted because I was hungry and lonely, but I felt a little uncomfortable and never quite knew when I should leave and go to Tante Marie's cold and dark house.

I told Herr Eisenbart that I had changed my mind. But he said that they all had second thoughts about it, too.

"A rectory is not a place for a child. I think we can find something more suitable for you."

It was Frau Eisenbart who came to pick me up and who took me to the blacksmith's home, Saturday, midmorning. She spoke calmly but convincingly to Tante Marie. Marie was sad to be alone. She wanted to keep my doll so that I would come to visit her, but Frau Eisenbart said, "That was a present from her Mama. She's so far away from home. Don't you think we should let her have the doll near her?"

While this conversation was going on, I realized that my aunt didn't talk like a grown-up. She sounded like a child. She was somewhat "simple minded." Tante Frida knew all of that, but she sent me to her because she thought that I was "not quite right" either! Her rejection of me was now even more hurtful, but in some strange way it made me feel protective towards Tante Marie, and I promised her that I would come to see her every weekend, and we left.

I carried the doll, and Frau Eisenbart carried my suitcase. It had rained. The unpaved road from Tante Marie's up to the highway was muddy and messy. As we got to the main street, which was paved, the sun shone on the puddles and threw off sparks of light. The world had a shiny, newly washed look about it.

The school and church were to the left of us. We walked the other way, past the big farm house where Irma, the only other girl my age, lived. I had never been in that part of the village and looked, for the first time, at several other farms, the Gasthaus and bakery on the other side of the street, and at the bottom of the hill, on the corner, a small farm house and next to it, the smithy.

Although the house and the smithy were also eighteenth-century vintage, the house had undergone some modernization. The living room had four large windows, two looking out to the street, and the other two facing the garden. As in most of the farmhouses in southern Germany at that time, the cows' stable, followed by the barn, were all under the same roof as the living quarters. The pig and the chickens were housed in another smaller building across the yard. The smithy was a separate building.

Frau Eisenbart opened the fence gate, and we entered the yard. The front door of the house was massive dark wood. She knocked, and a smiling lady opened the door, Frau Mack, who became Tante Lene to me.

I don't remember what was said between the two women, I was so interested in the house, and before I realized it, Frau Eisenbart had left, and Tante Lene was showing me around. The first thing I noticed was that the floor of the hallway was made up of large stone tiles, which were worn down where people had walked a lot. A very big, dark wooden chest stood in the hall. To the left was the light and sunny living room. I liked the lace curtains and plants on the windowsills. The room was furnished quite simply with a beige corduroy-covered sofa, a buffet, on which stood a radio and a clock, and some kind of cactus in an earthen pot. All of those things, of course, were set on an embroidered doily. On the wall between the two street-side windows hung a crucifix and a picture of Mary and Baby Jesus. The dining area was a wooden booth, large enough for six people. Around the three sides of the hearth, which was tiled in green, was a bench, with nice, soft cushions. There was one large braided rug on a shiny wooden floor, and in the corner by the door, a china cabinet, which did not hold anywhere near as many items as Tante Marie's did.

The master bedroom was across the hall. Again I saw massive, dark furniture that matched the chest out in the hall. Continuing along, next to that bedroom was my room. It was furnished with a bed, and a small wardrobe. There was also a door that led to the barn and the cows. Herr Mack walked through every morning, but he never woke me.

Across from my room was the kitchen, which also was large enough for a long table and several other things one has in a kitchen, including the stove and sink, of course. We had normal tap water, no pumps to prime, but the stove, which really was quite large, did require wood and coal.

By the time I had finished the tour and put my few things into the wardrobe, it was time for lunch. I helped set the table. There was such an ease between Tante Lene and I, as if we had known each other for a long time. Herr Mack came into the room just as everything was ready. He was large and walked with a heavy gait. His hair was white, and he had bushy white eyebrows and a mustache. He reminded me of a Santa Claus without a beard. He sat down on the opposite side of the table, looked at me and smiled in a man's kind of way, and said, "So, here you are. Tell me about yourself."

I started to tell him my name, age, that I had a brother and sisters, that I was born in America and lived there until I was seven, and that we now live in Essen, and that if I were in America I would be in fourth grade, but now I'm just in second, but I like the school here because I can learn more than just second grade stuff.

He was eating, but looked up when I stopped talking, and asked, "So, why did they send you away?"

Totally unprepared for that question, I could only say that I was very tired, and the doctor said I had to get out of the city and into the country.

Tante Lene put me at ease again.

"That's enough for today. You'd better eat before your food gets cold."

That afternoon, I learned not to be afraid of the cows, and walked between them to put feed into the trough for them. I also learned what kind of fruit trees were in the yard, and visited the smithy, which faced the street at the bottom of the hill. It was built into the hill. A corner of the orchard grew on top of the smithy.

That evening, as we were getting ready to go to sleep, I saw how long and beautiful Tante Lene's hair was. During the day, she wore it in a braid, then twisted it into a bun at the back of her head and held it there with big hairpins. In the evening, she let it loose, and it was like a cape all the way down to her knees. She never had her hair cut. It was a beautiful golden red color. She was really pretty. I didn't know how old she was then, but I knew she was older than Mama, but not as old as Oma, and she was quite a bit younger than Herr Mack. You could tell that on their wedding picture. He was a widower and had a son when they got married. His son was in the army now, but he was married and lived in a city somewhere.

I liked my room. The bed was very comfortable. It was actually a large sack of straw in a wooden box. I had flannel sheets, a feather bed cover and a wonderful, big, soft pillow. When I sat up in bed, I could look out of the window and see what was going on in the street. Down at the tavern on the corner across the street, I saw lights in the windows of the tavern and in front of the tavern door, too. It occurred to me that people didn't have blackout curtains in this village.

I reviewed the happenings of the day, and I remembered especially what Herr Mack had asked me. "So, why did they send you away?" I didn't know that I was not the only child in the world to be sent out into the country. I thought I was sent away because Erika died, even though I didn't think that anyone really knew what happened. It was all mixed up in my mind.

The truth, of course, is that many children in Germany, as well as in England, France, perhaps other countries, too, where there was war, were being sent out into the country to strangers. Many of those children were much younger than I was, and often the families didn't even know exactly where they would end up. Sometimes the families of those children would die in an air raid, or their house would be bombed, and they would have to move, and the children lost track of them. Some children from the German cities were sent to camps in East German areas, and as the Russians advanced, they had to flee and had no place to go and no one to look after them.

Of course, I should have realized that when I got a tag to hang around my neck, it hadn't been printed just for me. My thoughts wandered a bit longer, and I got situated just so, hugged my doll, which would sleep with me, and thought about Rose Marie and wondered if she had gotten a doll, too. And I thought about Essen, and our room, and the sea chest, and wondered if anyone had found the book. I tried to remember exactly what Herbie and Hannelore looked like, and was sorry that I didn't even have any photo of my family. I felt a little guilty about Tante Marie, but I told myself that she was without me all of her life, and anyhow, I would visit her either Saturday or Sunday.

When I remembered Onkel Josef, I just felt sad, as if he were already dead.

Tante Lene and I got along very well together. She never told me that I had to do anything, but I wanted to, and she let me experiment and try everything. She was unbelievably patient and good natured. I enjoyed being with her. She was a friend. I seldom thought about my own home, and tried to avoid all thoughts of Erika or the book and my guilt. Here I was an only child, and the only person I had to concern myself with. Just sometimes, when I was alone for a while, and I was playing with my doll, I would think about Rose Marie, who was with Tante Frida, all alone and much younger than I. And I would feel sad for Herbie and Hannelore being in Essen. I felt a little guilty that I was here, where there never was an air raid, but I didn't want to go back. I was really afraid to think about Erika. My heart would start pounding, and I would push thoughts of her away.

One of the two cows in the stable had a calf. I thought it was a truly beautiful little animal. Tante Lene gave me some milk that she said was very special and very, very healthy. I think it tasted rather sweet. When the calf was old enough to eat regular feed, it was sold to another farmer. I was sad, and so was the cow, and the calf. Both of them called to each other as the baby was taken away in a truck. Tante Lene explained to me that they didn't have room for another animal, and that the calf would be happy on the big farm, where it could play outside in the pasture with the other calves. Then she showed me a sack, and said that the farmer left something for me. She opened the sack, and out came a little fuzzy gray kitten. I called her "Muschi." Herr Mack was not really too crazy about having a cat.

He said, "At least it should have been a dog, but I guess girls like cats."

Muschi slept on the rug in the living room during the day. When Herr Mack sat and read the paper, she played with his shoelaces. He would look down at her and smile and shake his head, and go on reading. She roamed around all night in the barn or up in the attic, and when Herr Mack went to feed the cows in the morning, she came in, and when I woke up, she was sleeping on the feather bed, exactly where my feet were. I felt very well and a bit spoiled because both Tante Lene and Herr Mack were always nice, and I got not only their attention, but a lot of praise and affection. There was a routine to our days, and they never got angry with each other or with me, either. Sometimes I wondered why God was being so nice to me, I wasn't even good. Erika was so good, and she was dead.

I actually looked forward to being in school, mostly because Herr Eisenbart was the teacher. We really worked all the time, but it didn't seem like dull school work because he knew everything, and he did things so differently than my other teachers had done. He rigged up a telephone in our classroom, and all of the kids got to talk to his wife, who was upstairs. They had never talked on a phone before. There were only three telephones in the village. The priest, the teacher, and the mayor, who also owned the grocery store, had a phone. If anyone in the village had to call someone, or if they received a call, one of those three gentlemen would take care of it. There was no police, or fire department, or even a doctor in the village.

One time, Herr Eisenbart told us that the next day the inspector would be coming to see if we had learned anything. He moved some of our seats. When the man was there to observe, Herr Eisenbart called on all of the people who would know the answers to his questions. The inspector said that we were very bright, and Herr Eisenbart was very happy, although he didn't say anything to us, not even that we had been good.

My favorite activity in school was story reading. But I would get bored waiting for others to drag through the words and sentences and I would read ahead, and then when I was to read, I had to find my place. Then he would look at me and say, "Slow down! Don't show off!"

We didn't have much homework because most of the kids had to help on the farm right after school. Sometimes I would play with Irma, but most of the time I would go home quickly to be with Tante Lene. I liked to go out into the fields with her and help however I could. At times we did things around the house.

At other times I would go to the smithy and watch Herr Mack. That was great fun. The walls of the smithy were very thick. On them were lots of hooks and nails. Different iron things were hanging from them: horse shoes, iron rims for wheels, brackets, and many odd shapes to be put on wagons or other machinery. There was only one small window, way up. The front of the building had a double door, which was always open when the smith was working. There was a coal fire in something that looked like a big BBQ pit. To keep the coals hot, you had to step on the bellows. Herr Mack let me do that. I liked to see him shape the iron that had gotten red hot in the coals. He hit it with a hammer on the anvil. It sounded like a bell. Sparks flew off. After he had beaten it into shape, he took it from the anvil with the tongs he had been holding it with and dipped the piece into a bucket of water. There was a loud "tsh" and a cloud of steam rose from the bucket. While he was working, his shadow moved very large on the wall, since the source of light was the fire. Herr Mack said that it was too bad that I was a girl because girls can't be blacksmiths.

"You have to be very strong to do this kind of work," he said.

There was a watering trough on the corner outside of the smithy. I watched Herr Mack shoe a horse. When the hot horseshoe is put on, it melts the hoof bottom a little so that the shoe fits perfectly. Melting hooves smell bad. I walked over to the watering trough, and there at the bottom lay a small pocket knife with a mother-of-pearl handle. Herr Mack said, "Finders, keepers. You found it, it's yours."

Tante Lene didn't think a little girl should have a knife, but Herr Mack said, "You worry too much," and he brought me some wood and said I could make something out of it. But nothing I tried ever looked like what I had wanted to make. Carving wood is not easy.

During these months, while I was learning to be a new person in a wonderful and safe world, I heard, but very passively, some of the news on the radio. Herr Mack also received a letter from his son, who was in Greece. Mama wrote a letter to Tante Marie in which she told her that our cousin Heinz was a paratrooper, and Alois, who was in the Navy, had been in the Mediterranean on a ship, which was sunk by the British. He was rescued by them, and as they were sailing back to England, the Germans sank that ship, and he's back in the German Navy, having gone through two ships sinking without ever touching land. She also said that every other person in the service from the family was on the Eastern front—Tante Frida's husband Josef; Tante Marie's husband (of course, we knew that). So was Tante Sofie's son . . . also called Josef.

Herr Mack had a lot of old friends who came by in the mornings. They talked about the First World War, when they were soldiers. Herr Mack said that he's so glad that his son is not going to Russia because he knows what that is. At these times, seeing all of these old men, I realized that there weren't any young men in the village at all. Herr Eisenbart was the youngest, and he was older than my father.

The months went by, summer was over, and the quieter time was approaching. The village calendar was divided into agricultural seasons and highlighted by religious holidays. At the end of harvest time, we made a pretty bouquet of grain stalks and field-flowers and took it to the church to be blessed. It was hung on the wall to give thanks for the harvest, and to ask for a good one next year. As December approached, Tante Lene and I made an Advent wreath with fresh pine branches. We baked Christmas cookies together. I got to cut them out.

Friday evening, early in December, as we were taking the laundry from the lines, Tante Lene said, "See the sky, how red it is? The angels are baking cookies, too. It will snow tonight. I know because when ever it's going to snow, my old frostbite itches."

It snowed and got very cold. The whole weekend we were indoors. Monday morning, a friend of Herr Mack came into the living room with a newspaper.

"Look, the Americans are in the war, too, now. Those stupid Japanese started it, but you know that was all foreseen. America had to get into it somehow, some time. It's just a matter of time until there will be a declaration and we'll be fighting them, and the rest of the world. We're going to lose this one, too. When they get in, there's no chance for us. But, thank God, they didn't wait till the last minute, the way they did last time. Now maybe this thing will be over soon and we can go back to normal life."

Herr Mack said, "What do you mean, normal life? How do you have a normal life when you lose a war? You don't remember any more. In the attic I have a box of money from that normal life time after the last war. No, believe me, it won't be so easy. We can never live normal lives. They won't let us. And this won't be over soon, either. Our brothers in Berlin will hold on to the end and go out in a Wagnerian . . . *Götterdämmerung*

All it means is that more boys will be killed, more cities will be destroyed, more suffering for half of the world."

The war was so far away. I hadn't heard a siren since I came to Ohmenheim a year ago. I picked up my doll, and went to one of the windows while the men were talking. There were ice flowers on the windowpane. I remembered Milwaukee and Miss Smith, the schoolroom and the song we sang every morning: "My Country 'tis of Thee, sweet Land of Liberty . . . . Land where my Fathers died . . ." that line always bothered me. None of my Fathers had died there . . ."Land of the Pilgrims' Pride . . . those people, who wore black shoes with silver buckles . . . corn on the cob, pumpkins, turkeys, Indians . . ."

I didn't understand. How could Americans be enemies? They're regular people like us. This is wrong, they shouldn't be on the bad side, they should be our friends.

As I was thinking about these things, I realized that I had forgotten English. Since when? It seems that it was when I was so tired. I forgot what happened after I was so hysterical that night. I don't even know how long I was sleeping before I heard my mother in the kitchen telling someone about the doctor.

Somebody once said that you don't really forget languages you knew. Onkel Berthold said he really forgot Russian, but when he had an operation, he was speaking Russian when he was coming out of the anesthesia, but then he forgot it again. Maybe if I practice, I'll remember again.

I tried to name things in the room, but all I could think of were the German names. I tried to remember events. I could do that. There was a night when Papa and I were walking home. It was very dark out, but the sky was full of stars. I thought they were on the ceiling of the world. Papa said we were on the outside of the earth and all of those stars were like the sun, but very far away.

I remembered the Fourth of July. The whole school was at a big picnic at the park. Mrs. Smith gave her whole class boxes of Cracker Jacks (caramel covered popcorn), and we got Dixie Cups with vanilla ice cream, and when it got dark, we were lying down in the grass, and there were wonderful fireworks. I knew we were speaking English then. Why couldn't I remember any of the words? It wasn't so long ago. I had only been in Germany two years, but so many things happened since then. Before I dismissed this problem, I realized that I did remember words to songs. I knew the words to "My Country 'Tis of Thee," "Three little Fishies," "When it's Springtime in the Rockies," I even remembered that silly thing I learned on the ship about seeing London and France . . .

Christmas 1941 came and went. We had a lovely tree in the living room. I don't think we went to Midnight Mass, and I'm not even sure that I received gifts. I don't remember any. It must have been uneventful. I do remember spending one of the afternoons with Tante Marie, though. She said that a young woman, who was a refugee, would be coming to live with her. That was welcome news for me. Now I wouldn't have to feel guilty for having left her.

As uneventful as Christmas was, New Year's Eve was unforgettable. In the middle of the night I heard very loud cannon fire. I sat up in bed, terrified. I thought THEY had found me. Tante Lene came to my room in her nightgown and told me not to be afraid: "The old men are welcoming in the new year." It was now 1942.

On the sixth of January, Tante Lene and I went to church with a cup of salt and a piece of chalk. They were blessed. When we got home, she wrote over the door 19-B-L-M-42. Now the house was blessed by the Three Holy Kings. The salt was blessed to keep us healthy for another year. It didn't help Herr Mack, though. He looked really fine, but sometimes he would faint, and he also had a sore on his foot. The priest's sister brought a salve that she made from Marigolds, but it didn't heal that sore.

In February we had a blizzard. There was so much snow that no mail truck could get into the village. The people had a snowplow made of wood, a V-shaped contraption, with boards across it, on which every young person in the village sat. It was pulled by three teams of horses. It did pile the snow up on the sides of the road. We built igloos. The older kids, teenagers actually, built castles with stairways and towers. It was a fun time. No one did any work except to feed the animals and change the straw in the stalls.

Russia, too, had the worst winter it had in thirty years. German soldiers were freezing. They had won so much ground, but they were not issued winter clothing. It seemed to me that the war was getting harder to fight, and some of Herr Mack's friends started telling jokes about Hitler and Goering. They didn't like those two very much.

On Ash Wednesday we got ashes on our foreheads, and our throats were blessed with crossed candles so that you don't get fish bones stuck. Nobody in Ohmenheim ate fish. I got a sore throat once, and Tante Lene boiled potatoes and put them into a stocking, mashed them a little so they would be more flexible, and wrapped the stocking around my neck. It felt hot for a long time. My throat got better.

Herr Mack got so ill that he was lying in a hospital bed in the living room. He had lots of company. He was very popular, especially among the older men in the village. But, he had to go to the hospital. The doctors told Tante Lene that he had diabetes and they wanted to cut off his leg because it had gangrene in it. Herr Mack said he wanted to die because he couldn't be a smith with one leg.

He was put on a special diet at the hospital. He asked Tante Lene to make him his favorite cake. Tante Lene talked to the old neighbor lady, who said, "Give a dying man his wish." We baked the cake together: flour, butter, eggs, SUGAR . . . In German, diabetes is called sugarsickness. I wanted to ask Tante Lene if Herr Mack was supposed to have sugar, or not, but I didn't. When the cake was done, Tante Lene wrapped it into a special small table cloth that she got out of the big chest in the hall. Then she put it into her bag. She said she might stay the whole night at the hospital.

"If I'm not home by sunset, feed the cows, milk them, and close the chicken coop."

She came back before it was dark. She stopped to talk to the neighbor: "We ate the whole cake together and had a nice long talk about our life together. Then he told me he was tired, and I should go home."

Early the next morning, the priest came to the house. He had a telephone call from the hospital. Herr Mack had died last night in his sleep.

The earth was still hard from the cold. Herr Mack had died early Friday. The funeral was on Sunday. Many relatives came from the neighboring villages. The whole family went to the Gasthaus after the funeral. We sat at a long table. Tante Lene's family sat on one side, and Herr Mack's family sat on the other side. They talked about what she should do . . . close the smithy . . . the mayor could advertise for another blacksmith, but there probably won't be any . . . the property is hers, and from her it will go to Josef, Herr Mack's son, the one who was in Greece. We drank cider or beer and ate ham that was baked inside of a large loaf of bread. They only made it like that for funeral meals.

The saying was that if someone dies on Friday, he takes two others with him. A young refugee woman, who lived upstairs in one of the houses near the school, had a baby that died. Some of the girls from school went to see the baby. I went alone. I walked up the stairs and knocked on the door. A pale, young woman, dressed in black, opened the door. I didn't know what to say and nearly ran away, but she said, "You came to see my baby. Come in." I stepped into the room. The shutters were pulled shut, and two little heart-shaped cutouts let some light into the room. Two large candles flickered near the little white coffin. The baby looked like a doll with yellow skin. His blond head was on a white satin pillow, and he was covered with a white satin blanket. Crepe paper and white lilies were tucked into the corners. They looked horrible.

"Go ahead, you can touch him," she said.

I let my fingers glide over one of the little fists. It was hard and cold. Such a pretty baby, like the baby in Erika's book, like Herbie was when he was little. If Herbie had died, he would have been hard and cold like this, too. Erika and her brothers were . . .

The room smelled stuffy and sickeningly sharp and sweet. The young mother sat in a chair near the window. Next to her was a table. On the table was a picture of a handsome young man in an officer's uniform. There was a black ribbon across the corner and a medal hanging down from it. A wave of sorrow swept over me. I was gasping for air. I felt that I was drowning in my own tears. I ran to her, and, kneeling on the floor, I put my arms around her waist and buried my head in her lap. She stroked my hair. All I could manage through my tears was, "I'm sorry. I'm so sorry."

She looked so thin, so sad, so alone as I left. I never saw her again.

The daughter of the farmer across from the Gasthaus died. She had gotten cut out in the field. She died of lock jaw. We didn't see her body.

When it was still quite cold, the pig was butchered. Tante Lene's relatives came to help. The butcher came early in the morning and tied the pig up to the fence post. The pig was squealing. It was scared because it had never been out there before. The butcher stroked the pig to quiet it down, then, in a flash, with the broad side of an ax, he hit it on the forehead. It made no sound. It just fell over. Then one of the relatives ran over to him with a very large metal bowl. The butcher stabbed the pig in the chest. Blood gushed out into the bowl. The butcher was kneeling on the ground, and the pig's head was on his lap. I felt sad that the pig had to die, but I also thought that the butcher killed the pig, but not in a mean way. I also realized that I couldn't stand to see what would surely have to happen next. I turned away and went to school. I didn't feel very well that day. I had fed that pig many times and always felt sorry for it being in a small stall all by itself, just getting big and fat to be killed.

When I got back from school at noon, there were large kettles cooking on the kitchen stove. The family was making sausages, rending the lard, pickling the feet and ears of the pig. The bladder was inflated like a balloon. I guess that was to show that the pig was healthy. Big pieces of meat were put on hooks and hung into the chimney. Special pine and other wood branches were fed into the stove to get the first smoking of the meat just right. All of that work took several days. We were eating many of the things that couldn't be kept long. I didn't like the clear gelatin that the pig's knuckles were in. I didn't want to eat anything that was obviously from that pig, especially not that. It looked like slime, and it wiggled, but we had to eat it, or else it would spoil.

Perhaps it did spoil because I got very sick to my stomach and threw up all over my bed. Tante Lene fixed a bed on the rug near the hearth in the living room for me. She was still tucking me in when there was a loud knock on the door and men's voices were heard: "Open up immediately." Tante Lene went to the door.

I was sure that THEY, the enemy, were here at last. I sat up and waited for the end.

"We have information that you are harboring an American."

That's me, I realized. My heart was beating so hard, I could barely hear what else was being said. I waited, my eyes closed.

Tante Lene acted amazed. "An American? Here? That's news to me. If there's an American here, you better find him. I'm alone with this child. I certainly don't need any enemy around here."

"We have to search the premises," one of them said. Then he gave orders to some of the men with him to search the house and the stable and barn. And then he came into the room. He had on a black uniform, and he looked very tall.

"Why are you up at this time?" he demanded.

"She got sick. We just butchered a few days ago, and something didn't agree with her. I was just putting her to sleep here."

"Is this your child?"

"No, she is from Essen. She was sent with Mutter und Kind, I have her papers." Tante Lene went to her bedroom and produced the documents from the organization, as well as my ration cards.

"You understand, we have to investigate these reports," he said. "Come here, child."

I went to him. Perhaps he noticed how frightened I was. He looked at my face for a while. I didn't want him to look into my eyes because he might see the orange star. He looked at Tante Lene and then back at me and asked me how old I was. I told him. He asked why my hair was short when all of the girls around there have long braids.

Tante Lene said, "Because she is from a big city. She's not a village child."

I was wearing an undershirt and panties. He had been stooped down, so that his face was near mine. With his index finger, he pulled on the elastic of my panty and looked in . . . to check if I really was a girl. Then he told me to get back under the covers. Was I safe?

The men still walked through the house, up into the attic, the stalls and the barn.

Finally, the same voice said, "Sorry to have disturbed you," to Tante Lene, and they left. We didn't hear anything outside. Where did they come from? They must have come in a vehicle. Where was it parked, how could they just disappear into the night without a sound?

After they were gone, Tante Lene sat down on the rug next to me and asked, "Who knows that you were born in America? Who would want to cause you harm?"

Everyone in school knew that I was born in America. I told a lot of stories about America. But, then I remembered something else. A week before this visit, I had been reading to the class. Herr Eisenbart was with the first graders. Jens, a fourth grader, also a city boy who was staying with the mayor's family, who also owned the grocery store, had been acting silly and interrupted my reading. It was a little irritating, but nothing serious. Irma, however, wanted to be loyal to me and went to get Herr Eisenbart. He, in turn, without waiting for explanations, gave Jens several whacks with the pointer. I felt sorry for him. I thought the punishment was much too severe for the little foolishness. Several of Jens' friends told other girls that Jens said he hated me and he'd get even with me, and that he called his father on the phone. When I told Tante Lene about that incident, she said, "Hm, I see." She looked serious.

We finally settled down for the night. The fire in the hearth made interesting shadows on the wall and the ceiling. I thought about the fact that those men were German, but they acted like enemies, and Tante Lene protected me from them. She was so smart. She knew that they didn't know what they were looking for, and so she made them think that they were looking for a man, an American soldier or something like that.

I couldn't believe that Jens would do something like this.

"I'll bet he'll be surprised when I get to school tomorrow. Or maybe he doesn't even know that anyone was here. They were so quiet, and it was so dark," I said to myself.

Before she went to bed, Tante Lene said that I shouldn't tell anybody what happened.

The next day at school, I looked around the room. No one looked at me. Even Jens seemed to be unaware of my distress. Could it be possible that nobody heard anything?

A few days later, Tante Lene gave me a basket with eggs and a piece of ham. She instructed me: "I want you to go to the store and wait until there are no customers. Then give the basket to the mayor, and say, 'This is for my communion candle.' Do you understand? Repeat it." I did.

She said, "Good. You just say that and leave."

It was such an odd request, so out of character for Tante Lene to do anything in such a mysterious way, that I could not help but wonder what the payment was really for, and though I was not schooled in intrigue, or terms of law and its vocabulary, I sensed that this was a kind of blackmail to keep me from harm. It had something to do with Jens or his family.

We repeated this ritual for a long time, every Friday. Only the contents of the basket changed a bit. Sometimes it was a sausage instead of ham. More meat and eggs went into the basket than the two of us ate during the week. I resented it very much, but Tante Lene never acted like she did. Now, that I understand more, there was no reason for fear. By the German law, especially at that time, I was a German citizen. They didn't care where one was born, only what your bloodline was. Mine was German all the way. Those black SS uniforms, however, could intimidate anyone. They had complete power over everyone. That made Tante Lene's cool little act that night even more admirable.

A package from Mama containing several pieces of cloth arrived shortly before my tenth birthday. It included material for a summer dress for me, and a pretty blue cotton material for Tante Lene, as well as material for my Communion dress. It was a cream-colored linen.

The seamstress came and spent two days at the house. The Communion dress would have short sleeves because there wasn't enough material for long ones.

On my birthday, I got a boiled egg for breakfast, and for lunch we had lentil soup with sugar and cinnamon donuts. That was a special Lent meal. Another Lent custom in Ohmenheim was to take a bowl of flour to the Gasthaus baker on Saturday morning. In the afternoon we picked up our bowl full of big, soft pretzels. I thought it was interesting that we were supposed to do without pleasurable things during Lent, but we got pretzels and donuts that we didn't have the rest of the year.

On Easter morning I found two colored eggs in the nest I had built under Herr Mack's huge pear tree. He had brought the sapling from Russia, Tante Lene had told me.

He had been there during the First World War like Onkel Berthold. I didn't know that when he was still alive, or I would have told him about my uncle. I wondered if he knew Russian, too. Somehow, because the tree seemed to be from somewhere far away, and it was old and very big, I liked it. Soft, green moss and violets grew between the gnarly roots of that tree. That is where I had made the nest, not really expecting to find anything in it, so I was amazed that Tante Lene had managed to color eggs without my knowing it, and had found a way to place them into the nest as a surprise.

We took the eggs in a basket with a special Easter bread to church, where it was blessed. As with all the other things we had taken to be blessed, the front of the church was covered this time with baskets from every household. We ate the eggs and the bread after Mass and crumbled the shells of the eggs and spread them around the garden.

The priest was very busy because many things needed to be blessed. If your cows' chains were loose, and you didn't know why, or if your chickens had lice, the priest could come and bless the stable or the chicken coop. There were little witches or bad spirits that did those things. If your hair was snarled, a little witch lived in your hair.

Sometimes, the little bad spirits came to bother people while they were in bed. They sat on your chest, and when you thought you had heartburn, it was really the pressure of them on your chest that caused the pain. Praying to some special saints sometimes could help. Some old ladies in the village, who always wore black, knew a lot about different kinds of teas and salves and cures for sicknesses. Tante Lene and some of the neighbor women talked about those things in the evening when I was in bed.

In the mountainous areas of Europe, spring comes very suddenly. A warm wind blows over the mountains from the south and snow melts, ice cracks, little rivulets of water flow under the ice. The atmosphere is one of giddy wonder. The world is *sooo* alive.

It was such a day, actually some time before Easter, when I came home from school, and there in the living room was my mother and Hannelore, who by now was a toddler. After a long, warm hug from Mama, I took Hannelore for a walk in her stroller. We drew a lot of attention, mainly because no one in Ohmenheim had a stroller, and because Hannelore was so very blond and pale. It was a very strange weekend for me. I hardly knew this little sister of mine, but still I had a great affinity for her. I didn't quite know to whom I should address myself, however, my mother or Tante Lene. I felt so at ease with Tante Lene, yet somehow restrained towards my mother. She said she had come to take me home if I wanted to go. On the way back, she would be picking up Rose Marie. I did want to be with my family. Seeing these two reminded me of the others again, but thinking about going home to Essen, to air raids and to THEM looking for me, and death waiting down there in the basement, I said, "No, I'm fine here."

Mama said she was happy to see me so healthy and she knew that I was well cared for. And so the morning came when Tante Lene, Mama, Hannelore in her stroller, and I walked down the road to the train station in Neresheim. The air was crisp. It was foggy. The morning sun sent probing fingers of light through the haze. The train was in the station. Mama was wearing her coat from America, dark green, fitted to her slim figure, with a large fox fur collar. Her eyes were beautiful. As she held me and kissed me good-bye, the fur was soft against my cheek. And then she was getting on the train. The fog reminded me of Erfurt and the river.

"No, Mama, don't go! Don't leave me!" I ran to the train. But it started to move. I ran along side. I saw her fur collar through the window, but the train went faster and faster.

Tante Lene and I climbed the hill together, our shadows stretching out ahead of us. The fog had lifted. It would be a sparkling, fresh day. I felt raw inside. Something wild and unexpected had happened to me. I cared. I really still cared about my family. I had wrapped myself into a soft, padded cocoon while I was away from them. Just exist, don't think. It was so comfortable and easy.

"You are sorry that you didn't go, aren't you?" Tante Lene asked.

"No, not really. I don't want to go to Essen, but I miss my mother."

"Child, I would like to be your mother. You know I think of you as my own. Why don't you call me 'Muedr' and you'll feel better."

"I can't do that. I have a mother, but while I'm with you, I'll be your child."

Communion Day was the Sunday after Easter. A few days before, Tante Lene and I went to the mayor's store to pick out my flower wreath and candle. Several other girls and their mothers were there, too. Tante Lene paid for the candle and the wreath with money, like every one else. I wanted to say something about that, but didn't know what, so I had to be quiet.

As we lined up outside the church on Sunday, I was really self-conscious. I looked different than the others. First of all, I was the tallest girl and just built differently. I had longer legs and a smaller body than they had. My hair was light brown and shoulder length. Theirs was dark and long in braids. They all wore long-sleeved white satin dresses. I had on an off-white linen, short-sleeved dress. They were wearing long white stockings. I had on cable-knit knee socks. I remembered Mrs. Smith's chart. I was the orange star.

I knelt through the Mass, watching the candles flicker. What if one of them went out? Would that be a sign that your soul wasn't pure? Did I confess all of my sins? I didn't tell that it was my fault that Erika died. It didn't fit into any of the sins we learned about. How is it going to feel when I've had Communion?' These were the thoughts that went through my head while the Mass went on.

Finally it was time for us to file out of the pew and kneel at the railing. *Fold your hands under the cloth. In case the wafer falls, it will fall on the cloth, not on the floor. When the priest gets to you, you close your eyes and open your mouth. You stick out your tongue, but just a little bit!*

The wafer tasted like rice paper candy without sugar. It dissolved into a little lump. *Don't chew it, that would be like biting God. Why do you eat God? I'm sorry, I didn't mean to think that.*

Back in the pew I waited. *Something special will happen now.* I expected to feel saintly, or spiritual, or like an angel, but nothing happened to me. *It's because of Erika! God doesn't want to live in my soul!*

If the others noticed? I looked around very carefully. One of the girls was scratching her leg. Another one was yawning. Two boys were whispering. Someone was saying "ssh."

"You are the worst class that has ever had First Communion. That's what I heard about you from the people." The priest glared at us. It seemed that he looked a little longer at me than the others. One of the talking boys noticed that, too. "Yes, she and Irma were talking," he said.

"What," I protested, "Irma wasn't even near me. It was you, who was talking." This was followed by several children shouting at the same time, accusing or defending. Finally the priest told the two boys and Irma and me to step forward. He held the two boys by the back of the neck and knocked their heads together. Then he did the same to us two girls. It hurt. I had a headache. I didn't say anything, but he knew how I felt. I looked daggers at him.

After this, Irma wasn't allowed to play with me unless we played at her house under supervision. It seemed that her parents thought I was a bad influence on her.

I spent my time away from school either playing alone in my own yard, or going with Tante Lene to the fields.

At the lower end of Ohmenheim were some very wet meadows. There were a number of storks that had nests in little man-made shelters in some old willow trees. I went along the path through the meadow, intending to inspect the nests to see if there was any truth in the stories about storks bringing babies. As I was going along, I saw smoke pouring out of a barn. Quite a few people were already gathered nearby. I ran through the meadow to see what was going on. It was the home of the boy who had told the priest that I was talking in church. Someone was saying, "He was playing with matches in the hay loft." The barn was a fiery inferno. It kept on burning. There was no fire department in Ohmenheim. Already, the people were pointing to the boy as "the barn burner." He would have to live with that stigma all of his life. I was amazed how quickly God had punished him for lying about me.

Our world reached as far as one could go in one day with a team of cows and a wagon. For us, personally, it was as far as our fields lay from Ohmenheim. Towards the northeast, far from the village, was surely the worst piece of earth anyone would try to cultivate. It was up on a ledge. There were rocks and thistles and ants that stung your feet and legs and hands. Lentils were planted here among the weeds and misery. It was late in the previous fall when we picked the pods off the dry bushes. A cold, hard wind whipped over the field and kept on for hours. I felt like someone in a Bible story in a field that was cursed by God. We worked till three or four in the afternoon and managed to gather a large sack full of lentils. Tante Lene said that we'll go to visit some of her relatives now, since we're so close.

By the time we arrived at the farm, it had begun to rain. The barnyard and the house were very quiet. Although it was quite dark outside, there was no light on in the house. After knocking and some waiting, someone opened the door for us. We were shown into the Stube. Gloom hung over the room. We were to learn that a few days before, the father had stepped on the handle of the pitchfork out in the barn. The fork was propelled up directly into the face of his only child, his nine-year-old son. The boy was rushed to the hospital in Neresheim. The doctors told the parents that the boy would probably be blind for the rest of his life.

The wife talked about her husband as though he were not there. She blamed him. He was silent, all alone in his sorrow. I knew how that was. It was like I felt about Erika. Every thought of her began with "If only I had . . ."

It was still raining when we left that unhappy house. The wind howled and took my breath away, and I was cold and wet. I sat on the board of the wagon and cried, my tears mingled with the rain.

The everyday events of life in the country took on such importance for me, that there was no time, no room for thoughts about the war. Battles were something they talked about on the radio. Foreign names meant little to me, especially those in the East. When there was news about Japan, I remember that I didn't like the Japanese because when I was in first grade in Milwaukee we collected things to send to China for the poor children there. The Japanese were the enemy to the Chinese people. I also was annoyed when the news announcers told us how many enemy aircraft were destroyed in the air raids the night before. They never said how many homes were bombed, or how many people got killed.

The length of our school days depended on the season and the weather. If it was a day for field work, we would go home very early. If not, we'd come back for the afternoon. When the weather was very nice, and the potato plants quite big and strong, we'd have a field trip to inspect the plants of the various farmers. We were to look for plants that were unhealthy because they might have potato bugs on them. If we found a potato bug, all of the plants around would have to be destroyed.

"Germany had gotten rid of all of its potato bugs, but the Americans might throw some down from their planes." I always said a small prayer that we wouldn't find any because I didn't want America to be blamed for doing something so bad.

As we walked through the fields, everyone had his own row to inspect. We also got lessons on bugs, beetles, and all kinds of things one could find in a field, and once even the history of the potato, which according to Herr Eisenbart "is a native of America. Actually it is just one tuberous fruit from that continent. In South America, the Indians grow various foods high in starch . . ."

On the way back, one day, we passed a house that was newly built. Several people were just getting ready to tile the roof. Herr Eisenbart had us all get in a long line and we passed tiles. The whole roof was done before we left. He said, "The priest should have field trips like this instead of processions, sprinkling holy water into the dust, and spreading flower pedals around. God helps him, who helps himself. Remember that!"

A package arrived from Essen. It looked like a shoe box. It was supposed to have been for my birthday. It was under way a very long time. In it was a pair of roller skates, a bunch of radishes, whose leaves had dried up, and a letter. Josef, Herr Mack's son, was on furlough. I took the bunch of radishes, cut off the leaves and stems, rinsed them off, put them into a bowl and sat on the front door step with a salt shaker, a slice of bread and mustard, and proceeded to eat the entire bunch of radishes.

Josef came over and sat down next to me and said, "You're homesick, aren't you? There's no way anyone would sit and eat that unless he had some kind of a problem. Here, I've got something that would be more fitting for a birthday. He gave me a box of dried figs. "They're from Turkey. They're sweet and good" he said. "I bought them in Greece."

I remembered eating figs in America when I was little, a long time ago. What I remembered most from my mother's letter was "I'm so sorry to tell you now in a birthday letter that your Papa had to go to the Army . . ."

My father in the army! I didn't understand. Why would they put him in the army? They needed him as a steel molder. My family was in trouble without Papa to take care of them, but here nothing ever changed. Then I realized that Mama had sent this package before she came to see me, but she didn't ask if I got it, and she didn't say that Papa was in the army. Actually, we hardly talked at all. I didn't know what to say to her, and I was afraid to say the wrong thing.

I sat in the grass at the edge of the street and put on the skates. I was surprised that I remembered how to use the key. I hadn't had any skates on since we had come to Germany. It took a little practice to get confidence to skate off, but I managed it. The road was very good for skating down at the corner from the smithy, which had a big lock and chain on the doors facing the street, all the way to the mayor's house. As I got there, Jens was playing outside. When he saw me with skates, his face lit up, "Hey, wait for me. I've got my skates, too."

We two city kids established a common bond. We didn't talk much, but really found a kind of harmonious skating pattern and established a relationship bordering on friendship. The skates gave me a kind of light and happy feeling. But way back in the dark part of my mind I was sad about Papa in the army and being out of touch with my family.

Jens seemed to have no bad feelings towards me, and it was still puzzling how those SS men came without him knowing it. I was so curious to know the whole story, but I was afraid to talk about it. We never went to each other's house, but one of us would just skate around in front of the other's place, until the other one would join in. This activity, of course, set us apart from the village kids, who sat at the edge of the street in the beginning, watching us, and later, just glaring and making comments to each other. It didn't matter much to me. It was difficult to find common interests with them, anyhow.

At school I was on independent study, more or less. I was working with the older students' books. Herr Eisenbart told me what to do each day. Sometimes he would tell me to pay attention when he was teaching something new to the older students. At other times he would tell me to read something, or to write, or to do math problems. This special attention from the teacher did not make me very popular with the others, but it wasn't the only cause. I was an outsider, that's all. I would never be considered one of them. Time seemed to make the gulf between us grow. In school, I communicated with Herr Eisenbart. After school, I spent most of my time with Tante Lene.

It was April. I had been with Tante Lene more than a year. As time went on, I thought less of my former life and became more aware of the world in which I was living. I enjoyed school, which was a stimulating entertainment for me. But, what I really loved was being out in the fields with Tante Lene. There was a wonderful peace in riding on the wagon seat, watching the landscape go by, hearing only the squeaking and creaking of the wagon and the birds in the trees along the way.

Even the monotony and repetition of the work we did was a healing exercise. I let memories pass before my eyes as I worked. When Erika appeared, I no longer was afraid. I was just sad, like having my father in the army, Onkel Josef so far away in Russia, my cousins, who knows where. I worried about my family in Essen. Rose Marie was there, too, now. Mama had picked her up on the way back home that time. I prayed that they would be safe, that Erika's book would protect them, that THEY were after me, not the book. And when all those thoughts got too difficult, I would look up, across the land, and feel relieved. The earth was still beautiful and whole.

During that time, when I felt a kind of melancholic love for the land, there was one special day. A field that needed to be plowed lay to the west of the village. It was large, perhaps twice the size of the others we worked. I had never been to this field before, but I think it probably had grown sugar beets last.

Tante Lene set the plow down on the earth and put her weight on the handles. We began to plow. I led the cows down along the edge of the field. The shear began to cut into the ground, turning over a long line of dark brown earth. We went on, row after row, back and forth. The earth was wet and stuck to our shoes, and we had to scrape it off with a stick. Tante Lene let me hold the plow for a few rows. I held, pushed down, and the earth peeled off to the side. It was hypnotizing to watch. We took turns, and when I was leading the cows I could look out, away from the ground.

Our field lay in a valley. On the left side of us was a hill that sloped very gradually upwards. It was striped with fields of different crops in various shades of stubble-field beige, brownish green, to brown, where the plow had already been. Way up—it seemed so far away—was a man with a plow, pulled by a horse, and a young boy guiding the horse. Outside of us, there was no sign of any other human. The field was situated so that I could see very far in all directions. I had a feeling of aloneness that somehow made the occasion very solemn. With so much of nature to see, it was awesome and I felt small, but still a part of this beautiful world, and blessed to have this unique experience.

We spent a long time walking row after row on this very large field. I was getting tired, and so was Tante Lene. Neither one of us spoke. My mouth felt very dry, and my back and legs were beginning to ache. The man and the boy left. They were done, but we went on. I kept my mind on the ground, brown peeling away from beige. No thinking, it takes too much energy, just be, just go on . . . And finally, somehow, we were on the wagon. My neck, shoulders, arms, everything hurt. We got home at sunset. When I got to bed, I fell into a deep, deep sleep.

"My" field lay on a road that branched off the road to Noerdlingen. This road was not paved, but it was lined with trees. Most of them were apple trees. Along the road were many wild flowers: red poppies, blue cornflowers, and white daisies. The year before, there were sugar beets in the field, also four rows of poppies for poppy seed. The beets were pulled up and loaded on the wagon. When we got back to the barn, we cut off the green tops, which were fed to the cows. Some of the beets were taken to town, and Tante Lene got some sugar and *Ruebenkraut*, sugar beet molasses, and probably money, too, for them. Besides the very sour plum jelly we had, I liked *Ruebenkraut*. It tasted very good on rye bread.

Anyhow, while I was helping to cut off the leaves, I decided to try my little jack knife. On the first beet, I cut my finger. Half of the tip was just hanging by the skin. I pushed it against the rest of the finger and stuck my hand into the pocket of my jacket and went into the house. I was going to go to the kitchen to wash my hands, which were caked with soil, when Tante Lene looked up as I passed her.

"What do you have in your pocket?"

"Nothing."

"There is something bleeding in your pocket."

"Oh, I just cut myself a little."

"Let's see. Ja, just a little . . ." She washed it, bandaged it with a clean handkerchief and told me to go to the old doctor down the road, right away.

I objected, "He's a horse doctor."

"A horse doctor is better than no doctor. You have to get a shot. A tetanus shot. Right now!"

I walked down the road. I could see the abbey on the hill, and wondered where Onkel Josef was. Tante Marie and I never did get to see the picture on the wall. I'd better visit her this Sunday. Ever since that girl came to live with her, I didn't feel very comfortable there, but I did visit almost every weekend because I had promised. The girl was a lot older than I was, and she acted like Tante Marie was her aunt instead of mine, but Tante Marie always was really sweet and happy when I came to see her.

I was a bit nervous when I got to the doctor's office. I knocked on the door, tried the handle, opened it and went in. The old doctor, in a dark suit and striped shirt, growled at me something like, "What do you want?" I showed him my hand. He unwrapped the handkerchief bandage.

"Dirty mess. I should just yank the whole thing off."

When he looked at my startled face, he just grunted and then went to another room. He came back with an enormous needle and syringe.

"Don't worry, I'm not going to stick the whole thing into you," he growled.

For all his gruffness, he really was very gentle. I promised to return in a few days and to keep it clean.

As I was almost out the door, he added, "and get rid of that knife. Little girls shouldn't play with knives."

On Sunday, Tante Marie said the same thing. She insisted that I give the knife to her. I really didn't want to because it reminded me of Herr Mack, but I finally had to give in. She gave me a silver and porcelain flower basket from her buffet.

"This is for a girl, not a knife."

The girl didn't say anything to me. She just took some dishes and food into the kitchen. I noticed that some things had been changed recently. The red couch was gone. The buffet stood where the sofa had been, and a wide flat couch, or daybed, was now against that back wall where the buffet had stood. Although I thought it was a good change, I resented it, saying to myself that that girl was taking over Onkel Josef's house.

Poppies have beautiful pink and lilac flowers, incredibly delicate. After they had stopped blooming, it took a long time for the pods to grow and get dry. They had to sound like shakers before they could be broken off. We emptied the fresh poppy seeds into a bowl. You could also shake the seeds right into your mouth. They tasted very good. Tante Lene looked at me shaking seeds into my mouth.

"I think you had enough of that. You'll get drunk if you don't stop," she said.

I thought that was really funny, because I wasn't drinking anything. I laughed a lot.

This year the field was ready for wheat. It was Saturday morning. In the shade, the grass was still wet with dew. I spread an empty sack on the ground near an apple tree. The cows had been unhitched from the wagon and were tied with a rope to the tree. They were grazing. Tante Lene was getting ready to sow the wheat. She was raking the ground to make it smooth. I had picked some wildflowers and was attempting to make myself a wreath. The morning sun was shining softly. Tante Lene was wearing the blue dress from the cloth my mother had sent her. It was brighter than the village women generally wore. She had a light brown scarf around her hair and wore a sowing apron. She looked like a woman in a painting I saw at Tante Toni's house in the dining room in America. She looked really beautiful in a healthy, country kind of way.

After she was done raking the top of the ground smooth, she began to sow. There was a kind of majesty in the rhythm of her steps and the way her arm moved as she dipped into the apron and spread the wheat kernels in an arc in front of her. As she came towards me, I told her that it looked like it must be fun to sow. She asked if I wanted to do it. Then, when I said, "Yes," she walked along with me for a row and kept the rhythm . . . dip, swing, sow, dip, swing, sow . . ." and then she let me be. She sat down on my sack and watched and smiled. I felt exuberant. I had never before achieved anything that meant as much as this.

"I am sowing a field of wheat! It will grow and when it is tall and golden, the wind will make it wave back and forth and it will be my field, my crop. I'm making something live."

Our routine changed. We started to do a lot of visiting. We went by "my" field to see Tante Lene's brother in the next village. He was a baker and a shepherd. The house they lived in was very small. It was actually only one room and an attic, to which one found access only from the ladder against the house. The one room had a large stone oven in the corner. On top of the oven was a mattress, quilt and pillows, loft-style. There was a long table and benches along two walls, also several cupboards.

Tante Lene's brother liked her a lot. He laughed and joked around. It was nice to see a man. It was a surprise to see a healthy man not in uniform. The only young man left in Ohmenheim was Herr Eisenbart, and everyone knew that they would soon get him for the army, too.

Tante Lene's sister-in-law and their daughter, who was my age, were very quiet. The girl was so shy; she kept hiding behind one of her parents, and wouldn't speak at all. It seemed really strange to me. After all, we were ten years old.

The village seemed very far away from the rest of the world. At least Ohmenheim had a paved street with cars or trucks traveling between Noerdlingen and Neresheim, but this village was isolated, a dead end.

Tante Lene began taking day-long trips on her bicycle. Those were lonely days. I fed the chickens and the pig and the cows and played with the kitten and my doll and went to the orchard and looked at the big pear tree and then I felt lonely for Herr Mack. I went to the smithy by the side door, and looked at the things on the walls and the anvil and the leather apron hanging on a nail, and the cobwebs that were everywhere, and I felt angry.

"Why did you have to die? When you were here, there was life and fun. There were people, lots of people, lots of men. Now there are just a few grandfathers around, and they don't come to visit us. I want you to be here. I want the fire to be going and to hear the sound of the iron and see the sparks flying and watch your big shadow on the wall . . ."

"Ruth, I met a man, who is a widower. He has three children. They're older than you. He has a nice farm. He wants to marry me. He lives in a village on the other side of Neresheim. It's really a nice, big house. I want you to meet that family. Do you think you can ride my bicycle well enough to go that far? It's about ten kilometers from here, that's pretty far."

I set off in the morning after breakfast. The bicycle was big and I couldn't reach the seat, but it was faster and easier than walking. But, I had not prepared myself for the steep hill going down to Neresheim.

As I went along, I picked up momentum. I couldn't get myself to reverse the pedals and I couldn't move my hand from the handlebar to put on the hand brake, and so, with the wind rushing past my face, faster and faster, I went down. At the bottom of the hill was a mail truck going to Neresheim. In the middle of the road, an old man was sweeping the street. I steered for that side of the road. I just caught the man's apron a bit, and then I and the bicycle were in a soft, wet ditch.

The old man came running, his apron flapping.

"My dear child. I'm so sorry. I just didn't hear you. You know, I don't hear so good. Are you hurt badly?"

I didn't know if I was hurt at all. I was trembling so much that my teeth were chattering. The mailman came, too, and he determined that nothing had happened to me.

"You certainly have a fine guardian angel, my girl. You know you could have been killed. What's a little thing like you doing on a big bicycle like that anyway, and on a busy street like this. Where are you going?" and then, "that's too far. You are too little to go so far alone. You should go back right now."

But I didn't. I got to the farm at noon. I could have cried from exhaustion.

The visit was a disaster, although the youngest daughter liked me well enough. We were in the kitchen, talking. Then her father got angry because he wanted his dinner NOW. He frowned at me. When we were at the table, he told me to fetch something from the kitchen. I didn't understand him, but jumped anyway and then when I was in the kitchen, I didn't know what to get, so I peeked into the dining room, and the girl came to my rescue after he said something about idiots. I helped her with the dishes and left, knowing that her father didn't like me. The way back seemed very long. I got home as the sun was setting . . .

We sat in the red sunlight in the living room, and I told Tante Lene about my day, but not about the bicycle and the hill. She was quiet, and then she sighed and got up, made dinner and sat next to me instead of across from me. She stroked my hair and rubbed my back.

"You're tired, aren't you?" Yes, and I was sad, too.

We washed the curtains. The rugs went outside and were hung on the line and beaten. Tante Lene took things out of the large dark chest in the hall. There were stacks of folded linens around the bedroom. Even the cows in the stable were brushed. Someone came and talked to her about the dung-heap and the wagon. But my world was the same . . . The plum trees were full of blossoms. I lay on the moss and picked violets. The breeze stirred the branches and I was showered with flower petals. I made a May altar and got weepy when I said "Mother of God." I didn't really know why.

One day I was told to have lunch at Irma's house. I didn't understand why, nor why Irma's mother was so nice to me. She even told me I should stay a while and play. When I got back home it was late afternoon. A lot of our furniture was out on the lawn. A man was pointing to the sewing machine, and someone, sitting on one of our chairs, said something. Then the man said, "It's yours."

I walked through the group of people and finally found Tante Lene. She took me by the hand and led me to my room. It was bare. All that was in the room was my suitcase, my winter coat, and my doll. They were on the floor. The sun was shining its copper light on the doll.

"Ruthi, we have to say 'goodbye' now. My man just doesn't want to have someone else's child. I'm sorry. I'll miss you. You've been a good girl. I couldn't ask for anyone better. You can either go back to your Tante Marie, or maybe you would like to stay with my brother. You know, they already have a girl like you, and she would be happy to have some company."

Her voice sounded far away. I don't remember what else she said. I was not prepared for this. I should have been, with all of the preparations going on around me, but I had closed off my mind to it, and so I really was in shock, I guess. When bad things happen, they seem to be happening in slow motion, and I seem to be watching, not really being involved. It was something like that when I was hysterical in Essen, but that time I wasn't able to help myself. This time I didn't scream or cry. Did I say anything? I don't know. I knew I should go to

Tante Marie's but she didn't have any room for me, besides Ohmenheim without Tante Lene, without this home, was out of the question. So I had to go away. The auctioneer came to the door, and Tante Lene went to talk to someone. I didn't wait for her to come back. There was no point to it.

I didn't go back into the house to where the people were—I didn't want anyone to see me—to know that I was being sent away again. I went through the stable and barn, sneaked around the corner between the barn and the smithy and out onto the main road going past the mayor's house and store. There was no one outside to see me. Jens had left to visit his family, maybe even for good because he was going to a higher school in the fall. That reminded me that I hadn't delivered basket food ever since he had left. So it had to do with him, but he wasn't aware of it. Someone else, someone grown up, but I didn't know who.

Beyond the mayor's house the paved road turned off towards Noerdlingen. Mine went straight ahead. The sunlight was getting really red. The world seemed very quiet. I came to "my" field. The wheat was growing already. It was nice and green and even. There were no empty patches. But now no one would know that it was "mine." Who would harvest it? I'd never see it again.

I went on. My shadow was very long behind me, pulling back. There was another time, when we were leaving our home on 33rd Street. But that time, just three years ago, in another world, Papa was holding my hand.

I looked ahead. The treetops formed a tunnel. It seemed that they were very tall and dark, and the road was much longer than it was when we went this way with the wagon.

*   *   *

7

CROSSROADS

My arms hurt from carrying so many things. The village was farther from Ohmenheim than I had thought. The sun had set by the time I got there. On the street, I saw several groups of children with brooms in their hands, swatting at swarms of *Maikaefer* (June bugs). They were very loud—girls shrieking when the bugs fell on them, boys shouting and laughing. They swatted, dropped the brooms and raced together to pick up the bugs, which they threw into pails of hot water. Then they fed them to chickens that became very aggressive, fighting each other over the bugs.

I watched as I went along, and finally got to the house of Tante Lene's brother. I knocked and entered. The mother had her back towards the door. She was washing dishes. She turned to see who was coming, and turned back to her task. The father was reading a newspaper. He lowered it and smiled at me. The daughter, sitting next to him, slid closer to him, hiding, and peeking at me around his shoulder. The father was the only one who really talked to me. He was not surprised to see me. His concern was where we all would sleep. I supposed that they all had been sleeping in the loft above the big oven.

"It's probably best if you two girls sleep upstairs. There is a bed up there." He took my suitcase and carried it as he climbed the ladder. The two of us followed. There was a big brass bed in the middle of the usual cast-offs one stores in attics. The bed was not made. There were no sheets, no pillowcases, no blankets. The mattress was very dusty. The father looked around somewhat helplessly, and then just went down the ladder, saying, "Well, good night then." We got on the bed with our clothes on. She covered herself with some things that had been hanging around in the attic. They might have been table cloths or curtains. I curled up under my coat.

The girl was awed by my doll. She couldn't take her eyes or hands off her. She touched the doll's eyes and eyelashes, played with her hair and examined her dress. I let her hold her for a while and then I told her, "She can sleep in the middle, but we have to let her sleep, we can't play with her." I really didn't want her to touch my baby at all, but she was so pitiful, herself, I didn't have the heart to be really mean to her.

As I lay on that dusty bed, I realized how tired I was. I hadn't eaten since noon at Irma's house. That was so long ago, like in a different world, a different life. I should have said "good-bye" to Tante Marie and to Herr Eisenbart. I should have hugged and kissed Tante Lene, and not just run away, but I would have cried. For a tiny moment I thought about the night at the orphanage, but I told myself that I was too tired to think or cry. The door—actually it was a large shutter through which we had entered the attic—stood open. I could see the tops of trees, stars, and the shining moon. The voices of birds and crickets lulled me to sleep.

Far away to the north, the alarm sounded again that night. The RAF raided the city of Cologne in its first 1,000-bomber attack on German cities. It was May 30, 1942.

We got up without anyone waking us and climbed down the ladder and went into the house where I washed my face and hands at the kitchen sink. A back door led to a rickety old outhouse. The wood was gray and had holes in it. The whole structure looked like it would collapse in a strong wind.

Inside the house, the mother poured us barley coffee with milk, and cut a slice of bread from a round loaf for each of us. She gave us another slice of bread with bacon fat on it for school. She didn't offer to comb my hair, and so I went with the clothes I had worn day and night, and uncombed hair.

Six or seven children met us at the corner. Their ages ranged from six to twelve, perhaps. We went in a group together along a rutted country road. The children were peaceful and friendly. No one really made an overture to get to know me, but they didn't exclude me, either. A few of the little ones even gave me some wild onion grasses to chew along the way. We came to a village, which to me, seemed much farther away than Ohmenheim would have been. The school was a public library. There were stacks of books, a room full of books, several beautiful, large, polished wooden tables, comfortable chairs, and windows that went almost down to the ground. It was a new and modern structure that was completely out of place in the village. The teacher was a boy of about eighteen at the most. He had very pretty eyes, but a bad complexion. After he had gotten the other children settled to some assignment, he asked me to read for him. I read for a while, then I looked up at him. He smiled at me and said, "I don't think I can do much for you. I imagine you like to read. Go ahead and just pick whatever you like, and read."

I walked up and down the rows of books, reading titles. Some I took down and looked through, some I took over to one of the tables. I would read for a while and then pause and watch the shadows of the branches and leaves of the tree outside dance across the table . . . and I remembered my kindergarten class and the lanterns we made.

There were no more than a dozen other pupils in the room, and the teacher had a very quiet method of teaching. He was more of a tutor, going from one child to another, explaining or listening. I had a lot of time to think about many things: my life, or the stories I was reading, and those I had read in the past. I tried to think through, to understand what lesson I was supposed to learn from Erika's book, her death, and what was happening to me. I compared myself to the father in Erika's book. He could have saved the baby if he had known what was under the child's mattress. But he didn't. Even when he found it, he didn't recognize it for what it was. But, at least he did something. He made a baby doll's head, and in that way, the baby was not forgotten, because everyone has, or has seen, a baby doll. But how could I keep the memory of Erika alive with a book?

I had spent more than two weeks in this situation, and nothing happened. Each day I got closer to fear. I felt that I was lost, trapped in a place that the rest of the world didn't know anything about. I had run away, and no one knew it, and no one cared.

The visit to the "school" was precious time out each day, but we returned to a silent world, and physical neglect. Tante Lene's brother seemed to be the only person in that family who spoke more than a word or small phrase. Unfortunately, he was home very little because he had to be with his sheep most of the time. In the afternoons, I generally sat outside, somewhere around the wooded area behind the house. I conjured up people to talk to. The first one to pop into my mind was Tante Lene, but I pushed her away. I couldn't think about her yet. Then I'd go to Rose Marie. I could see her standing in front of me, with her hands on her hips, asking, "Why don't you like it here? I think it's really pretty," and I would feel dumb for complaining.

Oma would be better.

I'll tell her about all of this when I get home. She'll understand. I should have told her about Erika, she even knew about her because of the album with which she helped me. But, what if she thought that it was my fault that she died, and she wouldn't like me anymore?

It was the third Sunday I was spending in this village. I felt terribly lonely, and awfully uncomfortable and dirty. Everything I had to wear should have been washed. The only dress I still had, that was clean, was my three-year-old Shirley Temple dress from America. It was very short, and the pleats had long since been washed and ironed out, but I put it on. The family didn't go to church, not on any of the Sundays I was there. I was sitting in the grass, taking care of the geese, and having a conversation, one way, with Erika. I told her, "I miss you, and since you are in heaven, you know that I'm telling the truth. Would you please ask God to get me out of this place?"

A voice, above, behind me, said, "What are you doing here, child?"

I turned and saw a dress with purple flowers.

"Mama, how did you find me?"

"Oh, you poor child, what all has happened to you? How you look. You are so brown. I wonder how much of that is from the sun, and how much is dirt. Oh, well, come, we're going home."

She hugged me for a long time, and then we walked together with her arm around my shoulder. My mother, who appeared to me like an angel, had come to rescue me.

My suitcase was already packed and in the kitchen. There was also a shopping net for my mother with flour and a few eggs in the flour, and a crock of lard.

"We have to hurry to get to the train station on time. We have to walk real fast," Mama said after a hasty "thank you" and "good-bye" to my hostess.

We nearly ran, and as we were out on the road, I realized that I didn't have my doll or my coat.

"We can't go back now. We'll ask them to mail those things," Mama said.

I knew I would never get that doll back again, and began mourning her all the way home. I couldn't believe that I could forget my doll, my baby, just like I did with my baby doll in America.

We came to a small station in a town I didn't even know existed. The train was already there. As soon as we had boarded, the doors were shut, and the conductor blew his whistle. The train began to move before we reached our seats. It was a nice day, and I enjoyed having my mother all to myself. When I asked her how she knew where I was, she said that both Tante Lene and Tante Marie had written to her. I felt a little guilty again about Tante Marie. I should have gone to her, but then things might not have worked out like this.

As we reached the industrial area in the north, people stared at me as they passed the compartment. I realized why. They all seemed so pale and tired. I looked so disgustingly healthy and brown.

When we arrived in Essen, I was shocked to see how many more houses had been bombed. Some of them seemed to have tumbled into the street. I remembered the dream I had when I was sick with scarlet fever. Brick walls swaying, bricks falling . . . We had to walk around some of them on little paths. When we got to our block, it was still untouched. I was relieved.

Our flat looked luxurious to me. The furniture, the lace panels at the windows of our girls' bedroom were so different from where I had been. Oma was at home with Herbie and Hannelore when we arrived. Rose Marie was at school. Herbie still remembered me and smiled and let me hug him. Hannelore looked at a stranger that I was to her, of course. She didn't remember me from that weekend in Ohmenheim, and she didn't really know that I was a part of the family. She was only a year old when I left Essen. I had been gone eighteen months.

Rose Marie came home from school. She hid her face from me. I finally learned that she was ashamed of how she looked. She had lost her two front teeth. She was very thin and pale. I felt embarrassed by my health, but as we all sat down to eat, I knew that I belonged here with these people, and that they really were happy to have me back, too.

After our meal, Rose Marie and I went to our bedroom. I looked into the drawers and cabinet to see what treasures I had forgotten I had. Then I got to the trunk. I held my breath as I opened it. I looked in, and there was THE BOOK. I almost wished that it had disappeared while I was gone. The old fear started creeping up again, but I talked myself out of it.

"It's just a dumb book . . . well, not dumb, but it's a book, a story book, that's all. And no English people are coming over here at night to look for this book. Don't be stupid."

When the siren sounded that night, I was completely disoriented, but finally got out of bed and went through the old routine. Even though I had been gone so long, I was still conditioned to find clothes and shoes in the dark, to get Rose Marie ready and take the little case with our papers that stood by the door, down to the basement. Mama and Oma brought the little ones. I don't know how Oma managed carrying a child down the stairs. I was relieved to know that the lady downstairs from us helped her the nights that Mama was away picking up her children.

The basement had been fortified. There was a different door, too.

It had an air lock. Also, instead of a window, a kind of air vent was installed. The shelter was built not to collapse, even if the whole house would fall apart. Krupp had that done to their houses. I had complete confidence in its safety. Krupp made the best things.

That thought brought me to ask Oma why Krupp let Papa go to the army.

She explained, "They wanted him to work on top-secret work and join the Party. But he said that he had a big mouth and couldn't keep secrets and would be a bad safety risk. They got mad at him and he got called for the army. They were going to send him to Russia, but some officer said that would be dumb considering that he knows English and is used to heat from the blast furnaces. So they gave him all kinds of shots against malaria and other African diseases. They were going to send him there, but he ended up with the anti-aircraft flack in Holland."

I was glad to hear that. It didn't sound too dangerous; it wasn't like being in battle.

School was still in session. I was a celebrity. My classmates wanted to hear about my adventures and kept on asking me to say things in Schwaebisch. I had been gone so long that I really didn't remember the children living on our street anymore, and I don't think we played those same games we used to, either. I had no close friend. Without Erika, everything had changed.

When I was tested to see how much I had missed, attending a country school, I surprised the teacher and the principal. I had apparently learned skills beyond my grade level. The principal talked to me about the school in Ohmenheim. She asked questions about Herr Eisenbart, and how the classes were put together, and also she asked me school questions about math and German and science.

The next day I was called back to her office. There was a man and another woman there. I was asked to repeat many of the same things I had done the day before, including writing in both the old German script, and the Latin script, which had been reintroduced at the beginning of the school year. Then they talked together, and the principal showed them my report card from America. I didn't know that my parents had given it to the person who enrolled me. I had gotten all E's, which, in those days, stood for excellent. The American principal had written "summa cum laude" on the back of it. I remember that when I got it from Mrs. Smith, I was very upset. All around me the kids were telling each other how many A's and B's they had.

Mrs. Smith asked me, "What's the matter?"

I said, "I didn't get any A's or B's."

She smiled at me, "Don't be sad, what you got is much better than A's and B's."

I don't remember any kind of reaction from my parents at the time, and I had forgotten about it until I saw it again. At any rate, it must have helped to impress the trio, and I received a letter for my mother, which said that I was recommended to attend the Gymnasium, a college prep school, in the fall. It also said that I was exempt from the written entrance exam that had already been given earlier that year. But I did have to pass the family tree requirement. Not only did you have to be really above average in school, but you also had to prove that your family background was all "Christian" or "pure" German to be acceptable. Since both of my parents were born into Catholic families, the Church had all the baptism, marriage, burial records of several generations. We passed the test. I received my assignment letter to a Gymnasium. Oma was especially happy and really proud of me. It was a great honor and privilege, because only Gymnasium graduates could ever study at a university, and at that time, not many children were given that opportunity. My cousin Heinz in Erfurt and I were the only ones of our generation of fifty-four first cousins to have the opportunity to earn university degrees.

*   *   *

Family portrait after my 18 months in the country.

8

FRIEND OR FOE?

When vacation began, we were back on the train heading
south, once more to Ellwangen. Mama tried to convince
Oma to come along. She, however, refused again, saying that if she
were to go anywhere it would be home to Schlesien in the East, where
all of the Schwabe family's relatives lived. She said there would be
plenty of room for all of us because Opa's family owned a lot of land
there. But, Mama felt that that would be like going to another foreign
country, and she preferred the South, which was her home. And so we
came to Ellwangen, but this time we were able to live in the upstairs
apartment at Onkel Karl's house. Mama did have to cook downstairs in
Tante Agnes' kitchen, though. Tante Agnes didn't like us being there,
but there wasn't much she could do. Onkel Karl was Mama's older
brother.

Ellwangen could boast an old castle, two lovely old churches, a
Stukka base and an SS training school. There also was a military
hospital, serving many soldiers who had been wounded in battle far
away from this little town.

On sunny days the Stukka pilots would practice fighter flights.
They mostly did dives, which made eerie, shrill, shrieking noises.
That was pretty scary, but worse than that was the SS. They wore black
uniforms like those that had come at night in Ohmenheim.

Once I was in the grocery store. People were talking about the weather, their children, and who knows what. The door opened and closed. It was completely silent in the store. I knew, without looking, that whoever had entered was wearing a black uniform. I turned, and right next to me were the boots and the uniform from that night. I started to shake. THEY had found me again! I couldn't get myself to look up at the face of this black giant next to me. I was convinced that he was the one who checked me over so carefully that night. I stood in absolute terror. Strangely, I remembered the old lady in the butcher shop in Essen. She was afraid, too, just like this. But she was brave. She wore her star on her coat. I was even afraid to show my face and to look at the one that belonged to the uniform. But, nothing happened. The man in uniform just bought something and left again. He didn't even notice me. The normal pattern of conversation began again in the store, and I had to tell myself that I was stupid to be afraid of HIM or THEM. I had nothing to hide. I was German, I was allowed to attend a Gymnasium, so that really proved that I was German.

In September, I started as a student in the Gymnasium. Girls and boys were taught in separate sections of the building. This would be so through tenth grade. I was now in fifth grade. This time, finally, I was one of the youngest students again. Among my classmates was a group of five girls, who seemed a bit bigger, or older, and not from Ellwangen. They sat in the back of the room and were loud and fresh. They were daughters of SS men. I was told about that when I turned to tell them to stop talking, and the girl next to me said, "Don't do that! You can't say that to them. Their fathers are SS!"

I was a good student and really enjoyed my classes. The teachers had a completely different attitude towards their students than regular teachers seemed to have. They were friendly and actually asked for ideas or opinions from us. I was very eager and cooperative, I think, and that was not appreciated by the big five. What irked them even more was that the English teacher and I got to be good friends. We talked about America, corn on the cob, pumpkin pie, and lots of things. I was aware of the fact that I was annoying those girls, but I was so self-confident that I went out of my way to put them down. Once, when I corrected an answer of one of them, I realized from the silence in the classroom, that if they didn't know the answers, nobody else was supposed to know them, either.

Our animosity towards each other increased as time went on. I felt that I was waging a one-person crusade against those girls. They, in turn, found ways to torment me. In sewing class, one of them kept sticking me with a needle. When I tried to protect myself with my hand, the needle went under the nail of my thumb. It throbbed and became infected. It had to be lanced. None of the teachers were aware of all of this, neither was my mother. The girl, who sat next to me and had given me the information on how one is supposed to behave towards SS daughters, was the only one who seemed to see and hear everything.

One day, it was December by then, close to Christmas vacation, and the snow was very high already, that girl asked if she could come home with me. Since she lived in exactly the opposite direction from where I lived, I thought it was really nice of her, and I was happy to have a special friend again. We talked about school and our families on the way up the hill. As we had gotten to a place where we had a good view, she asked me to stop and look down at the town. I did, and suddenly I found my face down in the snow. Her knees were in my back and her hands were pushing down my neck. I struggled at first, but then there seemed no need for it. The snow was soft and I had no trouble breathing, so I just lay there quietly. After a while, she got up. I pulled myself out of the snow and faced her.

"What was that for?" I was puzzled.

"They told me I had to do it, or they would beat me up," she answered.

"Why? Why were you supposed to attack me? You know I could have died. If the snow had been packed harder, I couldn't have breathed. You could have killed me!"

"They said that you're an enemy," she said, lowering her eyes.

"An enemy! What kind of an enemy? Do you think I'm an enemy?" I was yelling by now.

She started to whine.

"I don't know what you are. I don't know if you're an enemy or a friend."

"Why would I be an enemy? Because I have the guts to give a right answer when they're too dumb to get it right?"

"No," she said, keeping her head down, "because you're always praising America. America does happen to be our enemy, you know."

"Yes, but . . ." I wanted to say things like "American people are nice, they're only in this war because the Japanese started it" but I realized that wouldn't make things any better.

I took another approach: "You know, I was so happy that you were my friend, and now I see that you were planning to hurt me."

She still didn't look at me, but said, "I did what I had to do. If you didn't deserve it, then I'm sorry."

I picked up my school bag and said, "Goodbye, Judas," and went on up the hill. After a while I stopped and looked back. She was looking up at me. I didn't wave. I went on, feeling numb. In a corner of my mind I saw Tante Lene sitting on the rug next to me, asking who all knew that I was born in America, and who would want to do me harm. And I realized that I had brought this on myself. I had a big, bragging mouth. I shouldn't talk so much. Still, was I an enemy? I didn't feel like one. I did love America, that was true. But I also loved Germany. *After all, I am German,* I thought. *It's just that I lived in America, and remember. It seemed better . . . but that's probably because there's a war here,* I reasoned.

I felt tired and sad. As usual, I stopped at the elementary school to pick up Rose Marie, and at the nursery school, where Herbie, Hannelore, and our little cousin, Monika, played with a great array of toys in an ultra-modern setting. The building was new, centrally heated, with marvelous murals on the walls and huge windows looking out to the road and the fenced-in play yard. Sometimes Rose Marie and I stayed a while to play with them before we all left to go home for lunch.

I didn't tell anyone about what happened that day, not even my cousin, Karl, who was my friend. Karl was two years older than I and very intelligent and creative. He should have been going to the Gymnasium, but he wasn't as fortunate as I was. No one did anything to promote him. Karl's special talent was for the theater. He made a shadow box theater and performed for us in the stable with the goats.

It was a secret performance. His mother didn't like him to play theater. She said he did that because he was too lazy to do real work, and it gave him stupid ideas about life.

Goats smell pretty bad, but their milk is very good for you. Taking care of the goats was Karl's job. He did that before and after school. Sometimes he would work on his theaters with a flash light in the goat stable.

My last school day had been on Friday. That weekend we had company from Nuremberg. Three other cousins and their mother came to visit. Their father, Mama's youngest brother, Fritz, was in the army, in Russia. The whole clan of kids went sledding. On Monday morning I had a sore throat and told my mother that I was too sick to go to school. I managed to be sick the next few days, and then we had Christmas vacation. I was truly happy to be sick because I was afraid to go back to school.

On the twenty-fourth of December, Mama sent me with the children on many errands. This was customary. It would give her a chance to decorate the tree. The weather was very cold, and we were all getting tired and a bit cross by the time we finally reached home. However, when we did, we had a great surprise. Papa was home on furlough.

Mama told me, "There I was walking home from the store with the groceries in the net, and behind me someone whistled and said, in English, "Look at those legs." Imagine here in Germany! Nobody does that here, only Americans do that. I knew it was your Papa."

The tree looked beautiful. Our presents were modest, except for the dolls that Papa brought from Belgium. He had brought three, one for each girl, but Mama gave mine to Monika. She said that Monika was little and needed a doll more than I did. Papa also brought a goose, which both families ate for Christmas dinner. But, the whole holiday really revolved around Papa. All of us were vying for his attention. He seemed to be exactly the same as I had remembered him during the two years I had not seen him. He had a quiet air of authority, which made everything run and hum smoothly, and made us all happy. But, he could only stay a few days, and got ready to return to his unit. He took twenty pounds of salt with him. He said he can trade it with the farmers for chickens and eggs. He did the cooking for his outfit.

And then he was all dressed in his bluish gray Luftwaffe uniform, and he and Mama went to the train station. I missed him more after this visit than I had before.

On the second New Year's Day, Tante Agnes and Mama got into a big fight. It was about me. I had taken the milk can to get the milk at the dairy and when Karl went after I got back, the dairy had already closed. Mama told me to say that I was sorry that I took so long. I said that I didn't take too long and I wouldn't apologize. Mama was angry with me, screaming at me, pleading with me, pulling my hair, and finally breaking the porcelain flower basket I had gotten from Tante Marie over my head. I remained unmoved. I didn't like Tante Agnes, I was angry at my mother for giving my doll to Monika, who already had dolls, and I didn't want to stay in Ellwangen anymore because I was really afraid to go back to school.

We were on the train to Essen the next day. I was escaping from THEM, but there was no way that I could tell that to my mother or anyone else. Mama hardly talked to me. She just couldn't understand what had come over me. On top of everything else, the three other children all were ill. They were coming down with mumps.

I sat in the corner of the compartment, staring out of the window, thinking about school, sad because I really liked my teachers, the whole atmosphere of the school, glad because I got away from THEM.

What will "Judas" say to them? When they realize that I am not coming back, she surely will be their hero. Will that make her happy, or will she feel guilty like I do about Erika?

During the six months we had spent in Ellwangen, many events took place on battlefields and in large cities. I learned about these things later. At the time, I was fighting my own little war, and I was oblivious of everything else.

While we were escaping to the South from air raids, others were also traveling on trains to the East. It was in 1942, I believe, that most of the deportation of the Jewish population of Germany, and other occupied countries took place. Somewhere I heard people talking about Jews being sent to East Prussia or Poland to live. There also was whispered talk about prison camps where people would have to go if they broke the law. One of the laws was listening to enemy radio stations, or getting or selling food on the black market, or being a spy, or unpatriotic in some way. You never knew whom you could trust. There were informers who would get a reward if they caught someone and turned him or her in.

The news we heard on the radio a lot was that about Africa and General Rommel's Afrika Panzer corps. Everyone loved to hear how wonderful they were. But, at the turn of the year, they had a defeat, too. The U-Boats were also praised, and endless statistics were repeated on the radio about how many ships and tonnage were sunk. They never said that the Germans lost any ships, nor submarines.

I don't know how well people were informed about the battle of Stalingrad at the time it was being waged, and which had begun at the end of summer and was going on and on, and would result in unbelievable loss of lives, not only of Germans, but Russians, Romanians, Italians, Hungarians. All together, just in this battle, which lasted from late August to the next February, 1.5 million people lost their lives, according to American sources. This particular time, the end of 1942 and beginning of 1943 was the turning point of the war for Germany. Its eastern front army was devastated. It took months, into the next Christmas season, for people to receive notices that their son, husband, brother was killed or missing in action. Eighty thousand German soldiers, what was left of twenty-two divisions, surrendered to the Russians, in February. I don't know how many of those survived and returned. I think it was around six thousand. My Onkel Josef did not return, nor did Tante Frida's husband, but Onkel Fritz and Tante Sofie's son, Josef, did make it after the families had given up ever seeing them alive again.

*   *   *

9

A Trip to Remember

We arrived back in Essen on the third of January 1943. Had I known how everything had deteriorated during the time we were gone, I might not have been so eager to return. There was a smell of gas and smoke in the air. The sun was obscured by brown wisps of smoky clouds. People, nature, buildings, vehicles all looked gray, closed in, silent, grim. It seemed colder here in the city than in the mountain snow. More buildings had been gutted by bombs, so that the landscape looked like old, dead ruins. I wondered where all of the people lived and where they were going. In some areas there wasn't a single building that wasn't damaged.

We got off the tram at our street and walked down the block. I was holding my breath. Happily, nothing had changed. Our block was still in tact. At the corner, however, a lot of people were standing in the street. Were they in line for milk at the dairy store? As we got closer, we could see what it was that drew the crowd. A bomb was stuck into the pavement. The body and tail section were standing up at an angle. It looked like a gray iron fish. It was a dud. Around noon an alarm sounded, and everyone was to take cover. The bomb was going to be disarmed. We went to the basement. Nothing bad happened, the all-clear sounded, and a truck came to take it away.

It was a very cold winter. We wore stockings and all of our

underclothes to bed. The only warm place in the house was next to the stove in the kitchen. Air raids came during the day and at night. I promised God many things if he would let us live. Everything we wanted to buy seemed to be scarce. There were lines in every store, even though everything was rationed. At the market, I stood for four hours to get six potatoes, one for each of us, and when I brought them home, Oma discovered that they weren't good, anymore. They had been frozen and thawed again. They were rotten inside.

Oma enrolled me in the Gymnasium, which was downtown. I had to go on two different streetcars to get there. Sometimes there were air raids and we'd have to get off and find shelter and get to school late.

The school was fine. The teachers were calm and precise about everything. They were also very understanding about our coming in late, and even let those students, who fell asleep in their seats, go on sleeping. Because of all these irregularities and our not always attending the whole class, sometimes missing it altogether, the teachers became tutors. Assignments were written on the board, and the teacher would spend the period assisting us individually with our work. Everyone behaved. There was no discipline problem. There was also no color or gayety in the school. Everyone was so tired, and the rooms looked dark and gloomy. Perhaps the grayness was from the weather outside, or maybe they were saving electricity.

One afternoon in mid-February, I was doing an assignment on the kitchen table when Mama came home from somewhere.

"Oma, we got it, but we have to be at the train station at six this evening. Do you think we can be ready by that time?" she asked.

Mama was excited. We were going to be evacuated. Mothers and children were being sent out of Essen to the country. Oma, again, refused to go.

"This is my home, and here is where I'm going to stay," she declared.

Into suitcases went enough clothes for each of us to manage with for a week or two. Oma would send the rest of the things. This time, after some deliberation, I decided to take Erika's book along. I put it into my school bag.

There was great turmoil at the station. Babies were crying, women were shouting after wandering children. Boys and girls were carrying bundles or brothers and sisters. It was a nervous flurry of activity with the always-present teams of nurses, and men in beige with big swastikas on their armbands, carrying clip boards with lists of names. Family names were called off, members of the family counted and assigned car and seat numbers. The cars on the train had the Red Cross symbols on the roof and on the sides of each car.

Inside the train were some wounded soldiers on their way to hospitals in the South. They left the compartments and settled on baggage in the corridor. We all piled into the train and climbed over bags and bundles to find our compartment. There, after everyone was seated, we also had baggage stacked up on the floor. We shared our compartment with two other women and four small children, who, like those in the rest of the train, were whining and complaining.

It had gotten dark outside by the time the train was finally ready to roll. Every corner was packed full of people and baggage. There was no way anyone could get through the corridor without stepping on or falling over a soldier or some bag. The soldiers were quiet. They seemed very tired as they looked out at the night.

It took some time before the children stopped crying and the mothers stopped scolding. Children, who had enough sense not to fall out but were still small enough to fit into the baggage nets above our heads, were put to sleep there. Some found soft bundles or coats to snuggle against, and eventually it started to quiet down, and the train rolled along with its hypnotizing click, click, clack . . . and I was able to dream about meadows and Heidi-like mountain chalets and feel happy. Our destination was Memmingen, a small town in the foothills of the Alps.

I must have been asleep. I nearly fell off the seat. The train's brakes screeched, and we came to a rather abrupt halt. Outside, just a ditch away, was a large searchlight shining into the dark sky. Several soldiers were around it, some of them shouting orders, others turning the light to different areas in the sky.

Beyond the light, a barn was on fire. People were running around, yelling. Pigs were squealing, cows mooing, horses were screaming. The fire was very bright, illuminating even the faces of people in the train. Babies started crying again, children of all ages were frightened. Mothers were giving orders to be quiet and sit down. Farther ahead in the city, one saw flashes of lightning and all the thunder of bombs and anti-aircraft, and above us were the planes.

I felt paralyzed by terror. *My God, we're trapped here in the open. There's no place to hide from THEM. We're so exposed and helpless. And that light and fire next to us. Surely all this will draw THEIR attention to us.*

Some of the soldiers in the train lit cigarettes. Mama said to one of them, "Don't you think they'll see the fire of your cigarette?"

He smiled, "Don't worry, they won't do anything to this train. They're English, and this is a Red Cross train."

They're English. I remembered some of my textbook English from school now. The English eat porridge for breakfast. Americans don't eat porridge, I knew that. The English sing a funny lullaby, "Baby, baby, bunting. Your daddy goes a-hunting, to fetch a little rabbit skin, to wrap his baby bunting in." How can a daddy be an enemy?

I looked out at the light. Two of the soldiers were very young, really just boys, like my cousins. They got an order to turn the light. I followed the beam up to the sky. The light illuminated the clouds. Another beam from somewhere else met our beam and suddenly, from out of the cloud, a little beige-colored airplane appeared. It looked so small and alone. The beams followed it and held it in their bright light.

"Quick, hide! Get in the cloud!" I was saying this out loud.

The soldier, who had reassured my mother before, jumped up and came to the window on my side. He watched with me.

"Don't feel so sorry for them, little girl," he said. "They're here killing children like you. Don't forget that."

He didn't know how well I knew that THEY kill children like me. I tried to look at the game of plane and light beams, but I was afraid to see what would happen to the plane, even though . . .

The air raid seemed to last a long time, but slowly the fury of it passed, and eventually the light next to us was turned off. After some time, the train began to move again. As it pulled into the city of Mainz, the smoke hung heavy in the air. It was evident that the station had received some damage, too. The glass from the roof was broken in many places and scattered all over the platform and tracks. People were clearing debris away with large brooms. They were talking to the soldiers, saying that the engineer was very wise not to have pulled into the station.

"Yes, and he also helped that searchlight crew. But, that was a pretty big risk he took to set the train right next to them."

Some ladies with Red Cross armbands handed us Zwieback and things to drink through the windows. They had big pots on a table, and they rinsed out baby bottles in one and then put them into another one, then filled them with milk. The mothers and soldiers and older kids got sweet tea with milk. *That's how English people drink it.* I thought that, but I didn't say it. It tasted good and warm.

The train left the station, and everyone settled down again. The warmth from my tummy spread through my body, and I went back to my "Heidi" dreams.

In the morning, the train stopped several times. I opened an eye and saw some of the families get off the train. From our compartment they were gone after the second stop. I closed my eyes and drifted off again.

In a dream a voice was speaking, but it didn't fit. It was speaking English.

"You must be sure that you and your children will survive this disaster. There may be a new, terrible weapon. I tell you this so that you will live. Don't go back to Essen again until this war is over. The Americans surely have this weapon by now. If they use it, it will be in the Ruhr valley, I'm sure."

Mama's voice was also speaking English, "Is it some kind of gas?"

The other voice said, "No, it's not gas, it's something else, but if it is used, nothing will be left alive. I believe you will be safe where you are going."

I realized that I was awake. I opened an eye. The shade was drawn almost all the way down. Mama was sitting across from me. Next to her was an officer. He was wearing a gray uniform with a coat and an officer's hat. He was a high officer. I could see that on the collar of his uniform. His arm was in a black sling. He had gray hair, and wore glasses. He was tall and slim. I pretended to be asleep because I knew this was the kind of talk like in our kitchen in the house with the gas light.

The officer got off the train at the next stop. As he left, he spoke in German, "You will like Memmingen. It's a nice little town."

Mama smiled. She looked pretty with her soft brown eyes and wavy dark hair. Her fur collar outlined her face and hair like a cameo.

* * *

10

LEARNING TO THINK GERMAN

It was nearly noon when we arrived in Memmingen. Not very many people got off the train. There were five or six families in our group, but none of them had as many children as we did. All of our luggage was loaded onto a horse drawn wagon. We went on foot to an inn a few blocks from the train station. It was called *Zum Roten Ochsen* I think the town of Memmingen was smaller than Ellwangen, and probably older. The area around the train station was new, but a few blocks down from there, the road continued in cobble-stone and got quite narrow. We passed under the arch of what had been a gate to the city. There were several of those still standing, and quite a few long stretches of the original city wall, as well.

We had been walking through some slushy snow, and some of it oozed into my shoes. I was glad to get inside the restaurant, which was warm and comfortable in an old-fashioned kind of way. The dining room we entered was furnished with lovely, shiny wooden tables and chairs. The windows were made up of tiny little panes set together. Antlers and deer heads and wooden plates with flowers painted on them were hanging on the walls. It smelled like roast beef and red cabbage, which is what they served us.

Several people came to talk to the mothers of our group. A man in a beige uniform with the swastika armband came and pulled up a chair next to Mama. I saw that he limped. I also noticed that he looked a lot like Adolf Hitler. He had dark hair, cut and combed like Hitler's, and he had a mustache like Hitler, but his eyes were dark brown. I think Hitler's were a lighter color. He introduced himself as Herr Hannes. He was the Gauleiter, which was something official, like district supervisor. He told Mama that there was a village about five kilometers from Memmingen, called Benningen.

"A farm there has a cottage, completely furnished, that is for the grandparents when they retire, but no one is retiring yet, so that house is empty and just perfect for a family like this."

Mama told him that I go to a "higher" school and five kilometers is awfully far for a ten-year-old child to go back and forth each day. He looked at me and smiled.

"You know, I have the perfect solution. My daughter is going to the Hoehere Maedchen Schule here. It's right around the corner in the old Spital building. She's also in her first year. You could stay with us during the week and go to be with your family on the weekends." And so it was decided that I would begin school on the coming Monday.

We were transported along with two other families to the village with a wagon that belonged to the farm where we would be staying. It was drawn by a horse, and had rubber tires. It was a long enough trip for me to reminisce about other rides I had, like the one when we had come to Ellwangen the first time, and Mama was so happy to be home again, and the sled ride to Ohmenheim, and the many times that Tante Lene and I had been together going to the fields. I wondered how she was, and if that mean man was mean to her, too. I really missed her, and I knew that she was thinking about me, too. I asked God to be very good to her, because she really deserved it. I told myself that I have to write to her and let her know where we are and that we're well. I didn't know that my mother was writing to her on a regular basis. Somehow my mother and I didn't really talk to each other the way Tante Lene and I did. It was easier to talk to Oma than it was to talk to Mama.

The little house was really charming. It was set into a little garden, enclosed by a picket fence. It had a living room, kitchen, and two bedrooms, completely furnished. It even had inside plumbing, not very modern, but it was a kind of place where one could live for quite a while. I knew that this time we would not be going back to Essen, not in the foreseeable future. I felt comfortable here. The people, who owned the farm, were very friendly and made us feel like relatives.

On Monday, Mama and I walked to town to take a few changes of clothes to the Hannes apartment, to meet the family, and to register me at the school. A grandmother from one of the other families that had come to settle in Benningen stayed with Rose Marie, Herbie, and Hannelore.

Memmingen was, and is, a picturesque town with a number of historical sites still in tact. The building in which the Hannes family lived was probably the newest of all those surrounding the market place. Across to its left was an old church, so old, that it had once been a Roman place of worship. Next to that was the city hall, and in the corner, a real building with seven gables. On the right side was a bridge over a little stream. Two narrow walkways and small footbridges across the stream led to tiny shops, where tall people had to bend over to enter them. There was a green grocer, a butcher, an ice-cream store, bakery, shoe-maker . . . The stream, more like a creek, moved very slowly, and there was a lot of moss, and slimy green plants on the rocks. The plants waved in the water, and some carp swam around them. They had a special carp fishing day every year, but not during the war.

Herr Hannes had a jewelry shop downstairs in the building where they lived. He had two lady assistants. One of them was also the family cook, governess, and female authority figure in the lives of his daughter, Helga, and me. She was some relative, but not very close, because Helga and I called her Frau Inge. Helga didn't look much like Herr Hannes. She was big boned, and fairer skinned than her father. She was easy to get along with, calm and practical. She was really talented in art, and was also a good and serious student.

Frau Hannes, her mother, stayed on a farm most of the time. She came into town on weekends, when I was gone, and I never got to meet her until late in the school year when Helga invited me to spend a Sunday with her on the farm. Her father couldn't come along because he had some official business to attend to.

I don't remember how we got to the farm. It must have been by train. The farm was bigger than any I had ever seen. The barn was as big as a church. There were four different floors on which the hay, straw, and grain were stored on both sides of the wide-open gates, through which one could see a loaded hay wagon from the street. Before we got to the house, Helga took me to the barn, where we climbed ladders to the top floor. The floors were tiered, and we jumped from one level to another, and then we also jumped down into the wagon of hay. I knew that this was very foolish, but Helga did it first, and I was her guest.

The farm was so neat and well kept, it didn't seem like it was a real farm. The floor of the barn was swept clean. Outside of what looked like a cow stable, the walls were whitewashed, and the shutters were blue. The windows were closed, which seemed very strange to me, considering it was daytime, and it was warm outside. Shouldn't the animals have some fresh air? There were no chickens running around, no dogs barking, no cats, no dung heap that I could see or smell. It was also very quiet, as if no one was anywhere around. I did not feel comfortable, and I was glad to get into the house, where Frau Hannes, also a rather large woman, was directing two farm maids on various tasks. One of the girls was very pretty, I thought. She didn't look like a local girl. I thought she reminded me of Ivan, who was a Russian prisoner of war working in the farm in Benningen. The girls carried some large pots out of the kitchen. Frau Hannes was scooping some homemade butter into a dish and then proceeded to form it and decorate it with a teaspoon so that it looked like a fish with scales. I was impressed.

The big kitchen had huge pots and pans hanging around an over-sized stove and oven. It seemed to me that everything in Bayern (Bavaria) was bigger and stronger than in that wind-blown, harsh, but beautiful Schwaebischen Alb, which so often still seemed to tug at my heart.

We spent some time in that kitchen, got something to eat, and then we were on our way again. Did someone drive us back to town, did we go back on the train? I don't know anymore. I just remember that it was a very strange farm, and I kept thinking about a perfectly clean floor in the barn. Blue shutters on a stable wall and closed windows, no sight of, no smell of, any animals. It looked like a farm from the street, but it wasn't a regular farm. What was it? I said nothing about this to Helga, nor anyone else. I was learning to think German.

In town, the Hannes apartment was on the second floor. The kitchen, in a Bavarian country motif, was furnished with modern appliances. They were all electric and shiny white. They also had modern bathroom plumbing. My bedroom looked very sterile. It had super-stiff white sheets on the bed. There was a small wardrobe, a desk and chair, and a sink. The mirror hung behind the desk so that you could look at yourself while you were thinking. We did our homework right after lunch each day. Both of us went to our rooms and worked alone although we were in all the same classes. Sometimes I would look up at the mirror to see if the girl from America might have come along with me after all, but this one had a different look in her eyes. This girl's eyes didn't look so soft. I didn't want to get into the mirror anymore, either. Inside, behind those walls, around a corner might be Death, or Erika and her little brothers with their blond hair standing up and their mouths open and their blue eyes staring at me.

The kitchen was a nice, warm, safe place to be. We usually spent the latter part of the afternoon there. Helga drew paper dolls and clothes. I cut them out. Or we played some board games. We didn't talk about feelings, or our lives. I never learned what she would want to do someday, or where she had been, or what she had done when she was little. My experience in Ellwangen had taught me that America was a taboo subject, so I had very little to tell about myself, as well.

Our school was situated on what was formerly called the flower market. Next to the school was a church, but it was not used as a church. It had become a depot for grain. I though that was a sin. It reminded me of the bible when Jesus drove merchants out of the temple. But I had learned not to say things like that, too.

The school building had originally been a Catholic hospital, and was more than 100 years old. It was an interesting building. The rooms were built around an open area, which in earlier times had boasted a Spanish fountain and garden, but now there was no one to take care of the fountain, which was dry, and there were no plants, either. Our classroom was in the back, off the alley. The music, art, sewing, biology, physics, and chemistry classes were taught on the second floor. Other classrooms were scattered throughout three floors. The office was in the front, of course. It was a girls' school. On rainy or cold days, all of the students would walk around the promenade on the second floor during recess. When the weather was nice, we would be out front and walk up and down under the huge chestnut trees. The atmosphere of the school was warm, gentle, caring. My classmates were nice, polite girls. The teachers were real professionals, who were also human beings.

Frau Meier, who was a Lutheran minister's wife, taught us German, history, and sewing. She was very old. She had been retired and came back to teach because there was no other teacher available. She wore a black dress every day, but the lace collars were different. Her glasses hung on a black ribbon around her neck. She held them up to her eyes when she read, and let them hang when she talked to us. When we stood at attention as she entered the room, and all together said, "Heil Hitler," she would just smile at us and say, "Good morning, children."

When we started to get restless, or sleepy, she had us do stretching exercises right there in the classroom, which really did help. I still remember the lines we said while moving our arms forward, up, sideways, down: *Turnen ist die beste Medizin/Alle Grillen treibt sie aus dem Sinn/ Staerkt die Muskeln, streckt die Glieder aus/ Und dann geh'n wir alle froh nach Haus . . .*

The verse said that exercise drives nonsense out of your mind, strengthens muscles, stretches limbs and gets you happily on your way home.

The content of our German course was awfully grim—long poems and plays by Goethe and Schiller, Germanic Mythology, Greek

Mythology. It was all death, darkness, gloom, treachery, revenge, and destruction. In our classroom was a bookcase with pretty books locked behind glass. I asked Frau Meier once why we couldn't read those books, and she said, "Because that's the way it is."

I can't really remember what kind of history we had. It might have been Roman, or some other ancient civilization. I know it didn't have anything at all to do with our lives, or our world. We did have a very slim and new modern history book, which remained in our desks. We did not take it home. It began with *"Adolf Hitler ist geboren am 20. April, 1889 in Braunau am Inn."* It just gave Hitler's birth city, not the fact that it was in Austria.

I think we had history like that only around the time inspectors were coming to school. We always started with the first chapter, each year, and never went beyond it.

In sewing class we learned how to make a French hem, how to mend a sheet, how to make the different embroidery stitches, and how to crochet. I didn't hold the crochet hook like a lady, according to Frau Meier. Our big project was to sew, by hand, baby shirts for hospitals. When they were all done, Frau Meier packed them into a box and put mine on top. It was gray from the sweat of my hands, and the seams were uneven and lumpy.

"They will see that this was a real labor of love," she said. But she smiled at me as she said it, and I couldn't feel offended, though I wished that I could be more graceful, like the other girls. She made me feel like a little kid.

For math we had a younger teacher, whom we called Kobra. I'm not sure how she got that name, but she did wear snake skin shoes, her piercing gray eyes behind large, thick round glasses, and the fact that she had a spooky way of raising her head at the slightest sound during a test, and finally the henna rinse on her hair, which produced an unusual shade of red, all helped to create the cobra mystique.

Kobra liked me because she saw me during her frequent visits to Herr Hannes. She was a very patriotic type, who thought it was noble for fathers to be in the army and mothers to have at least four children, and I was the youngest and the smallest in the class, so she thought I must be very bright. She never noticed that I neither understood how nor why I had to do algebra. I sat at my desk once, working on one of the problems when she walked by and watched for a while.

I complained, "There must be some shorter way of doing this."

And she said, "Why don't you try. Who knows, you may discover something wonderful. That is the history of the German people, always searching, and finding solutions to problems."

Kobra was transferred to Muenchen during our second year. Fraulein Rosamunde took over math. She was our English teacher, too. She was large, rather heavy, around forty years old. She had a clear, powerful, impressive, soprano voice, which demanded attention and respect. She was my nemesis, forever critical and picky, deriding, correcting my efforts in class. She had studied and taught in London, and told us many interesting stories, including some about London fog and getting lost on your own street.

Though she was very hard to please, I liked her. Her class was fun, and I liked English.

One morning at breakfast, a few months after we had arrived in Memmingen, Herr Hannes told me that my mother had left for Essen because our house was bombed.

"And she had to take care of some formalities. An elderly lady is taking care of the children in Benningen. By the way, your grandmother is well. It was an incendiary bomb, so there was just fire. She is with your uncle's family."

He said this while he was putting honey on his bread. He never looked up from the bread. I felt as though I had been hit in the stomach. I was angry, furious! I hated the war, I hated the English! I started to cry. Our things were burned, furniture, clothes, toys, and our pictures from America. Everything . . . Oma had never gotten around to send those things she had intended to ship by train. My beautiful dolls, all of the things I loved, all gone. We didn't have a home anymore. We could never go home again!

I said all kinds of things, like "why our house?" and many angry things, as well.

Herr Hannes said, "You must be brave. This is war. You are doing this for the Vaterland."

I snapped back, "How does a burned house help the Vaterland?"

He looked at me as though he were going to bore holes into my head with his eyes, and said, "You watch your mouth."

I knew that I had overstepped the boundary, and said, "I'm sorry." But I really wasn't.

He said, "That's better." We finished the meal in an awkward silence.

That day we had English during first period. We were to make up dialogs. I volunteered.

"This is between two English women." Helga was my partner.

I began, "Oh, hello, Betsy. Wasn't it lovely last night? All those bombs? Ha ha . . . I love to see the fire and to hear the bombs explode, don't you?"

Helga just stood there and stared at me in disbelief. Some of our classmates giggled, and Fraulein Rosamunde swooped down on me,

"That's enough! Sit down! How can you be so insensitive? Bombs and dying are nothing to joke about. You are a disgusting child."

I didn't care what she said. I just smirked. I was in a mean mood.

Back in my seat, I had plenty of time to think. The others were doing their dialogs. That would take up more than the period. I visualized our home. My bedroom. I listed all of the things that had been there, and were no longer. As I got to the trunk, I remembered Erika's book.

I had it with me. It wasn't there. It IS a charm! As long as it was there, they didn't bomb our home, but now they could because I had the book. That means that as long as I have it, nothing will happen to me. The book will protect me.

A little voice said, "Erika would have been protected if she had had the book."

I wasn't going to be caught in that trap again, and answered, *Yes, but she gave it to me before she died. So, it's mine. Besides, I wouldn't have kept it if I had known that.*

I watched my classmates and felt sad and angry, and suddenly very lonely. I was alone in this experience, and there was no one to cry to, and on top of it all, I had made myself look ugly. I was the orange star again.

At the Hannes house we never heard anything negative about the war, but somewhere, perhaps in a store, on the radio, I heard about the Afrika Panzer Corps in trouble, and about Americans in combat with Germans. People, like Hitler and his propaganda people were giving lots of speeches about love for the Vaterland, for the German people, for spirit and unity and glory. I didn't like their speeches. They were always screaming and angry. It seemed like they were scolding us.

I was getting used to the routine of spending school days with the Hannes family, and walking to Benningen on Friday afternoon, returning to school on Monday morning.

One thing I learned from living in a rural area was that the natives never walk along the highways when they go to other villages or towns. There's always some short cut, some back way. In the weeks I had made the trip back and forth from Memmingen to the village, I learned about the shortcut through a bog. There were signs posted at the two ends of the footpath,

"No hoofed animals allowed. Hoof and Mouth Disease." No one knew how long those signs had been there. And nobody remembered the disease. The path was, for the most part, a bit raised and sandy. But right next to it were soft, swampy places, even, they said, some quicksand. At any rate, it looked eerie and foreboding, especially since there were so many dragonflies, which were not really seen very often anywhere else, and when the weather was cool, there were small patches of fog that moved around out there. I didn't know anyone who would be crazy enough to see if there really was quicksand or not. I stayed on the path, as I imagine everyone else did, and enjoyed the imagined danger and mystery of the area. What I found really fascinating about it was the little chapel about one kilometer outside of the village, right in the bog, on a sandy, solid island along the path.

The farmer's wife told me that the chapel was built by a former owner of a large flour mill nearby. The murals on the walls depicted a story: There were two brothers. One inherited the mill from his father, and the other one was jealous. He decided to give his brother bad luck.

He went to church and to Communion on Sunday, but he didn't swallow the wafer. He put it into his pocket. Then he went to his brother's mill and put the wafer between the millstones. The next day, when the miller began to grind the wheat, blood flowed from the stones. The story ends with the bad brother having all sorts of family disasters, including his house being swallowed up by the swamp, and the good brother building the chapel to break the spell of bad luck for the family.

The school year was progressing. We received our mid-term report cards. I had a 5(D) in English. I was so surprised, shocked, that I was sure it was an error. I asked Fraulein Rosamunde why I had gotten such a grade.

She answered in an icy voice, "It is obvious that your class of people does not belong in this school. You will nevah learn English."

The disdain and arrogance in that statement stung and touched a nerve that would never let me forget it. I had hurt myself more than I realized that day when I was lashing out at the English because they burned down my home.

When my mother saw that grade, she arranged a conference with my teacher. They sat together in the classroom after school. I sat on the steps to the alley and waited for Mama. It was a Friday, and I would walk back with her to Benningen for the weekend. I don't know what they talked about, but after the conference, Fraulein Rosamunde talked to me in a softer tone. Sometimes I was aware of her trying to make amends, but I did not have the social skills necessary to accommodate her, and I couldn't forget what she had said that day. All I really wanted to do is prove to her that I could, indeed, learn English.

Shortly after that, I had another disappointment. It had to do with Herr Braun, who was our biology and music teacher. He was very special to us all, being the only young man in our lives, and he had a way of making everything really fascinating. We were learning botany. The subject had become a passion with me. I spent hours doing watercolor diagrams of flowers. I collected leaves, and memorized Latin terms just to please him.

In music we were practicing folk songs and cradle songs. The folk songs were for a visit to the Lazaret, the soldier's hospital. And then, on a very beautiful, sunny day, Herr Braun spoke to us in the music room, "This will be the last time I will be with you. They have decided that I must go to war. I do not want to go. I do not feel that I can shoot at anyone, yet I must go. You will probably not have music anymore, and so I've been told to test you and give you a grade for the year.

We went in alphabetical order up to the piano and told him which song we preferred. I sang well. He gave me a 1(A). I wanted to hug him and tell him that I didn't want him to go and that he was my favorite teacher, but we're not allowed to do things like that, so I made my curtsey and returned to my seat. When we were all done with the testing, he played soft, sweet, sad melodies on the piano. The bell rang. He closed the piano, and we never heard it played again. We didn't have science class the rest of the year, nor the next school year, either.

Frau Oldenburg, who would be one of the three teachers we had left, was our P.E. and art teacher. I think she was even older than Frau Meier. She was very, very thin. Her skin hung on her in folds. For P.E. she wore the white T-shirt and black bloomers we all wore. We were barefoot, but she wore black tights and ballet slippers. The tights were very loose and wrinkled around her thin, bird-like legs. She carried a long stick, like a staff, which she would tap against the floor to demand attention, or she would wave it in the air to keep rhythm during gymnastic exercises. She'd touch us on the shoulder to tell us to stand up straight.

"Shoulders back, tummy in."

I had been ill with some kind of intestinal bug for some time and had become anemic. I was very thin and tired easily. Frau Oldenburg worried about my health, and when the class did strenuous exercises, she told me to sit and watch.

In art class we really had fun. We did only fantasy drawings with watercolor and ink, painted pictures for children's fairy-tale books and learned to make toys out of wooden spools, cardboard, pieces of very thin wood, and yarn.

In Benningen, Papa had come on a short furlough. I didn't see much of him because I still had to go to school. He made his mark on the village, though. The farmer's bull got loose one day and was running up and down the village street. People were in their gardens, behind fences, watching him run. Papa went into the house, came back out with a red-and-white-checked table cloth and waited for the bull to come his way. As the bull was approaching him, Papa stood in the middle of the street and played toreador with the tablecloth, calling "Aha, Toro." The bull stopped running and stood, looking at the checkered cloth. Ivan, the Russian prisoner of war who worked on the farm, came and put the rope back on the bull and took him to the stable.

Mama said that Papa was crazy for doing that, and that everybody in the village was talking and laughing about it.

Papa said, "Well, the bull stopped, didn't he?"

I loved seeing my father in a light and happy mood. He seemed to really enjoy being out in the country, and I know that he felt we were safe, which was a relief to him. I had no chance to talk to him about anything. Everyone else needed his attention, too. He returned again to the coast somewhere; Holland, Belgium, or France, I don't remember which it was.

A few weeks after Papa left, our summer vacation began. By the time I came home to Benningen to spend the summer there, I was very ill. I coughed endlessly, and also got terribly nauseous. I couldn't smell anything without heaving. Some of the older ladies thought I might have been bitten by a mosquito, others, including the doctor, thought I had hepatitis, but finally I was diagnosed as having pernicious anemia. I was supposed to get B-12 injections, but there was none available, so I had to swallow pure cod liver oil. It is revolting to swallow that stuff when you are well, it is nearly impossible to do so when you are already horribly nauseous. Mama said that I had to take it because I would die, otherwise. She had a unique way of getting me to take my medicine. She came at me with a tablespoon full of oil in one hand, and a wooden spoon in the other one and calmly said, "You're going to swallow this, and if you dare to throw up, I'm going to beat you with this wooden spoon."

I held my nose, opened my mouth, gagged and heaved, but I held my mouth shut, and somehow managed to swallow it. We went through this production twice a day until the bottle was empty.

Another part of my cure was to lie out in the sun every day for two weeks. I also got to eat apple cake with lots of raisins and a thick sugar coating. That was made by the farmer's wife. It was a wonderful cake, but any kind of smell, good or bad, made me heave. At first I had to hold my breath while I ate it, but by and by I was able to taste and to enjoy it, and I recovered.

It was during our summer vacation that Mama found an available apartment, closer to Memmingen, outside of yet another village. With the papers she had gotten in Essen, she was allowed to buy new furniture. It was a poor substitute for what we had lost, but it was ours. Our new home was on the third floor of the tallest of three houses on an unpaved road. It was not far from town. From the market place, one walked about two blocks to another old city gate whose tower was completely

RuTH S. OZAN

intact, and on the outside wall one could admire a cannonball which had hit and remained imbedded in the wall for centuries. Beyond the gate, the street became a highway, which led to the mountains, to Lindau, and the Bodensee. There were still buildings, houses, a grocery store along this street. It was less than one kilometer from the gate where our road turned off, right before the grocery store. A bit down the road was a small wooded area on the left, and on the right were three man-made ponds, stocked with fish. The house we would live in stood across from the third pond.

Our family shared this house with Frau Dauer and her two daughters on the first floor, Frau Grosse and her daughter on the second floor, and Frau Edelstein and her daughter, Iris. We lived on the third. All of the men were in the army, but Frau Edelstein's husband was somewhere else. All of the women, except for Mama and Frau Dauer, who was pretty old, went to work during the day.

Iris was the only child outside of us. She was a year younger than I and went to the village school where Rose Marie and Herbie would go in the fall. German summer vacation is not as long as it is in America, but they have a week in late fall, two weeks for Christmas, three weeks for spring break and a number of other holidays, and Summer vacation lasts about six weeks. At any rate, we still had a few weeks of free time, and we enjoyed it by exploring our new environment. On sunny days we would walk to the forest, which was within walking distance even for Hanni. Most of the time Iris would also come along. We picked wild strawberries and raspberries, listened to the birds and the wind sighing through the treetops. I told fairy tales and made up stories. Rose Marie and I pretended to see little dwarves or elves to intrigue the little ones, and we would spend our time in make-believe worlds. Iris tolerated this play, but did not really participate. She had a very complicated personality. There were times when she would not talk for, what seemed to me, absolutely no reason. I can't remember her ever really laughing about anything. She seemed to be unhappy. I don't think she had other friends. I know that she loved her grandfather, though. He lived in the village, and her last name was the same as his, it wasn't Edelstein.

One day it was raining, and Iris invited me over. Their kitchen was upstairs, on the opposite wall of our kitchen. Their bedroom was on the second floor. We shared the bathroom. So, anyhow, her mother wasn't home, and she decided to show me some pictures of herself and her family. She showed me a picture of her father. He was a tall, slim man with dark hair and dark eyes. He had on a very nice suit and a hat, and a Star of David on his lapel. She probably had not been aware of it before, because as she saw it, she quickly put the picture away. I pretended not to have noticed. Actually, if I hadn't lived in Essen in the Jewish neighborhood, I wouldn't have even known what it was. That evening I told my mother about the picture. She acted scared.

"Did you tell anybody else about this?" she asked.

"No, I just saw it a little while ago." I answered.

"Good," Mama said. "Don't ever, ever tell anybody else! Do you understand?"

"Yes, I know. But, why is that so terrible?"

Mama said, "Jewish people are considered enemies. They are arrested and put in prison."

"Is Iris' father in prison?"

"I don't know where he is, no one has told me. But, most likely he is."

"And, if they knew that Iris' father was Jewish, they would put her in prison because she would be an enemy?"

I remembered my night with the SS and the day when I was told that I was an enemy in Ellwangen.

Mama shook her head and sighed, "You always ask me questions to which I don't have answers. Please, just forget that you saw what you saw, will you please?"

I promised her I would never mention it again. I reminded myself to keep my big mouth shut about this and about America. I felt closer to Iris, but I didn't tell her about America, not even that I knew her secret.

School started again. Our classroom was the same, on the first floor, in the back, by the alley. Our teachers were Frau Meier, Frau Oldenburg, and Fraulein Rosamunde.

We didn't have geography, nor science, nor music. In German we learned old Germanic stories and poetry, which also took up history class, as well. English was the only subject that seemed to be alive and have some connection with the present and reality. I didn't like math, even though Fraulein Rosamunde taught it. It was still just numbers, minus, plus, powers, brackets, and always had to be absolutely perfectly correct, with no room for creativity and imagination. I don't think Fraulein Rosamunde liked it very much either, she couldn't tell any stories about numbers, and nothing funny or interesting ever happened in math.

Since we now lived close enough to school for me to come and go every day, I no longer slept at the Hannes' apartment. Helga was still the classmate I associated with most, and on days when the weather was very bad after school, or on Wednesdays, I would go home with her for lunch. My presence there was understood, and I never felt that I was not welcome.

This school year, we went to BDM meetings on Wednesday afternoon. BDM stood for Bund Deutscher Maedel, loosely translated as Association of German Girls, which was the girls' part of the Hitler Youth. Since we were not yet fourteen years old, we were not "real" BDM members, but what the older boys and girls called *Kueken* (chickies).

We met in a room in the tower of the city gate through which I went every day. It was very exciting to climb the old stairs and come to the room with thick stone slabs on the floor, little windows in very thick walls, and to sit on old wooden benches at long, dark wooden tables among the ghosts of hundreds of years of history.

Our group leader was a very pretty, tall, blond young woman, who went to the Gymnasium Oberstufe. That means that she was in at least the eleventh grade. Our school only went from fifth through tenth. After that, the girls joined the boys' classes at the Gymnasium. We were now in sixth grade.

The BDM meetings offered us a variety of activities, so each meeting was anticipated all week long. It was an afternoon of crafts, music, and fun. We learned old folksongs, painted wooden toys that the older boys had constructed, went on field trips out to the forest.

Along the way, we learned to march, and sing marching songs. In the forest we picked raspberry leaves for medicinal teas. We finally even went to visit the hospital and sang to the soldiers.

After we finished singing, we were supposed to talk to the soldiers and cheer them up. I thought it would be terribly depressing. So many of them looked like my father and other men I cared about. I felt like crying. I was aware, again, that there were no young, healthy men around. But, somehow, I ended up at the bed of a man who looked a lot like my father. I had no idea what I should say, but he helped to break the ice by asking me a lot of questions about myself. I think I must have told him my whole life story. He listened very patiently, and kept me going with little questions. Then he told me that his family lived in Schlesien, where my father's family was from. He said he wished they were here in the South. He was worried about them. He had two sons, aged ten and eight, and a little daughter, whom he had never seen. He sounded very sad when he talked about his family, but then he turned to me again, and told me that if I believe that everything will turn out well, then it really will. He said that things always look much worse than they are. Before I left, I told him that I hope he doesn't have to go back to the war again, that they will let him go home.

He smiled, and said, "That would be very nice."

One day, during that fall, as I was on my way home, walking along the highway, I saw a convoy of tanks and trucks rolling toward Memmingen. There were tanned, smiling and cheerful young men aboard. They waved back at me. It was the remainder of the Afrika Panzer Corps. After their defeat in Africa, they had landed in Italy, and were returning to Germany and other assignments. I don't think anyone knew that they were coming. They had been the darlings of the nation, but they had lost not only the battle, but very many men, as well. The government didn't consider them heroes anymore, I guessed. I felt sad for them, and also happy to see that there really were some young men still alive. They reminded me of Heinz, who was my idol. He was a paratrooper, which made sense to me because he was so athletic and I thought that one ought to be that, to jump out of planes and land safely. I also knew that it was terribly dangerous because they were so exposed and always had to jump into dangerous places.

Perhaps it was my memories of Heinz and Erfurt, the cool, damp, dark leaves on the ground of the park, or maybe I was just getting older and more sensitive to weather conditions. As I walked along on the little road to our home, I felt my feet getting wet from walking through the rotting fallen leaves, and I became aware of a sadness, a dark melancholy that seemed to lie over everyone. When children were loud and laughing, someone would tell them to be quiet, that there is a war and that there is nothing to laugh about. Everyone, including Mama, was quiet and pre-occupied. The sun seemed to have left our part of the world. It was gray and damp every day.

As on every school day, I would come home, eat lunch and then do my homework, while also taking care, more or less, of my siblings. This was more of a job when the weather was nice, and I did my work out on the table under the lilac and mock orange bushes. Towards evening, Iris and I would walk to the village dairy with our family milk cans, stand in line, get precisely as much milk as we were rationed to get, and then walk back home. Sometimes we would tell each other about things that happened in school. Often we just were silent, daydreaming.

We also went together to pick up the ration stamps, which were given out at the beginning of the month on Sunday afternoon at the village school. The stamps came on different-colored sheets of paper, one color for bread, another color for dairy products, another for meats, staples, etc . . . It also depended on age groups. Small children got more milk, people who did hard labor got more meat.

On the radio, ladies would talk about diet and how one could use the various products to have a good and nourishing meal. But rations were really low, and Mama found it difficult to feed us adequately, and so we joined the many others in the activity called "hamstern." Simply put, it was "going begging." I usually went with all of my siblings from one farm to the next and ask for milk, an egg, some flour, or lard. Most of the time we were refused, but there was one farm where I knew we would get something, although the price seemed very hard for me to pay.

The farm was on the other side of the three ponds near our house. Mama worked at that farm on occasion, especially in the potato fields.

That's how she got a sack of potatoes for us. The woman knew us, too. She was very fat, and although she was terribly grumpy, she did have a heart, somewhere.

We picked late afternoon for our visit. It would be after the milking had been done for the day. The fat lady sat in the kitchen with one of the maids, who also looked very well fed. The conversation usually ran in exactly this way:

"So, you're here again. And what do you want?" she would begin.

My line was, "Some milk, eggs, anything that you have."

She would go on, "I can't believe that you can come here again and again like this. Aren't you even a little bit ashamed to go begging like this?"

I didn't answer.

"Well, what do you have to say for yourself?" she badgered on.

"I'm not begging. I do have money to pay for the food," I protested.

"Money! You can keep your silly money. There's nothing to buy for money. If you brought me something worthwhile, I could do business with you . . ."

"You know that everything we had was burned in Essen," I replied.

"Yes, yes, everybody comes and cries the same old song. I should feed the whole world."

I stood silently looking at the ground. The little ones started to hide behind me. The ordeal was almost over. She started to feel bad.

"Look at you, standing there like that. It makes me sick to look at you!" She turned to the maid, "Here, take this milk and fill the cat's bowl and give the rest to them so that they can leave."

What was left over was usually about a cupful of milk.

I said "Thank you."

She grumbled, "Tell your Mama she should be ashamed to send her children begging."

Each time on the way home, I told God that I hated to beg and if I could, I would steal, but I didn't know how.

Pretty soon Mama realized that we weren't getting very far locally, and decided that we might have better luck if we visited people we knew. She took the train to Ellwangen and visited Tante Sofie and came back with a pretty good haul. When that was gone, I got on the train to

Neresheim. I was supposed to stop in Ohmenheim and visit my former friend Irma. Mama thought they might be willing to part with some food. But, as I got into the village, I decided to stop there on my way back. I felt like a total stranger walking down the familiar street, and as I got to the bend of the road where the old house and smithy used to be, I saw only a little rise and neatly cut grass. The house and the smithy had been razed. The trees, even the big pear tree, had been cut down.

As I stood, looking and remembering, a young boy from the house across the street came to stand behind me and jeered, "That's a surprise, isn't it? Your old dump isn't there anymore. It's out of our lives and out of our sight, just like you are, so why don't you just go and get lost."

I didn't even answer him, or look at him. I was shocked that my precious memory had just disappeared, and that I was greeted in this hostile manner.

I went on past the mayor's house, out onto the road that led to Tante Lene's brother's house. At least, I could try to retrieve my doll and my coat. The road to the village seemed to have gotten narrower since then. I tried to find "my" field, but since other crops were planted, I couldn't.

I arrived at the house around noon. It was Saturday. Bread had been baked that day. The room smelled delicious. Several village women were sitting on the benches. They looked up when I entered, and then went on with their conversations. The girl was sitting near the oven. She was stroking the doll's hair. When she recognized me, she tried to hide the doll behind her. I went to her quickly and pulled the doll from her and then saw that it was no longer the baby I remembered. She had a finger broken off. Her hair was tangled. She only had her underclothes on, and they were a grimy gray. The eyelashes on one eye were cut. The girl grabbed the doll from me and clutched her to herself, and I knew I wouldn't take her away.

The women were leaving as all of this was going on. When they were gone, the mother came over to us and said, "As you can see, I couldn't take that baby away from her. She needs it more than you do." I understood, because I realized that this girl was always going to remain a speechless, wild child who loved that doll more than I ever could.

I told the mother that I had come to get the doll and my coat.

"Your coat isn't here. I gave it to my sister for her girl. It would be too small for you, anyway."

"But, I don't have a coat. All of our things burned in Essen, and my coat was here when we left, so I didn't have a coat. Besides, even if it were too small for me, my sister could wear it."

"Well, there's nothing to be done about it now. I can give you some bread, though."

"We do get bread with our ration cards," I said. "What we need is lard and eggs and meat."

"I'll see what I have here," she answered, and went to a cupboard. "We'll send a rabbit when my husband gets back. He went to the heath with the sheep." Sending a rabbit sounded ridiculous, but she was getting some things out of the cupboard. She brought a sack of flour over to the table. I had brought my little suitcase along. She put flour into a paper bag, and placed two eggs into the flour. Then she packed a cup of lard and some vegetables from the garden in, too, to fill up the other space. She gave me a piece of fresh bread with lard, and an apple for the road, and I was on my way again.

I wished that I could have avoided going through Ohmenheim on the way back, but it had to be done. No one I knew saw me. I did not go anywhere, not even to Tante Marie's house, excusing myself with the thought that I might miss the train home. I tried to feel some sort of sense of belonging, but I couldn't. It seemed that the happy time I had spent in this village was very long ago. I let the tears flow while I was walking down the hill towards Neresheim. I cried over my doll most of all.

On the train I had to stand for a long time. It was very crowded. I was worried about the suitcase. It was made of Ersatz material, and sometimes the snaps just popped open. If that were to happen, I would be in very bad trouble. Hamstering, as was obvious from the contents of the suitcase, was a very serious crime. But, I got home all right.

Mama said, "It's a good thing that we don't have to worry about having wasted the money for your train fare. What you brought here is definitely not worth all the trouble and money it cost, but it doesn't matter, we can't buy anything with our money, anyhow."

I felt that I had lost more than the train fare. My wonderful village life with Tante Lene and my doll were gone. They only existed in my mind like so many other memories.

Life was getting harder in many ways. The stores were empty. Christmas was coming, and there was nothing at the department store that didn't require stamps or some other official paper. There were only bookmarks, napkin rings, and very old postcards. Clothing was rationed, if there was anything to buy. We got one pair of shoes a year, but in the late years of the war, they were wooden-soled sandals. There were no new socks or underwear, and certainly no coat. Iris' father used to run the department store. I heard a neighbor tell that to Mama over the fence. She said that he was on a big farm somewhere not far from Memmingen and that Herr Hannes used to know him real well, that they grew up together, and that he fixed it so that Iris' father wouldn't have to go far away. Everybody knew that Iris was his daughter, but she had her mother's maiden name, and nobody told.

I heard the whole conversation, but two words just stood out: "farm" and "Hannes." I knew! I knew what farm she was talking about. I knew it wasn't a regular farm! It was . . . What was it? It was strange. I guess some sort of farm work was done there, but the people who worked there were special. I knew a very big secret, but since I wasn't supposed to have heard the conversation, I couldn't tell. I wondered if Frau Edelstein and Iris knew. I would have liked to tell Iris, but how could I? She shouldn't know that I know . . . I didn't tell Mama, either, because I didn't think I could explain why I felt that there was something strange about the farm. She always got very aggravated when I tried to tell her something that I was thinking about. I wondered if Helga knew. She must have known, but what?

It was getting really cold already in November. One Sunday afternoon Iris and I went to the school to pick up the food stamps. A fine, chilling rain had been falling for days. The leaves on the ground were still rotting. The wet was seeping through shoes and socks again.

Our clothes were heavy with the moisture. On the way home, we heard airplane engines up above us. We looked up. Two fighter planes were flying very close together, practicing maneuvers. Suddenly they touched. One wavered and flew off, the other stalled, choked, sputtered, started to smoke, and came tumbling down. It was falling, head over tail, sideways, tumbling, tumbling down into the woods. From then until the end of the war, the plane was stuck, nose down, in the soft wet earth, and a soldier stood guard near it. Shortly after that accident, they closed the flight school, which was on the other side of Memmingen.

Winter came early and hard that year. It was very cold. Our school ran out of coal. We sat in our classroom with coats and gloves on. Finally, they told us we would have Christmas vacation a little early, and they closed the school.

The Christmas season was more religious and solemn for us than it had been before. We didn't have Midnight Mass because we had to observe the black-out, but on Christmas Day the church sparkled with candles and green branches, pretty shiny stars, angel hair, and tinsel.

The children had been hoping for some wonderful surprises, perhaps a big package in the mail.

The postal clerk was very busy with deliveries. She pushed her bicycle from one house to the next, the mail in a basket in front of the handle-bars. She was not delivering packages or holiday greetings. She was delivering telegrams from the Ministry of War. It seemed that all of the men from the village had been in Russia, and died or were missing outside of Stalingrad. It took so long for the families to be notified. With the telegrams came rumors about many of the soldiers having frozen to death, about them eating the flesh from the horses. I thought about Onkel Josef and knew that he was there, dead, probably very close to the skeletons of his horses. I hoped that he didn't have to watch the others eat the horses' flesh. Eventually we found out that he, and Tante Frida's husband, Tante Sofie's son Josef, and Onkel Fritz were either dead or missing.

That horrendous tragedy in Russia was the fatal wound to the psyche of the German people. Everyone felt a very deep sorrow and a dark hopelessness that didn't go away.

The women in the three houses got together. Although none had received a telegram, they all had husbands, brothers, other relatives in the army, and they worried about them now more than ever. The family in the first house had geese. They butchered, and we all had a taste of Christmas goose. And very quietly, the new year, 1944, began.

In *The People's Chronology*, a Henry Holt reference book, I read that by May of 1943 the Germans had lost the war in North Africa. On July 9 and 10, British paratroopers and American airborne forces had invaded Sicily. On July 19, 500 US bombers raided Rome. Benito Mussolini resigned July 25. Allied armies took Messina August 17 and crossed the straits to invade Southern Italy. The Italian regime signed an armistice at Algiers. September 8 was the official day of the Italian unconditional surrender, but the Germans, stationed in Italy, resisted the Allied advances. The U.S. Fifth Army landed at Salerno on September 9, and took Naples on October 1.

Heavy bombings of industrial centers in Germany, and occupied France began in January of 1943 and proceeded on a continuous basis.

In Russia, supplies and new troops relieved Leningrad's seventeen-month-long siege in February, but the Germans blockaded the narrow corridor to the city 1,200 times through the year, and starvation continued. Germans lost 500,000 men in three months of winter fighting as the Russians took back Kharkov and other key cities, but the Germans recaptured Kharkov, March 15. The Battle of Kursk began July 5 and involved 6,000 German and Russian tanks and 4,000 planes. It ended after a week of heavy fighting in a victory for the Soviet Fifth Army. The Germans lost 70,000 men, 2,000 tanks, 1,392 planes, and 5,000 vehicles. The losses were probably equally as high for the Soviets.

The Soviet forces retook Kharkov August 23 with the help of supplies from the U.S. Smolensk, and Kiev on the Dnieper River were back in Russian hands by early November. The Moscow Conference in late October established a European advisory commission on terms of German surrender, separation of Austria from Germany, and destruction of Italy's fascist regime.

France's Pas de Calais area was attacked December 24, Christmas Eve, 1943, by 3,000 Allied planes that included 1,300 from the U.S. Eighth Air Force.

In Poland the Battle of the Warsaw Ghetto began Passover Eve, April 18, and ended six weeks later with 5,000 German troops killed and wounded, but 5,000 Jews were also killed defending themselves against German tanks and artillery. Some 500,000 Jews had been locked into an area that formerly accommodated half that number. Thousands escaped to join the Polish resistance, but 20,000 were deported to death camps such as Auschwitz, Birtkenau, Belzec, Chmelno, Maidenek, and Sobibor. Jews at Bialystock, Tamow, and other Polish cities offered resistance, but few survived the genocidal Nazi Holocaust.

On October 4, in a speech to his *Gruppenfuhrer* (lieutenant generals), SSfuhrer Heinrich Himmler is said to have made the following statement: The plan for the extermination of the Jews is well advanced (despite pleas to spare this or that "exceptional" Jew.) . . . while we will never speak of it in public, the destruction of the Jews will remain forever an unwritten and never-to-be-written page of glory.

In Denmark the SS began rounding up Danish Jews in October, after having left them untouched since 1940, but the Danes helped most of their Jewish compatriots escape to safety in Sweden.

All of these events took place since we had come from Essen early in 1943. I try to remember what I heard, what I knew. I knew that the

Americans were in Italy, but that still seemed very far away, though from where we lived Italy was actually not that far away. I know that I heard about Monte Cassino, which actually happened in February of 1944. The reason I remembered it is that they talked about it a lot on the radio. They said that the Americans bombed their own men, and they destroyed that historic Benedictine abbey. I didn't hear, or would not have understood, that Polish troops came to the rescue of the Americans.

We heard a lot of scary propaganda about savage and cruel Polish resistance fighters, this mostly through a kind of gossip in stores, or among neighbors. I don't know if our parents knew about what was going on in Warsaw, that Jews were being sent to death camps. They certainly never discussed it in front of us if they did.

I was sure that every soldier who had to go to Russia would die there. If anyone told me that her father, brother, cousin was in Russia, to me that was like saying he's dead.

There were reports about air raids of all of the large cities, and always they listed how many enemy planes were supposedly shot down, but people in the stores, or across the fence, talked about how many thousand people died, and that they were making mass graves because they couldn't bury all the people individually.

I was, like everyone around me, wrapped up in my own life drama, of being cold and always a bit hungry and tense, waiting, waiting to see what terrible thing would happen next.

Papa's last furlough came at the beginning of March 1944. He brought a short-wave radio. It was against the law to listen to foreign broadcasts. He also brought some olive oil, which he had gotten in a trade for salt, and a can of meat, which looked like army food. The weather was wet and cold and dreary the whole time he was at home. He was tired and quiet, but he did many things around the house to help us all. He chopped wood for all of the women, he repaired appliances, caulked windows, and dug a trench in the backyard, covering it with branches and dirt. He said that if there is fighting or heavy bombing, we should go into the trench, not into the basement because the basement was not safe and the house was big and an easy target. I heard what he said, but dismissed his statements as just other gloomy things adults were saying.

One day we went shopping together. It was wonderful to walk down the street, holding hands with my father again. Sometimes, a man would salute "Heil Hitler" as he went by, and Papa would put his hand to his cap. On the way home, an older man saluted him "Heil Hitler" again, and Papa turned to me and said, *"Ich hab' ihn doch nicht krank gemacht."* I didn't understand. "What did you say, Papa?" I asked.

He replied, "The man said 'Heil Hitler.' Well, 'heil' means both 'hail' and 'heal.' I said that I didn't make him sick."

I was aghast, "Oh, Papa, that's bad! You can get into trouble if you say things like that."

Papa looked down at me for a moment, and then led me to the fence at the side of the road. He stood, looking out at the field. I got up on a board of the fence, so that I would be at face level with him. He turned to me and said, "Child, you must not be so afraid of everything. You have to trust and believe in yourself and in those you love. I have to leave, and I don't know when I'll be back. You have to be sensible and strong and help your Mama now. You are a smart girl. I want you to use your head. You can't be a child anymore. Your mother has to be able to rely on you."

Then he was quiet for a moment, and continued in a way as if he were giving me advice for the rest of my life. "Whatever happens, remember this: Behave yourself. Always be a lady. If you act like a lady, people will treat you like one. Be kind to everyone. Think of others, not just yourself. Put yourself in their place. People will respond in the same manner. You get back what you give. Remember what I've said to you."

Back home, he rigged an antenna for the radio with wires along the window sill and ending with a spoon tied to the end of the wire which dangled against the wall behind the sofa bed. Then he told me to go next door to Edelsteins and stand near the sink to see if the radio could be heard. I knocked on the door and pretended I needed to know how far several of the villages were from Memmingen, that we were doing a geography lesson in school. That was my excuse for coming over. Frau Edelstein gave me her guesses, while I leaned against her sink. I didn't hear anything, but just to be sure, Mama would stuff a rag into the drain and the faucet, and roll a big towel and put it on the floor in front of the door to our apartment. Frau Edelstein would probably have been the last person to have anything to do with Nazi authorities, but one couldn't take chances. She or Iris might accidentally say something to someone else. Listening to foreign broadcasts, especially enemy broadcasts, was considered an act of treason.

The precious days our father was with us flew by. On the day he had to leave, it was so dark and stormy we had the light on in the kitchen. It was really dark outside. Papa was grumbling about boots and big woolen coats that are more trouble than help in weather like this, and he wished he could get rid of that disgusting gas mask canister that just is so much more baggage to be carried around. He told Mama that he didn't want her to go to the train station with him because she would just get wet and catch cold and he'd have to worry about her, too. But she went anyway.

The gloom and silence hung like a black cloud over us, who were left behind. The fire in the stove nearly died. I put some wood in and blew and blew to get the sparks to catch.

On my twelfth birthday, a few days later, the sun was shining again, and Helga had a surprise for me. A friend of hers gave me her BDM uniform that had gotten too small for her. It looked like new, and fit me quite well. I loved it, especially the jacket, which was wonderfully soft velvet. I was at Hannes' and put it on upstairs, and came downstairs, to show it to Herr Hannes. He looked annoyed. "Why are you wearing your uniform?" he asked.

"I'm going to have my picture taken," I answered.

"I wish you girls wouldn't walk around in those uniforms so much . . . All right, go get your picture taken and then get back and change into your regular clothes," he growled. I didn't understand why he would say that. He used to wear his uniform a lot . . . although not lately.

Slowly, the weather got milder, and one morning we woke up, and spring had arrived. The sky was clear and the world sparkled. Day by day everything became green once more. Fruit trees bloomed, and life seemed to be sweet. Rose Marie made her First Communion in a white satin long-sleeved dress and long white stockings, and both of us had our confirmation. The bishop didn't come to Memmingen every year, so several age groups were confirmed together. Mama let me wear my hair unbraided for the occasion. Old Frau Dauer disapproved. She said I looked wild. Apparently the bishop thought so, too. When he reminded me of the fact that I may have to suffer for my faith, he definitely slapped my cheek, but he just patted Rose Marie's.

And then came May, so unbearably beautiful with blue skies and showers of blossoms from the lilac bush and the mock orange tree in the yard. I did my homework at the picnic table under the branches of those trees, and kept my eye on the younger children. The flowers smelled heavenly. All that beauty made me feel lonely. There seemed to be no person in the whole world with whom I could talk about feelings, ideas, anything. I would alternate from giddy joy and wild energy to dark and tear-filled despair. Sometimes I would talk to Erika. I wasn't afraid of her anymore. Since our home was bombed, too, I felt that the book was a gift from her that would protect me. I wanted to believe that she had really been an angel all the time. Remembering the sun shining on her hair and that of her brothers, they really did look like angels. I could understand that sometimes angels appear as people, but I couldn't justify their deaths. No matter how hard I tried, I couldn't make myself believe that angels would have to suffocate in order to become invisible again. And so I would just leave that part of my flawed fantasy out and continue to speak to her as my friend and companion angel.

But, it wasn't enough to feel that there was an angel spirit who heard me, I needed . . . I needed something earthly, human love. I went on a reading binge. I read my mother's books from the library, all in secret. I read a love story between a German girl and a French young man. The love was doomed, of course. Very conveniently, the young man was killed in an auto accident and the girl was set free from her enchantment. She returned home to her own country where she belonged. I was angry at the author. I didn't like that ending. I liked the young man, and I would have been in love with him, too.

Another story took place in a strange, dark world. The story was about an Egyptian girl, her hashish-addicted father, the man who supplied the dope, and the hero, nationality unknown, who paid the father's debts and rescued the daughter from the clutches of the dope dealer. I couldn't relate to that story very well.

I read these books by moonlight, sitting on the windowsill. I took them with me to the wood shed, the toilet, the basement, and the attic. Mama couldn't understand why every errand took forever. Sometimes, I even forgot what I was supposed to do. She became very frustrated with me, and screamed some colorful names at me. I took that in as just another part of my great suffering, though most of the time I was in the world of the book I was reading, and was living the life of the heroine, drifting through the real world with my mind somewhere else.

And so I drifted into June. The weather was mild, the windows were open at night. There was a full moon, but high in the sky. It gave off a pale, cool light. Everything was silent, no sound of birds, crickets, all was still. I looked at the landscape below, and the eerie light gave the silent world a disturbing appearance. It seemed that nothing outside was alive, and I felt a great need to talk to God. I prayed, out loud, I guess.

"Dear God, make the war end soon and protect every one, especially Papa. Please, take good care of him."

Somehow, I felt that my prayer had gone to where it was heard, and I felt at peace. Herbie told me later that he had heard me pray.

Mama was listening to BBC when I got up in the morning. She was nearly in shock. "They've landed. The Americans and the English.

They're fighting. Richard must be right there. His last letter was from Calais. They were moving them up the coast."

Night after night she listened to endless lists of names of German prisoners being read on BBC. She never heard Papa's name. She wrote him letters. They were returned. "Whereabouts unknown." Neighbors said that was good. It must mean he's still alive. "No news is good news!" I didn't think he was dead either. First of all, I had asked God to take care of him, and also, I just didn't feel that he was dead. I knew that Onkel Josef would die, and I knew that he was dead, but I didn't feel that way about my cousins, or about Papa.

There had been occasional air raids. Mostly they were at night. Often we didn't even hear a plane. But now, the raids came with more regularity. Still, no bombs were dropped on us. We did get up and generally went to the basement. When the weather was pleasant and there was moonlight, we would go to Papa's trench. Although I was almost certain that Erika's book would protect us, I wasn't absolutely sure and was always relieved when we could crawl back into bed and nothing had happened.

At the end of the summer of 1944, we started to get daytime raids, as well. I wasn't afraid during the day. I never thought of dying while the sun was shining. Death hides in shadows at night.

The three ponds between us and the fat lady's farm were rectangular. Not only were they used to breed fish in the summer, but in the winter, when they froze, the nearby brewery chopped the ice into big slabs and took it for storing beer in its caves. We used to have a lot of fun standing on the slabs, pushing our "boats" like gondolas around the pond, with poles made from tree branches. We could only do that when the adults weren't there to see us, of course.

On a cool, sunny day, we had an air raid. It was Saturday, and those of us who were at home went to the basement because it was warmer than Papa's trench outside.

I was sitting on the floor by the chimney near the window toward the street. Suddenly we heard some planes flying very low, and then there was a lot of noise, and dirt and rocks flying against the house and the window. Frau Grosse got down on her knees, her large behind in front of my face. "O God, spare us, we're innocent," she pleaded. The sight, and the fact that this woman, who was mean and always told our mother what terrible things we had done, like picking apples before they were ripe, that she would plead "we're innocent," struck me as very funny, and I couldn't help laughing.

Mama thought I was hysterical and started slapping my face and saying, "It's all right, nothing's going to happen to us."

This seemed even funnier to me, but I stopped laughing when I saw that her eyes had filled with tears and she was really scared that I had flipped out. I said, as calmly as I could, that I was fine. I tried very hard not to think of Frau Grosse, and concentrated on what had happened outside. The bombs had hit the water. The ponds were quite shallow, and that's why dirt and stones went flying, too. The ponds must have looked like something else from the air. I did think about what Papa had said. What if the house had been the target? Or what if they didn't aim well, and they hit the house? We should have gone to the trench, but they could have hit the yard, too!

Throughout this time, one thing remained unchanged. On every Wednesday afternoon we had regular BDM meetings. We had many movie sessions during the earlier part of 1944. They consisted of a very long newsreel about battles and how brave and strong the army was, followed by a movie on themes of loyalty and duty, and noble sacrifices for the good of others. The movies were nice to watch because the good person always was loved and appreciated and was the winner in the end.

BDM provided the only entertainment available to us. It was an afternoon away from home and school. All tasks were easy. There were no reprimands, and every effort was rewarded with praise.

One weekend our group went camping. We rode on the train for a short stretch and then marched to a large farm, where we all got to sleep on hay in the barn. During the day, we learned how to braid straw and we made a lot of straw soles for slippers that would go to the soldiers' hospital. We also had sausages and potatoes grilled on wood fires, and got fresh milk from the farm.

In the evening, when it had gotten dark, we went to serenade in the village, singing a lot of folk songs. At one of the farms, a grouchy old man came out and yelled at us to quit that howling because he had to get some sleep. So we moved on to the next house after our group leader apologized for disturbing him and wishing him a good night.

We returned to the not-so-comfortable barn for another night's sleep.

On Sunday morning, to the sound of the church bells, we trampled the grass in a meadow, picking wildflowers to take home on the train. They were wilted by the time we did get home. Mama asked me what she was supposed to do with those wilted weeds. I, personally, was glad when it was time that I could go to sleep in a bed again. But, it had been fun.

A four-day trip into the mountains was much better. For this, only those girls who needed sunshine and fresh mountain air got to go. They asked who had been ill, and they looked to see who looked pale, thin, and tired. I qualified.

I had to tell the village teacher that I would be gone for four days because he had to adjust my food rations. He asked me, "What does your mother say to this?"

I told him she was happy that I could go to the mountains because I had never been before.

He said in a grumpy voice, "Well, I don't think it's a good idea, but I guess in four days not much can happen."

I had no idea why he would say that. I also thought he took away too many stamps.

The train trip was to Kempten and from there on with another train we got to Oberstdorf, which really seemed to be at the top of the world. I was awed. We were definitely in the mountains. Looking out ahead and around, tall gray mountains stood like giant walls. The air was very fresh, like in the Schwaebischen Alb. It was more beautiful than anywhere I had ever been. I felt a rush of pure love for this beautiful land, as I did in the forest near Tante Sofie's house that summer, and out in the field that Tante Lene and I were plowing.

I thought of a song we had learned in BDM, which said that Germany was blessed beyond all measure, and that her lakes, forests, and mountains were holy. We were told that love for the land was our Germanic heritage, because Germans have always loved the beauty, goodness and purity in nature, and that we are obligated to cherish, nourish, and protect the land.

The setting of Oberstdorf was breathtaking. Around the train station were many trees, the little town was to the right, and to the left of us were woods and a gradual, long way up. I was so awed by the magnificence of this world, I just kept on looking around. After everyone had gotten off the train, and gawked enough, we started our hike up to the camp, which was in a chalet way up above the town. A small path led up to it through meadows in which the grass got shorter and thinner as the path went on. We climbed nearly an hour with short rest stops every now and then. Everyone was huffing and puffing, out of breath.

At the chalet, the girls were separated into two groups, little girls in one dorm, big girls in another. We little girls were there strictly on vacation. We did have to make our beds, but after breakfast we were told to go out and lie in the sun or read or sleep until lunch. After lunch we had a nap and went out again till it was time for dinner. The older girls had to do the cooking, cleaning, and had lessons. I imagine it was sex education because one day we came in for lunch, and a chart of a pregnant woman's body was still on the wall. It was quickly rolled up and put away.

We were served wonderful, rich food, surprisingly good for those times when all good things had disappeared from our diets. After supper, all of us sang folk songs and listened to German legends and folk tales. Ursula, the woman who was in charge of the camp, was really beautiful with dark hair, braided and wrapped around her head like a crown, and she had lovely blue eyes with long, dark lashes. She looked like a movie star. She always wore Bavarian Dirndl dresses and was very feminine, warm, gentle, and entertaining. I thought she was everything I'd like to be.

On our last night, we all sat outside in the starlit night, and she told us the stories of the constellations. It was a perfect night for stargazing. The sky was deep black and the air was clear and the stars were so bright and compelling, I felt hypnotized by them. It was about 2 A.M. when we went to bed. I didn't sleep right away, because the sky with those big stars reminded me of an evening walk with my father in Milwaukee when I learned that the sky wasn't the ceiling of our world even if it looked like that. I remembered how many stars were in that dark sky that night. I missed my father and wondered where he was and how he was, and wondered if he had looked at the same stars I saw because they were also shining on him, wherever he was, and they would shine on America, too. I fell asleep remembering America, something I had not done in quite a while. It was confusing because I never loved Germany as much as I did up on that mountain, and I was remembering America. Maybe just having such strong feelings of love made me remember other things and times and places I loved, too.

The night was very short and we had to have everything ready before we could go downstairs to eat. But, right after breakfast, the whole lot of us went tearing down the mountain to the town and the train station and home.

My wonderful memories of this vacation were somewhat spoiled a few days after I had returned when Mama discovered the reason for my itching head. I had picked up lice. She tried all sorts of methods to rid me of them. She cried, too. Finally, she brought a bottle of kerosene from somewhere, and poured it over my head. I nearly suffocated from the fumes, but it did kill the lice.

The summer flew by. With autumn came refugees. They came by train, on foot, walking along on the roads with little wagons filled with their belongings. I had no idea where they were coming from. During Christmas vacation, our school was turned into a refugee center.

Christmas was very depressing. Mama bought a small tree in a clay pot. She wanted something that was alive. But the tree died. It was cold outside, but it rained. We didn't know where Papa was. Herbie was sick and lost more weight, and we worried about him. Mama and I made a little caramel candy in the frying pan. It turned out to be a funny interlude. Mama was standing in front of the stove, stirring the butter and sugar with a wooden spoon.

She said, "Bring me a glass of water."

I did. She continued,

"Well, give it here." I didn't know that she wanted to test the "candy" by dropping a bit into the water. I thought she meant for me to pour it into the pan. She managed to get the glass away from me before too much had hit the pan, and very seriously and calmly, she poured the remaining water over my head. I remember it so well because I think that was the only funny thing my mother ever did during those years. The candy, by the way, wasn't a total loss. It just got to be more of a crunch, rather than a caramel.

Each of us did get a gift. They were all things that had been made of wood: a cradle and a small baby carriage for the girls. Herbie got some sort of wooden train, and I got a lovely box, painted with happy flowers. Mama apologized to us for having nothing "better" to give us, but I really loved my present and remembered it more than any other, except my doll . . .

Nineteen forty-five began with endless speeches on the radio by leaders, especially Hitler, who seemed just to scream all the time. Even the music was sad and depressing.

When vacation was over, our school was closed because of the refugees. I decided to go with my siblings to the village school. The teacher didn't mind. I sat in on the upper level classes and learned some things I had not learned in my school.

We had geography, which I hadn't had at all. We read interesting, contemporary stories from an anthology. Once a week, the village priest came to instruct. We learned about the lives of saints. One day we were reading about St. Elizabeth, my favorite saint. She was a queen who disguised herself as an ordinary person and left her castle at night in a hooded cape to nurse the poor and sick.

I enjoyed reading out loud, and I liked this story, so when it was my turn to read, I just kept on reading until the story was done. When I looked up, the priest and the teacher were looking at each other. I felt a bit embarrassed, realizing that I had hogged the whole story to myself, but they didn't say anything, and it didn't seem like the other kids minded.

The teacher, whom I had met several times before in regard to ration cards, was about the same age as my first grade teacher had been, but he didn't say bad things about Jews and gypsies. He was Iris' teacher, too, and he had been in that village for a long time and knew everything about everyone. I enjoyed the time I spent there.

In February, we were told at a BDM meeting that our school would be opened again. There were a few rooms downstairs, including our own classroom, which could be used. We went to school and sat in all of our outdoors clothes, and our teachers took turns talking to us and giving us weekly assignments, and then dismissed us again. On the first day, as we were on the way home, there was another air raid. Those of us going in the same direction ran back to the school because we didn't know where else to go. We sat on the basement floor with a lot of refugees who lived in our school on the second and third floor.

A few times after that, we had class at the inn Zum Roten Ochsen. It was nice and warm there, but weird to sit in big cushioned chairs around a huge dining table and concentrate on schoolwork.

During those early months of 1945, we had two unusual political indoctrination sessions, which were held in a large meeting room of a hotel. A lot of boys and girls my age, from the district schools, were there. A team of young adults, mostly women, but also a few young men in full Hitler Youth uniforms, would drill us on such information as titles of Goering and Goebbels, names of generals, the boundaries of the Third Reich, the victories and battles won by the various armies, and on and on. It was terribly boring, and the tempers of our instructors sometimes showed their frustration at our restlessness, apathy, and ignorance.

During the second of those meetings, Ursula came to inspect.

She was now the assigned area coordinator and would be stationed in Memmingen. She recognized some of us who had been at the chalet, and talked to us, asking where we were going to school. She told us that we should organize the girls at the local schools and see if we couldn't get some slippers made.

I went back to the village school, full of purpose and eager to please my idol. The teacher did let me meet with the girls one afternoon, but they were more interested in playing games. Nothing was done. The next week, when I wanted to call another meeting, the teacher said, "These girls don't have time for this foolishness, and I'm not going to keep the school building open for you to run around and make a mess."

So, that was the end of that effort.

On the last Wednesday in February, on a cold afternoon, we had a group meeting upstairs in the old tower room. Our group leader was wearing her uniform, which she had not done very often. She asked us to stand in a circle. Then she began to speak, "I have sad news for you. Due to many other important things that have to do with the war, we will have to stop our regular meetings for a while. We must all prepare ourselves for some trying times ahead. But, we are brave, and strong, and intelligent, and we know who we are, no matter what. It is possible that you will hear some terrible lies about our people. Don't believe them. Remember that one of the ways in which the enemy tries to destroy us is through propaganda. Should you hear evil things, remember they are the enemy's lies.

"Whether we see each other again or not, remember who you are. You are German. You have been taught to be noble, wise, and pure. It is your duty to see that your country remains beautiful, that the world and its people are good. These are, and have been, the ideals of your forefathers for many, many generations.

"And now I am going to ask you for your solemn promise, your oath, to always remember that you are German. I am going to shake your hand on it. If you feel that you cannot keep this sacred promise, then don't take my hand. Nothing will happen to you if you don't. I will understand."

Thoughts were racing through my mind. I remembered from the legends and stories of the old Germans that your sworn oath was like binding your soul to your promise. You would never, never break that promise. So, what were we promising? To always remember that we are German. We can do that. We are German. Who would forget that? So, why do we have to promise it?

As I was thinking this out, she was already going around the circle, shaking hands. I don't think that the others understood the whole meaning of this promise any more than I did, but I knew that I certainly would not refuse to shake her hand. "Nothing will happen to you" sounded very ominous to me. Everyone in the circle shook her hand. When she got to me, she looked right into my eyes, and for a split second I wondered if she saw my orange star. Did she know that I was born in America, and even if it was Germany's enemy, I couldn't hate that country? But she went on to the next person without anything to cause me to panic.

When she had completed the circle, she stood stiffly, almost like a soldier at attention, and she said, "You may leave."

She seemed like a different person than she used to be. We looked at each other uncertainly, and then we filed out and went down the stairs. I think we were all afraid to talk about this because we didn't want to appear ignorant or confused to the others, and so we just went on our way home. Most of the girls lived in town. I went my way, alone.

I never was up in that room again, but each time I passed under the arch of the gate tower, I would look up at the little windows and remember the times we spent there, and wonder if anyone was there now, and when we would meet again. I missed the happy afternoons we had spent there, singing, painting toys.

The grocery stores got a new shipment of soap. It was different from the heavy, gritty kind we had been using. It was yellow with a slight tint of green. It was light, oil based, instead of slimy sand. While I was waiting my turn in the store, I overheard a girl tell her friend, "My mother's friend told her that the new soap is made from dead bodies."

When I got home, Mama was giving Hannelore a bath. She was full of white foam and Mama was scrubbing her with gusto. I watched the soap dancing on top of the water.

"A girl in the store said that that soap is made from dead bodies," I blurted out.

Mama stopped and straightened up to look at me. "Why do you do things like this? Do you get some sort of pleasure out of these macabre statements? This is the first decent product we had since we've been here."

"I'm just telling you what I heard," I replied.

"Well, what am I supposed to do about this now? It's the first time since this child was born that she gets washed with soap and not sandstone," she yelled.

"So use it." I yelled back. "It's probably just enemy propaganda, anyhow. They told us at BDM that we would hear a lot of lies like that."

I went to the bedroom, thinking, *There had been so many big bombings. In Dresden, one hundred thirty-five thousand people died in the bombing. The British did that. They used napalm, and the fire was so hot that the air caught fire. They said it was a fire storm. Everybody burned to death in that fire. Hamburg was bombed, and eighty thousand people died. The city didn't burn though, but there were so many dead people, that they couldn't bury them fast enough, and because they were afraid of a plague, they burned the bodies. And, maybe they did that in Berlin, too, and in all the big cities that were bombed. Maybe, when they burn bodies, the fat runs out . . .*

It was a gruesome thought, and I shuddered. *Mama was right. I have a macabre mind,* I thought. *It's probably plant oil, like margarine,* I finally decided.

Still, the seed of suspicion had been planted, and I really had an aversion to that soap, even though it did everything soap should do, while the old soap was like a bar of kitchen cleanser.

Around this time, we started getting a lot of air raids, again. They came during the night and during the day. People said that the English bomb at night, and the Americans do it during the day. Other people said that the Americans did all of the bombing now. Although we weren't really the target for any of these raids, it nevertheless was disrupting our lives and especially our sleep.

One night Mama took us to the basement instead of joining the others outside in the trench. It was drizzling, and the ground had gotten all muddy, the children had colds, so we stayed indoors. We were sitting together on a bench near the stairs. The one dim light bulb, hanging down from the ceiling, cast dark shadows through the basement. The ground water was running under the house to the drain, and somewhere in the shadows was a steady drip, drip, drip . . . It was cold and damp.

Mama sat with Hanni on her lap, Herbie was cuddled up against her. I sat next to them with Rose Marie's head in my lap. Mama was talking to herself: "This is like a tomb, as if we're already buried. My God, how much longer is this going to go on? I can't take this anymore. This has to end."

It was the first time I really heard my mother complain. She seemed so tired and depressed. My father's words came back to me. He told me that I should be my mother's strength. I like to think that it was that night that I started to be aware of others' problems and stopped being so absorbed in myself.

Our nighttime raids had been rung for the time it took the planes to fly over us, strike their target, and return again. The sound of the loaded planes was a deep hum, like bumble bees. On their return they sounded lighter. They never bombed us at night. Daytime raids were different. They often dropped bombs on us now, but they were scattered, either probes or leftovers.

One sunny March day, Mama borrowed Frau Dauer's bicycle to go hamstering in Benningen. It was noontime when the alarm sounded.

The children were at the first house, near the woods. I ran over there to fetch them. But we were all herded down into their cellar where we stumbled over potatoes, cabbages, and other things. The trap door was just pulled down by the woman when we heard a terrifying whistling sound and then several tremendous blasts. The small window in the cellar was blown in, and I was hit by it. They told me later that I was unconscious. I don't remember that, or of waking up. I do remember being out on the road and seeing trees and dirt from the little woods all over the road and two enormous craters in the soft ground.

Someone said they were chain bombs that had made those holes. That meant three bombs chained together. No one knew why they had wasted them on the woods. There was nothing around that should require such force to destroy it. There was nothing that was worth even one bomb. At home, our bedroom windows, with frames, had been blown across the room. Glass was all over the beds. Otherwise, nothing had been damaged.

I was worried about Mama, and waited several agonizing hours until I saw her walking the bicycle past the trees and dirt. She was still in Benningen during the air raid, and said that she really was scared about us when she saw what had happened to the woods.

It took a long time to clean the bedroom, and still, we weren't sure that we had gotten all of the glass particles. Mama said that she hoped it wouldn't rain until we got the windows replaced. They wouldn't be replaced, not even after the war. A carpenter came, and nailed some boards across the window openings. You could see some light through the cracks.

A few days after the bombing of the woods, all of the inhabitants of the house were outside in the yard. The women were planting. We saw a plane flying very low, just skimming the roof of our house and the trees that lined the road. It was a plane with stars on its wings. We could see the pilot with goggles and leather cap and jacket. The plane didn't make a sound, and we realized he was going to crash. Ahead of him was a long open space of fields. He could land there. We were shouting for him to land. He kept on coming down lower and lower, and finally it seemed that he was on the ground, but he kept on going, right into the farm house which seemed so far away. A big ball of yellow flames obscured the house. It seemed to burn a very long time. By that evening, rumor had it that the pilot had flight plans and information in his boot that told of a large bombing mission on Muenchen (Munich).

Soon after that, one morning when we got up, the fields, yards, roads were covered with leaflets that had been dropped during the night. We didn't have any air raid that night! How did this happen? The leaflets announced a large-scale bombing of Muenchen at 2 P.M. of a specific day, and told civilians to leave the city.

On the predicted day, there was a great exodus into the forests by residents of Memmingen and the surrounding villages. We joined hundreds of little groups of mothers, grandmothers, and children, little wagons, baby carriages, going along the roads through the fields leading to the forest.

I insisted, though, that our group stay at the edge of the forest. I didn't want to take the chance on being burned alive in the forest if they decided to drop a few incendiaries on us.

At 1:30 P.M. the planes appeared in the sky. They were coming from the southwest, heading towards Muenchen. They came in perfect chevron formations. The whole sky was full of planes, squadron after squadron. Their bellies were filled, they sounded heavy. They moved on against a blue sky, uninterrupted. There were hundreds of them. We watched them pass over. Mama said, "Those poor people." Frau Dauer crossed herself, and we all stood quietly, imagining what would be happening. The bombing could be heard by us, more than 100 kilometers away. It sounded like a thunderstorm in the distance.

By and by, the planes returned, in perfect chevron formations. It was a beautiful, clear day, but everyone was very quiet and sad as we returned. Watching those planes, undisturbed, in the middle of the day, was such a humiliating experience for the German me, I couldn't feel any love for America because this show of power, and deliberate, senseless destruction of that lovely city didn't seem good and nice, the way I remembered America.

The sun was setting in a glorious spectacle of gold and copper as we got home. I couldn't understand how that bombing and this beautiful sky could both be directed by God.

After that day, there was a long lull. We had no raids, day or night. It was almost spooky. Everyone was just waiting for the next thing to happen.

Another attempt was made to get classes started again at our school, but only half of the girls showed up. The teachers didn't really seem to know what to do with us, and we had gotten out of practice, too. Besides that, there was no paper to be found anywhere, so we couldn't write anything.

As this half-hearted attempt went on for several days, fewer students showed up each day, and finally I gave up, too. Somewhere during this time, we also heard that Mr. Roosevelt had died on April 12.

The women said, "Well, that's the first of them, which one is going to be next?" They were talking about Churchill, Stalin, Hitler, and Mussolini.

I felt at loose ends. I didn't want to go back to the village school, and no one from my school lived anywhere near me. Helga had left for her mother's farm, and it seemed that every other person I knew had just vanished. It was a day in late April when I walked by the Hitler Youth offices, and decided to visit Ursula. I thought I should tell her that I didn't get even one pair of slippers done, and also I missed seeing people I knew.

The offices were in a building behind a gate that opened to the street. I had never been there before, but I was hoping to find her. The gate was very heavy, but not locked. I pushed one of the gate wings just enough to squeeze through. In the courtyard was a wagon with a team of horses. The wagon was full of straw . . . a rather strange thing to have in this courtyard. Some big boys were carrying boxes and putting them into the straw. Ursula was telling them what to do. She seemed agitated. When she saw me, she looked almost frightened.

"What are you doing here, child?" she asked.

"I came to say 'hello.' I haven't seen you in a long time, and I also thought I should tell you that nobody wanted to do anything in the village, and they won't even let us get together again," I complained.

She looked at me for a moment in astonishment. Then she bent down to me and held my face in her hands.

"You have no idea what's going on, do you? Do you see what we are doing here? We are moving these things away and these offices will be closed. You will understand why very soon. But now I'm going to ask you to go home, and in the future, you're going to walk past this building like any other one, and you'll never tell anybody that you know what used to be here. Now go out the same way you came in, and go home. Stay well. Ade."

"Ade" was a final farewell. I felt confused and sad. I squeezed through the gate, remembering her pretty dirndl, and how she had her hair braided around her head. She was nice, and gentle, and smart, and pretty. I really loved her, and wanted to see her again, and hoped that I would make her really proud of me someday.

The drifting, waiting time continued. I ran, no, I walked errands for my mother. I played with the little ones and told them stories. And then one day, the women in the house decided to get on with living. The carpets were put outside and beaten. All the bedding was on the window sills, except for our room, where the boards were still across the two openings that were once windows.

The painter came and whitewashed the walls inside and with a crumpled rag, dipped into a rose-colored paint, he dabbed a design onto the walls. It was interesting because each dab was a little different, and one could imagine all sorts of pictures and stories.

The painter was also a spiritualist. He told my mother that someday I would be a very good medium. He could see it in my eyes. From then on I avoided direct eye contact with him, but I was fascinated by the subject and the thought that I had some special gift made me happy, and so I was really sad to see his work come to an end.

The day after the painter had finished, the air raid siren sounded in the morning, but we ignored it and went on with normal activities. Around noon, Mama realized that we didn't have anything at home for lunch. I volunteered to go to the store up the road, and borrowed Frau Dauer's bicycle. It was a warm day. I had on my light blue dress, which I had gotten after our house was bombed in Essen. I had grown. The waistband was sitting on my ribs, and the skirt came way above my knees, but it was the only summer weight dress I had.

I rode past the craters in the woods. They said that there could be bodies in there because people along the way often went into the woods during an air raid.

"Someday, if there's a good rain, and some of that dirt is washed away, you might see an arm or a foot sticking out."

The little kids in the neighborhood liked playing around there now. I kept telling Herbie that it was dangerous. I don't think he really believed it, but he was in our yard much more often. The boys had made Papa's trench their fortress.

When I got to the store, several people were standing around listening to the radio. A lady was giving the weather report. It was going to get cold again. Then they played the song about the soldier on the Volga shore who asks God if He had forgotten him, because he's so lonely, and he asks God to send him one of his angels. *"Hast Du dort oben vergessen auf mich . . ."*

An old man said, "There may be a soldier on the shore of the Volga, but he's not one of ours."

"Unless it's a ghost," someone else said.

I got a small piece of liverwurst. The lady behind the counter warned me, "You know there's an air raid?"

"I know, but nothing's happening," I said very flippantly as I left the store.

I got on the bike. As I reached the corner, I suddenly seemed to lose my grip and was knocked off the bike. Something had hit me so hard that I went flying. I heard a very loud noise, but didn't see anything. I didn't feel hitting the ground, but I was lying on my stomach, and in front of me, the wheel of the bicycle was turning. But something else caught my eye just a foot or so beyond the wheel. Pebbles were jumping up in the air in a line from one side of the road to the other in front of me, and shining in the sun were copper—and gold-colored bullets— big, long ones. My ears were ringing, and above me I heard the roar of very loud airplane engines. Then I saw two low-flying planes with stars on their wings. It seemed that I could hear the pilots talking to each other. When they were over the field next to the road, they climbed and flew off.

After some time I managed to get up, but I was really shaking. I found the liverwurst package ahead in the road, past the jumping gravel line. I pulled the bicycle up by the handlebar, but I didn't have the strength or desire to ride it. I walked it home. Shiny lights and dark spots passed in front of my eyes. My body ached all over, and somewhere in my head a thought was stuck behind a door. I kept seeing the jumping gravel. How can gravel jump up in the air? What does that mean? And what was it that hit me so hard and made me fly off the bike?

As I neared the woods, I saw Rose Marie and Herbie running towards me, and down closer to the house was Mama, too. Rose Marie came up to me first and asked, "Do you know that some planes were shooting machine guns at something?"

I heard what she said, but it didn't sink in. I asked her to take the bike. She pushed it along. Herbie took my hand. When Mama saw me, she asked, "What happened to you?"

"I fell off the bike," I said. I was too tired for anything else.

"We'd better clean you up. Look at you. Are you sure you're all right? You are so pale."

Frau Dauer was in the yard, too, and she said, "Well, that will once and for all show you that that bicycle is too big for you kids. And don't ask to use it again!"

Though I felt very weak and ached all over, I wasn't really hurt. I didn't even have a scraped knee. That night I went over the whole scene again, and when I saw the gravel jump, and the bullets, I realized that those planes had shot at me. *They shot at me, but I didn't die! I didn't even get hurt, even though I flew away from the bicycle and landed on the gravel road. Something, someone pushed me off the bike. An angel! An angel saved my life! That means that God doesn't want me to die yet. I'm going to live through this war. He's not going to kill me. Still, that doesn't mean that I can just forget about everything. I will have to pay for Erika's book, I know.*

My idea of Death as a skeleton in a hooded cloak, touching one's shoulder with his bony fingers, was definitely no longer valid. I realized that dying was possible at any time, anywhere, giving me a deeper respect for life, I would say. Everything around us became more focused. I felt that time was running through an hourglass, yet I didn't really know why I felt that way. Mama was spending hours at night listening to English radio. I used to be very nervous and worried when she did this before. Now I didn't mind. I watched her standing at the kitchen window, staring out into space a lot, and I knew that she was thinking about Papa, where he might be and if he's well. I knew that he was alive. I never doubted it. I could feel it. But I wondered where he was, too. I'm not sure that I realized that the Allies were closing in on us, and that the women were worried about that final day when they would arrive in our little corner of the world. It could be the French or Americans. I think they were all hoping for the Americans, I know that I was. And so the days crept by.

One day it was May. We heard rumors that things were bad in Berlin, that the Russians were very terrible to the people in the eastern parts of Germany. We also heard that Poles had taken over Schlesien and killed or took prisoner every German male. We could have been there, if we had listened to Oma. Or we could have been among the refugees, who were burned to death in Dresden. We also heard that Hitler and Eva Braun had committed suicide, and that Benito Mussolini had been killed, and his body was hung up and people spat at it. I didn't believe that Germans would do that to their leader, no matter how much they hated him. And, we also heard that the Americans had gotten to Nuernberg, where Onkel Fritz's family lived. We heard all of these accounts in the stores, or in our yard as people passed by and gossiped with the women of our house.

We had a couple of days of late frost, and with the frost came a horde of foreign men. Prisoners? Workers? Were they released? Had they escaped? Who were they? They came from somewhere and swarmed over the land. They roamed across the fields and pounded on the heavy house door. They seemed cold and hungry.

The women in the house were afraid of them, yet they pitied them, too, and so it was decided to boil a lot of potatoes to feed them. A fire was lit in the laundry stove in the basement, and potatoes were put into the hollowed-out stone bowl, in which one generally boiled white or soiled laundry.

Since the women were afraid to face these wild men, I was elected to take a bowl full of warm potatoes to the door when they knocked. I was the least attractive of all the females in the house, I guess, the most expendable. But I really didn't object, either. I felt it was my responsibility. Since I felt that God wanted me to live, I wasn't afraid. I imagined myself wrapped in some kind of magic shawl, and waited behind the closed door until they knocked. Every one else went upstairs.

Mama and Frau Edelstein were in the hallway on the second floor. There was a knocking on the door, I opened it and held the bowl of potatoes out to them. I did that with two groups. The first ones were just eager for the warm potatoes in their hands, they even bowed their heads and smiled at me.

In the second group, one of the men looked at me in a scary way. He had a bad smile on his face, and he looked at my legs and looked for a long time at the bottom of my very short dress, and then he looked farther up at my face. I know that I looked scared, because his smile got meaner. But then somebody in the house made a noise in the stairway, and he looked beyond me and then to the stairs, and I knew that he was a little afraid, so I looked back at him like I knew something that he didn't know. He just took a potato and backed off. I slowly stepped back, too, then ran behind the door, slammed and locked it. My heart was beating very hard, and I thought about what a stupid idea it had been to stand there like that. Who knows who these people were and where they had come from. After that, I just put the bowl full of potatoes out in front of the door, when no one was there. By late afternoon the last groups had passed, and I was very relieved.

On the morning of May 5, a convoy of German soldiers, in trucks, came down our road and stopped under the trees in front of our house. They got out of the trucks and lay down in the grass. They looked very dusty and tired. The children, of course, went to see them. The soldiers asked them to bring some water, and gave their various utensils and water bottles to be filled. I helped, too, and we all ran in and out of the house to fetch the water. Mama and the other ladies came to the fence and asked if there was anything they could do. Finally they decided to cook more potatoes, since the soldiers only had that dry, dark cracker bread that tasted like cardboard. And once more the wash kettle was put to use. By noon enough onions, a bit of bacon, vinegar and our olive oil were scraped together between the three houses, so that all of the men got potato salad for lunch. Their surprise and gratitude made tears well up into my eyes. They were like big kids, not tough soldiers.

I sat down in the grass next to a group of really young-looking soldiers and began to ask them a lot of questions. One of them was called Robert. I mentioned that that was an English name. Mama shushed me. I explained that Robert was a popular name in my English book. Robert told me that he had gone to a Gymnasium at home, and as a matter of fact, the whole group sitting together came from the same school. They would be in twelfth grade this year. Looking at the whole bunch of them more carefully, I realized that they all were young, except for the officer, who stood nearby and looked around at the sky all the time. One of the women asked him what he was looking for, and he answered, "Fighter airplanes. They know we're here somewhere."

I felt like saying, "I saw them a few days ago," but I didn't have the chance.

He continued, "I really don't want to endanger you, but the boys needed a rest. They'll need all the energy they can find by tomorrow. The Americans are not more than two days from here. We should meet them tomorrow, and then it will finally be over. For you here, I'd say the day after tomorrow, unless the French cross the river. But I don't think they will."

I couldn't help but say, "If it's going to be all over, then why do you go on? Why don't you just turn around and go home. You might be killed on the last day of the war, for nothing."

There was total silence. Mama got very nervous.

"Oh, excuse the child," she said, "They always have such simple solutions to everything. She, especially. You know she goes to a "higher" school, and they just let them say anything they want to."

One of the young men in Robert's group said, "You see, besides it being our duty to go on to the end, it's also the only way we can ever get home again. There's no place for us to go. They're everywhere. This is really the last corner of the country that hasn't been occupied yet. If we're lucky and survive the confrontation, they'll eventually send us home. We have to go through the process or be hunted and homeless all of our lives."

The officer just walked to the corner, his head down, his hands folded behind his back.

At the corner, our road continued on to the village, and another went through the fields, past the fat lady's farm and then along the forest. The officer came back and asked the women about the surface of the roads and whether they were tree-lined and about woods or other kinds of shelter. Frau Dauer had lived in this area all of her life. She knew every farm, every road. They talked together a long time.

After the men had eaten their potato salad, and rinsed their mess kits at the garden faucet of our house, and washed their faces and hands, they lay down to sleep in the shade of the trees. We left them and went back to the house. The officer sat against a tree and marked maps and wrote. Around four in the afternoon, they packed up and drove off on the back road towards the forest. Our good wishes and prayers for their safety went with them. I still thought it was awfully risky to go out to meet the enemy. Why not wait until the fighting is over, and then surrender?

Early the next morning, a woman came by on her bicycle. She stopped at our garden fence, and shouted into the yard, "They're opening the warehouses! People are just grabbing whatever they can. It's wild in town, but you'd better go and see what you can get. Who knows what will happen next."

Mama got to use Frau Dauer's bike. She rode off fast and came home about noon.

"You can't believe what it's like. The train station is just spitting out people with suitcases and bundles. At the army warehouse, they're fighting over skis. They are just the boards, nothing on them. They're running around with arms full of ski poles. What are they going to do with them, I'd like to know. I did find these blankets, though. Maybe we can get some coats made from them." She had two gray, wool army blankets.

"But I tried to find some bread. There was none left in any of the bakeries. Finally, I got to the dairy, and the girl gave me this."

It was a whole wheel of Swiss cheese. Well, anyway, we'd all have potatoes and cheese for some days.

Mama and I went to the store at the corner and traded the stamps we had for all the staples we were allowed—dried peas, flour, and sugar. People were talking about Hitler and Eva Braun and that the Americans were outside of Berlin, but they let the Russians take the city, and that it was really horrible there.

Before it got dark, Mama started putting things together near the door: The case with important papers, some blankets, some pillows, a cooking pot and some groceries . . . She kept on walking around, looking at things as if she were deciding whether she should add them or not.

She made us all go to sleep as soon as the sun had set.

"Who knows where we'll be sleeping tomorrow night."

I woke up several times during the night. Mama was listening to the radio.

*   *   *

11

MEETING THE ENEMY

I heard a noise, a familiar noise. It sounded like fireworks at the park on the Fourth of July. I opened my eyes. From the cracks between the boards at the window, I could tell that it was morning. I got up. Mama was in the kitchen. The window was open. She was looking out. In the sky were a few small puffy dark clouds.

"I guess that must be cannon fire," she mumbled. I thought about Robert and his friends and hoped that it was not directed at them.

"I suppose we'd better go to the basement. Memmingen is a Red Cross city. They're not supposed to fight, but God only knows what will happen today. I hope . . ." She didn't finish her sentence.

I knew she was worried and afraid. But I was very excited. Finally something important was about to happen, and I told her, "Mama, it's going to be a good day. The war is going to be over."

We moved our things downstairs. The other families did, also. And then, several long and boring hours passed. All of us were sitting around in the basement. We children tried to amuse ourselves by telling each other what we would do when the war was over.

"I'm going to eat six sausages."

"I'm going to have all kinds of different cakes with whipped cream and hot chocolate to drink, with whipped cream in it, too" . . . and on and on. And when the waiting got too boring, we went outside to see what was happening. We saw nothing, no one.

Finally, in the early afternoon, a German car went along the bigger, paved street behind our house, a wheat field away. The car came from Memmingen. It had a white flag flying, and the German flag facing down to the ground. On the other side was a Red Cross flag.

I watched it go down the road. I was both excited that something big and important was happening, and also sad to see the German flag like that. I understood what it meant. All those ideals, all the years of war, all of the people I loved who were gone, Erika and her brothers, our home in Essen, the nights of terror, for nothing. I remembered the newsreels of German soldiers marching into Paris and other places, how proud they were and how strong Germany seemed to be.

The car disappeared, and I prayed that the French wouldn't be our victors. They would act worse than the English or Americans because they would have to make us pay for their humiliation and defeat. But they would be better than the Russians.

We waited and watched, and finally the car returned with the Red Cross flag and the American Stars and Stripes. It looked so beautiful flying in the breeze. It was the Fourth of July to me. I was so relieved, and unexpectedly happy. I ran into the house and yelled down the stairs, "It's the American flag, the Americans are coming!"

Someone asked, "How do you know it's American?"

I laughed, "Because I've seen hundreds of American flags."

Mama called from the basement, "They must be close by. Everybody back down here. Hurry up."

We waited in the basement. Frau Dauer, who had gone up to her kitchen to fetch something, was talking to someone from her window. Frau Grosse stood on a chair downstairs, and peeked out of the small basement window that faced the village.

"It's Elke," she reported. "She says they killed her grandfather." He was the mayor of the village. "He went to the door to open it for them, but someone got scared when they heard him, and shot through the door. She's going to get her aunt because her mother also got shot in the leg. She's running up the road. She has a sheet with blood on it and she's holding it over her head. It looks like giant wings."

That news was sobering. It meant that they ought to be coming around the bend in the road any moment now, and it also meant that they were dangerous.

Frau Dauer came down the stairs. "They're coming! There's a tank coming down the road!"

My heart started to pound really loud. This was the moment. I would see the enemy. The window facing the street was covered by a little bush, but one could see through the foliage. I got on a stool and stood at the window.

Mama pleaded, "If they see you, they'll shoot! Why do you have to do this?"

"They won't see me, but I have to see them." I had to see the enemy whom I had feared for so long.

And then I did. A tank rolled very slowly along. Around the tank, so close to it, it seemed they wanted to melt into it, were young men, boys, in khaki uniforms and strange round helmets, holding rifles in front of them. They looked petrified. I could feel their fear.

At my feet, the others were pulling at me, "What do you see?" they wanted to know.

I turned from the window, and sat down on the stool. I was stunned by what I had seen. I could only summarize my thoughts and feelings by saying, "Enemies are frightened boys with guns!"

I didn't have much time to ponder this profound discovery. Outside, after a few tanks went cautiously by, jeeps and trucks followed, and their pace quickened. Eventually, the ladies decided that it would be a good time for children to cautiously appear in the yard . . . in view, but not too close to the road. So we sat on the edge of the vegetable patch, and watched the military vehicles go by.

On the street behind us, troops were moving, too. As the sun was getting low on the horizon, they started turning their trucks in on to the fields, and they began to pitch big tents.

The wheat in the field behind us was about a foot high, and as I watched it being trampled, and the trucks making deep grooves in the field, I felt that I was witnessing a great sin. Something sacred was being destroyed. I remembered the field I had called my own.

Within an hour, there was a city of tents and trucks and people all over the place. The children lifted the barbed wire and joined others from neighboring houses, who were watching the soldiers. I joined them, feeling a little embarrassed because I was older than they, but I was also curious.

One soldier was working alone, pounding a stake into the ground. He called to several others and they came immediately. Then I noticed that his uniform was a bit different—he was an officer.

He stood up and looked at us and said, "Look, kids, I don't have anything—nix chocolate, nix gum."

I answered, "We want no chocolate. We come to see."

"Hey, you know English?"

"A little, I am born in America."

"Oh, yeah, really? Where?"

"In Wisconsin."

"You really do understand, don't you? You live around here?"

"Yes, in that house."

"Your parents live there, too?"

"My mother."

"Where's your father?"

"I don't know."

"In the war?"

"Yes."

A look of sympathy, a sigh, a little softer tone followed.

"Does your mother speak English?"

"Yes."

"Who else lives in the house?"

"Four women and children."

"Listen, do you have a bath tub?"

"Yes, in the cellar."

"Can you heat water?"

"Yes, in the washing place."

"OK. Listen, tell your Mom that my buddy and I would like to take a bath. Tell her to please heat some water and as soon as it's dark, we'll come over, OK?"

"OK." I ran to tell Mama. I was delighted that such an exciting thing was happening to us, but Mama was not pleased at all.

"How can you invite them to take a bath here? Soldiers, enemy soldiers! What will people think?"

But no one in the house thought it was so bad. They all pitched in and got the old bathtub near the laundry stove. They rinsed the big stone bowl, in which they had boiled potatoes for other men, and filled it with water. Eventually, everything was ready for our visitors.

As announced, two officers appeared and after some time, they finished their baths. The friend went back to the tents, the other came upstairs and sat at our table, drank tea and talked with Mama for hours about the war, and what's been going on in the United States and Germany. He told about movies and a lot of famous people. I was amazed that I had no trouble understanding what he was saying, yet I just couldn't speak beyond what I had learned in school.

I was getting very tired. We had been up for such a long time. I asked Mama if I could go to bed, but she said, in German of course, "You invited him, and you're staying up until he leaves." He finally did leave, saying that he would send someone over in the morning with some rations.

When we got up in the morning, the trucks, tents, soldiers were gone from the field.

The following days were a kaleidoscope of sights, events, impressions. The end of the war wasn't at all as we had imagined it to be. No one ate sausages, nor cakes. Food had suddenly become a really crucial problem. We were not allowed to leave our streets. Every shop was closed. We had no milk, no bread. For our first breakfast, we had water-cooked cream of wheat with jelly. We wondered how long it would be before things got back to how they used to be.

The first day, in the morning, a jeep stopped in front of the gate to our house, and several Americans got out. Frau Dauer opened the front door since she lived on the ground floor, and soon she called up the stairs for Mama. The Americans wanted to evacuate us and use the building for their headquarters because the house was large and they needed the space. Mama told them how many people would have to move somewhere else. She also let them know that we were born in America. As a final touch, she showed them the rather primitive bathroom facilities of the old house. They said that we could stay. They asked Mama, though, if they could call on her for interpreting and translating. She said, "Yes, of course," not realizing what a big task she had taken on.

Several times that day Mama had to interpret mostly problems involving farmers' care of live stock, vehicles blocking access to roads or fields, and other traffic problems.

The radio was on all day. People were giving instructions on detours, but also told about Hitler's suicide, the capitulation done by Admiral Doenitz. And a word that I had never heard before kept on coming up in the newscasts. It was *KONZENTRATIONSLAGER* (concentration camp). I asked Mama what that was. I meant "what does one do in a *Konzentrationslager?*" The only concept of the word *Konzentration* I had, had to do with focusing one's mind on something.

Mama said, "That's nothing for you to listen to."

"Why?" I wanted to know.

"Because it has to do with political prisons, and they are saying that those prisoners were treated very badly."

I thought it was a strange name for a prison, and wondered if this was some of that enemy propaganda that we had been warned against. But I didn't dwell on it very long, because three very drunken foreign men were throwing hand grenades into the pond across the street from us. When they exploded in the water, dead fish floated up to the surface, and the men gathered them up. All of us were very glad to see another jeep drive up to our house. When the "fishermen" saw the American uniforms, they went away.

Towards the late afternoon, one of the jeeps carried the chaplain of the occupation group. He asked Mama if she could iron his altar cloth.

All of this activity in our small apartment was exciting and kind of fun for us, but Mama was getting tired. No one paid her, and no one thought of bringing food for us, either. I was just amazed at how our lives had changed. Suddenly we had so many men around, and though they were supposed to be the enemy, they acted just like they belonged there and treated us the way they would have done at home, and best of all, I understood them and they didn't speak the way Fraulein Rosamunde spoke, they pronounced things in American.

When it got dark, Mama turned on the lights and didn't close the shades. I got so scared, I ran to the window to close up. She laughed and said, "The war is over. You don't have to do that anymore."

"But there could be someone, who doesn't know," I worried. She patted me on the head, and said that it really was safe. I finally relaxed and enjoyed the view and the breeze and seeing other lights in other houses.

On the second day, I ventured into town to the closest baker late in the afternoon. I got a half loaf of bread, but it wasn't baked right. The lady told us that the baker was taken to some place along with all the other German men. The Americans had to find out if they were Nazis or war criminals. I also heard that Herr Hannes had committed suicide the morning of the day the Americans came into town. I wondered if he had poisoned himself with that black tar-like stuff that we were told never to touch, and I was sad because he had been good to me, and I didn't know of any crime he would have committed, or why he would be that much afraid of the Americans.

After I got home, I went to the dairy in the village. Iris was living at her grandfather's house. Her mother had not been at her apartment in our house in the last two days, either. I missed Iris' company on my way. As I got to the dairy, I sensed a slight difference in the other girls and women towards me. It wasn't exactly hostile, but they regarded me as someone who was not in their group. I realized it had to do with our association with the Americans. My orange star was showing again, but it didn't make me as uncomfortable as it had previously. I was different now that the Americans were among us. I accepted that.

There were two groups among our occupation forces. One group had tigers as their insignia, and another group had something to do with Texas. I heard some of them talking about being in Casino in Italy and being bombed by their own guys because the bombers thought that the Germans were still there. Mama told them that we heard about that on German radio.

One afternoon, one of the officers had some photos he showed to Mama. He wouldn't let us see them. He said that those were pictures taken at the concentration camp of Dachau. Mama was really shocked by what she saw, I could tell. The officer said that was a camp where mostly Jewish people were. He also told Mama not to let us go into town the next day because they had orders to sweep the streets and get everyone who's outside into the movie theater to show some really gruesome footage of the camps. He said, "Your kids don't need to have nightmares about that, too."

I met a girl I knew from school a few days later. She asked me if I had seen it, and when I said "no" she told me about it. She said that it wasn't a movie, but just scenes of piles of skeletons and striped clothes and dead bodies and really skinny people, and that it was very long, and she closed her eyes and tried to think about something else while it was being shown.

I wondered where they could have found so many skeletons and dead bodies. Was it a trick? Did they keep on photographing some artificial bones and skulls? I was sure it was enemy propaganda because Germans would never do things like that. I couldn't understand why nice Americans had to tell such lies about Germans. It did not enter my mind to believe, even to have a doubt or suspicion about what I heard. I simply did not accept it. I believed what I had been taught: Germans are good and noble, and enemies are bad and sneaky and dishonest, and kill innocent people, and they will do anything to destroy Germans. The only troublesome portion of this belief was the way the Americans, who were the enemy, too, behaved. They were as I had thought they were, just normal people. But I was still convinced that the Russians, and to some degree, the other victors were bad. I held on to these beliefs for some time.

The weather through all of these days was unbelievably mild and clear. The lilac bush and mock orange were heavy with flowers. The neighbor's strawberries were ripe. It was evening. Since it hadn't rained for a while, the dirt road in front of the house had become very dry. Every time a truck or a jeep passed by, it would raise a large cloud of dust. I was watering the street with the watering can, more to be doing something than for a long-time effect. The neighbor was picking strawberries. I was hoping she would offer me one, but she didn't.

Two Americans came walking along from the side road, on their way back to Memmingen. I just stopped sprinkling the road, and said "Hello" in English. They stopped and started talking to me. One of them was the handsomest man I had ever seen. He looked a lot like my cousin Heinz, but this one was even better looking than he was. I learned very quickly that his name was Hamilton, and he was from Oklahoma. The other man, an officer, was a doctor. I asked them if they would like some strawberries, to which they said, "Yes, of course."

I told the neighbor, "They would like to know if they could taste your strawberries." She seemed very willing to share her berries with them, and still didn't give me even one. No one thought of offering me any.

How I managed to keep these two men from moving on is a mystery to me. I was so smitten by Hamilton that some nearly predatory aspect of my personality took over. I was very glib and full of energy, and somehow, by the time the sun was setting, I had convinced them to come up into the garden where the lilacs and orange blossoms filled the air with their perfume. By and by the others joined us, and we sat on the benches and spoke in broken phrases about many things. The moon was full, and the sky sparkled with millions of stars. The breeze sprinkled us with flower petals, and I was in love.

The doctor spoke German really well, and discussed medicine with the women. He wanted them to explain the health care system during the war and what kind of health problems were most common during that time. I sat next to Hamilton, and pulled out all the English I could get together to keep his attention on me alone.

Finally, they did get up to go. There was a curfew, and fraternization was strictly against the law. As we were starting off towards the gate, Hamilton saw the search light of a patrol car. He quickly managed to get us both down on the ground. He threw his jacket over me, so that they wouldn't see my light colored dress, and the car went on. I was in heaven. Could anything be more romantic?

At the gate, he promised he would be back tomorrow evening and he would bring us oranges and other food. Food, real food, was still the great priority in our lives, and would be for a long time.

That night I slept very little. The wind, that suddenly tore across the roof tops and beat tree branches against the house, seemed an extension of the wild longing joy and sadness within me. I did, however, fall asleep, and woke up to another glorious day, a special day for me.

It was market day. Since Mama was still called on, occasionally, to interpret, she decided to stay home, and I went to town to do the shopping. It was a fresh, sunny morning, and I didn't even think about the craters in the woods, but just about seeing Hamilton again in the evening. As I got to the main street, at the corner of the grocery store, I saw an old woman cross the street. A jeep came along. The driver swerved, deliberately hitting the woman, and then just kept on going. Several people were in the jeep and they were shouting something as they drove on. The woman was trying to push herself up, but her leg was limp, hanging in her black stocking. She was crying. Three old men, who had been talking together on the sidewalk ran out into the street and tried to help her. I stood, frozen, not knowing what to do. Finally, I ran to the store and told the lady that there had been an accident. She called the hospital. I was very confused and upset. I couldn't believe that the driver of that car would deliberately hit an old woman and then just drive away, and I felt so sorry for her. She was dressed all in black, probably someone she loved had died within the year, and now this.

I went on into town. No ambulance had come before I left, and I didn't meet any as I was going along either. I wondered how they would take care of that lady.

Near the old city gate stood a large government building. A dark-skinned American guard was standing sentry. Everything about him was polished and shiny. He stood very tall and proud and looked really fine. In front of him, in the ditch, sat a German man without legs. He had slid off his little cart that looked like a wide skate board. It had roller-skate wheels attached to it on the bottom. The guard reached into his jacket and pulled out a pack of cigarettes, put one into his mouth, put the pack back into his jacket, lit the cigarette and started to smoke it. The German man watched. After he had taken two puffs of the cigarette, the guard dropped it on the ground. The German man stretched and reached for it. The guard stepped on it and moved his foot back and forth, so that it would really be gone. My senses were still raw from the accident. Seeing this humiliation made me feel angry with the German man for having put himself in that position for a stupid cigarette. Somehow I understood the dark man, but a pain like the twisting of a knife was in my gut. I wanted to go to the German man and be kind to him in some way, but then I thought it would probably be kinder if I just went by, acting like I hadn't seen what happened. I felt sad because I realized that victors can do anything they want to do, and though most of the soldiers were very nice, some of them were not, and they wouldn't be punished for any bad things they did because they won the war.

Some blocks down the street, another soldier was sitting on the steps of a house, surrounded by children. He was peeling oranges for them. Oranges! This man knew what those children needed. The children were leaning on him, sitting on his legs and having a wonderful time, and he was smiling, too. There was such a stark contrast between what I had just experienced and this scene. The oranges looked beautiful. I hadn't eaten an orange in five years, easily. But in the evening Hamilton would bring some.

I continued on into town. At the market place I walked by Herr Hannes' office. I was sorry that he was dead. I wondered who worked in his office, if the two ladies were still there, and who lived upstairs in their apartment. I suppose I could have just gone into the office to see who was there, but I didn't have the courage.

The market was set up, though there were only vegetables for sale, like radishes, beets, carrots, kohlrabi, and cabbage. I got whatever they gave me of each. The shopping net was quite heavy because the cabbage was rather large. The farmer still took the Hitler money, though there was talk about occupation money, but no one had any.

I walked along the different tables to see if there was something I had missed, when I heard some men joking and laughing, and speaking English. And then I saw him, Hamilton! Several of his buddies were teasing him.

"Ham's got a girlfriend."

"How old did you say she was?"

"Thirteen," someone else said. They all laughed.

Hamilton protested, "Come on guys, she's not my girlfriend. She's just a kid."

"Some kid, I'll bet," One of the guys answered. They all laughed again.

I wished I could be invisible. I had to get away, unseen. They couldn't see me. I felt again how short my dress was, how bony my knees looked, how stupid I looked with my braids, how absolutely ridiculous the whole situation was.

Turning my back to them, I slowly made my way back to the street, being careful to keep my face down so that I wouldn't be recognized by him. I got home surprisingly fast. I had lost all self-confidence and almost dreaded seeing him in the evening. Although I tried to tell myself that he doesn't expect to see a young woman, I wanted to look like one and moaned and groaned and complained all afternoon. Mama suggested that I try on my confirmation dress. "It's white. It looks like a party dress. We could let your hair hang loose. What do you say?"

I tried on the dress. It was longer, and fit better. My hair was passable. I looked somewhat better. Evening finally came. I got dressed and went down into the yard. Then I went out into the street to see if I could see him coming. Then I went to the fork of the road and walked along the dirt road, up to the main road and back again. I stopped on the little bridge across the creek. I waited a long time, but Hamilton didn't come. I went back home and sat on the bench under the lilac and orange bushes. It was dark when I went upstairs.

Mama was reading when I opened the door. She looked up. There was a look of sympathetic understanding in her eyes. To my relief, she didn't say anything.

Days went by. I never saw him again. Life went on in its boring way.

One day, my cousin Horst appeared. He had ridden a bicycle all the way from Essen through the borders of the different occupation zones to get food. Essen was in the British zone, and since everything in that area was industrial, they had no food. He said that the British were very experienced occupation forces. They were neither especially friendly nor mean. He said that someone was gutting the Krupp factories, taking out the machinery that hadn't been destroyed, and that Oma was well and staying with them. Their home was still standing. He spent two days with us, going to the various farms and coming back with more than I ever did. He took our rabbit along to Essen. Rose Marie cried that her bunny was gone, but Mama said that rabbits are kept to be eaten, and she didn't think that we would want to eat that rabbit, so it was better off with Horst, who would keep it to raise others, because they had a really nice rabbit hutch.

Rose Marie believed her and was consoled thinking that someday she would visit and see a whole family of rabbits there.

Although we had had more than enough money during the war since Mama got Papa's salary from Krupp, as well as money from the army, she wasn't sure what would happen to those payments in the future. So, she decided to look for a job, and she got one very easily at the UNRRA camp, which was set up at the former flight school. The camp held all kinds of displaced people, all foreign, of course. She went there for about two months, and then got a job working for the American Occupation Forces as a kind of housekeeper for the officers in a big villa they had taken over. The job she did most often was ironing. Of course, she also interpreted over the phone, or whenever there was the need for it on the grounds or with anything that had to do with domestic matters.

I went to visit her at work at least once a week, whenever the officers had some kind of special meal. Then I would help the cook in the kitchen by drying a lot of glasses. He was a very skinny, energetic, dark man, who talked with a funny Southern accent, and called me "honey-chile." He always managed to find some leftovers for me to take home. He wasn't supposed to do that, so he would wrap up the food in kitchen towels. Then he'd hand the "package" to me, go to the kitchen door, and look out, then he'd motion to me and say, "Coast is clear. You better git now."

Once, as I was going around the corner of the house, I passed two soldiers standing near a truck. One of them told the other, "Hey, you know, that is a really spooky kid. I swear she understands everything you say."

I turned and smiled.

He said, "There, you see! See what I mean?"

I had to laugh. That was really great fun.

I only knew the name of one soldier at the house. That was Tony. He was the aide to the senior officer. He mostly ran a lot of errands. One afternoon, towards the end of summer, I was visiting Mama. She had taken our laundry to work that day, and I was to take it home and hang it to dry. But before that, Tony was supposed to get an iron repaired in town. Since he didn't know German, I went along to interpret.

We rode in an open jeep, which I enjoyed immensely. Tony was very easy to talk to because he was very young, certainly not more than eighteen, and he was rather small, as though he still had some growing ahead of him. I directed him to the appliance store, though I had my doubts that there would be anyone who would actually fix the iron.

When we entered the store, two girls who had been sitting on the counter, quickly slid off and stood behind it. I recognized them as students at my school, but a few years older. As we approached the counter, one of them said, "I had no idea that these guys were that desperate."

I started to feel uneasy, but I told them that we wanted to see the repairman. They giggled, and made other stupid remarks. Tony guessed what was going on, and asked, "Are they giving you a hard time?"

I said, "Yes, and there's nobody to fix the iron."

He told me to ask for a screwdriver so that he could open up the iron and see what was wrong with it. I had to search my memory for a while to remember what screwdriver was. Finally, I talked around it, and one of the girls brought a toolbox. I didn't look at the girls, just concentrated on what Tony was doing. He opened up the iron as though he had done it often. He poked around, crimped something, tightened something else, and finally put it all back together again. Then he smiled and said, "Tell them 'thanks' and let's get out of here." He grinned at my sigh of relief when we got back into the jeep. Although it was late summer, the sun was shining and warm, the sky was clear and blue, and I felt happy, though I hadn't quite wiped away the memory of those girls' ridicule.

Back at the house, Tony gave Mama the iron. She told me to wait a little while more, the laundry hadn't come back yet. Tony told me to follow him, and we went upstairs to the sitting rooms. We sat on a very soft couch and began talking about where he was from, which was New York, and that he was Italian, and we talked about languages and many different subjects. I felt very comfortable talking to him, because he asked questions that didn't require complicated answers.

I don't know how we got from the difference of how Germans and Americans write the letter 'I' and a real grown-up kiss, my first kiss, but I remember his hand on my knee, and my realization that this was leading to something that I was not ready for. I pushed his hand aside, and moved back, away. He was confused.

"What's wrong?" he asked.

"I'm too little for this." I couldn't look at him.

"I'm not big, either," he answered.

"No. I'm thirteen!" I was angry at myself for my lack of language. I couldn't remember the word "young," which is just about exactly like the German word "jung."

"You're what?" he demanded.

"Thirteen." I felt like a bug.

He jumped up as if he had been shocked. He started to speak very loudly, "You're thirteen?! Damn! I didn't know. Jesus Christ! You're right, you are too little! Holy Cow! You don't seem that young. I really had no idea. Why, you're just a kid. Oh, man! You'd better get back down to your Mom."

If I had known how to say it in English, I would have said "I'm sorry," but I didn't. On the way down the stairs, I felt the waist of my dress cutting into my ribs, and the hem touching my butt. I wanted to disappear . . . again.

I was relieved to see the basket of laundry ready to be taken home when I got downstairs. Mama didn't notice that I was upset, and so I was quickly on my way home.

The warmth of the earlier afternoon was gone. The sky had become cloudy. It was cool and windy. The little wagon, with the basket of damp laundry squeaked behind me. I was reliving the afternoon as I was walking along the street. Suddenly, an egg-shaped ball came bouncing into the street in front of me. I went to pick it up and took it over to the hedge from where it had come. A young man, an American in a khaki T-shirt, stood on the other side of the hedge. I handed him the ball.

He said, "Thank you."

I answered, "You're welcome," and turned to go.

He called after me, "Wait a minute. You know English!"

"A little."

"Are you learning it in school?" he continued.

"Yes." I didn't want to talk.

"What are you, about twelve or thirteen?" he asked.

"Thirteen."

"I'm a teacher back home," he said. "I taught kids your age. I haven't seen you around here before. Do you live here?"

"No. I live out of the city."

"So, what are you doing over here?"

It was hard work to explain that I was taking the laundry home, that I had not washed it, that my mother worked over here, and that I didn't know where my father was.

He was so very nice, like Herr Braun, our science and music teacher. His eyes were warm and friendly brown.

"Why don't you come in and I'll make some hot chocolate for us." I would have loved hot chocolate, but I had to look away, because I was about to cry. I didn't know how to react to this kindness. It had been a very difficult day.

He interpreted my looking down the road as being afraid and asked, "Are you scared the other kids will be mad if you do?"

I couldn't talk, or even look at him, so I nodded my head. It was an easy way out.

He looked sad, and said, "Well, then, maybe another time."

Tears filled my eyes. I knew there would be no next time.

He said "goodbye."

I waved my hand and didn't look at him, I just turned to pick up the handle of our squeaky little wagon. When I was on my way again, I just let the tears flow. There was no one to see them. The road home seemed much longer than before. The sun was on the horizon by the time I got the laundry on the line. It would never dry before Mama got home.

During these summer months, while Mama was working, my grandmother from Benningen came to stay with us. She slept on the couch in the kitchen. We liked her a lot. She was very gentle, cooked what food there was, listened to the radio, mended socks, played board games with the younger children. She wasn't as interesting or knowledgeable as Oma, but it was comforting to have her there.

I had barely been in school the whole previous school year, the summer seemed endless, and there was no news about starting school again. I really felt at loose ends and missed having something to read or something to do with my mind. When the weather allowed, I was outside with my siblings, often walking out into the fields and the forest, where we had found our own "secret" place. It didn't have a magic spring, but it was by some moss-covered rocks and berry patches, and it was very still. The elves and good fairies lived in little castles in the rocks, and always watched over us. We made up stories, played them out, pretended to live in an enchanted world in which we were princesses, and Herbie, of course, was always the young prince who had some special task to perform for the king, and we would possess the magic powers to help him. I tried to have each child feel like the hero or most loved in these stories. When Iris was at the house and would join us, she also took part in these plays, depending on her mood. Sometimes she would just sit and watch.

Several incidents during that summer, which happened in town, have remained in my memory: One day I went to a grocery store and was surprised to see our BDM troupe leader, with her hair in a long, blond braid, and wearing a white apron, standing behind the counter, waiting on the customers. I was so happy to see a familiar face, that when it was my turn, I beamed a happy "Guten Tag" at her and told her how nice it was to see her. She looked at me with the coldest eyes, and asked me what I wanted to buy. I was childishly surprised that she didn't recognize me, so I told her my name. Her expression did not change. She just said something like, "I didn't understand that. What did you want?"

I just handed her the grocery list Mama had made out, and stood completely bewildered. It was obvious that she didn't want anyone to know that she knew me. But why? Did this have something to do with the promise we had made? But what did this have to do with remembering that we are German? Why was she denying that she knew me? She was afraid! But why? She didn't do anything bad. I couldn't imagine that Americans would consider painting toys and picking raspberry leaves, or teaching us folk songs, or even telling us that we were special and that we had an obligation to take care of the earth, as something to be afraid of.

Her attitude reminded me of the uniforms that were swimming in the creek after the Americans had come. All kinds of Hitler Youth and other German uniforms had been dumped into the water by their owners. When Mama saw them swimming by, she thought we should throw my BDM jacket in, too, but I refused to part with it. It was the only warm thing I had, and it fit me and was so soft. So she decided that she could dye it, which she did, and I wore it in navy blue. I thought the whole thing was silly. The Americans knew that people belonged to the Hitler Youth and BDM, and I couldn't understand why one should have to pretend that it wasn't so.

On another day that summer, I had a far worse experience. I had, for some time, had an ache along my jaw line that would come and go. It was around a tooth that had been filled a few years before. I woke up that morning with a swollen cheek and a really bad toothache. Reluctantly, I went into town to the dentist's office. The regular dentist wasn't there because anyone who had had a license from the Nazi German government could not practice. So, this person was not a licensed doctor. I didn't know that at the time, and even if I had known it, I had no choice. So, I climbed into the chair and let him take a look.

He decided that he had to pull my tooth. There was no painkiller. He clamped onto the tooth and began to wiggle it loose, and then, apparently, the crown broke off. I vaguely remember him wanting to say that he wasn't done yet, but I considered the ordeal to be finished, and got out of the chair and left. It took a good week for the swelling to go down, and the gum to heal, and I thought that was the end of it. (Several years later, another dentist found the roots and a ball of pus on which they had been sitting all that time.)

One day in August, I watched a few very drunken American soldiers drive a tank around the market square, pouring beer from bottles and shouting something that I finally learned was that the war with Japan was over, too. Other people, who were outside, just stood and watched the spectacle, prompted by something so important to Americans, but which made absolutely no difference to our lives.

Somewhere I heard that the department store was being redecorated, or perhaps even restocked, and that Iris' father was back in town. I never saw him. If they met, or were together, it was not in the house where we lived.

On a gray Saturday afternoon, Iris knocked at our door. I answered and she told me that there was a fair in town. We children got ready to go very quickly. It was the first time that Iris would come to town with us, and the first time in a long time that something enjoyable was being offered us.

The fair grounds were close to where Mama worked, which was far for Herbie and Hannelore to walk. Even Rose Marie complained a bit. But, when we got there, all was forgotten. Next to the entrance was a huge market table, stacked with sandwiches, lox sandwiches. We were very hungry. We were always hungry. I turned to the woman sitting next to the table and asked who would be eating those sandwiches, and how one could get one. I didn't have any ration stamps with me.

The lady was quite old. She had a lot of wrinkles, but her hair was a very deep red color, and she had a lot of make-up on her eyes, her cheeks and her lips. She spoke with an accent, and smilingly said, "You don't need stamps. If you have some money, I'll take that, but if you don't, that's all right, too."

I had ten occupation marks that Mama had given me. She didn't take the money, and said, "You don't have to pay, just go ahead and eat. I know you are hungry."

Her voice was sweet, but her smile and her eyes were not. Other children were eating sandwiches and enjoying them. Hannelore and Herbie were looking at me with big eyes. Iris was already eating, and Rose Marie was taking a sandwich. I looked at the woman, and she said, "Don't be afraid, there's nothing wrong with them." I finally nodded to the little ones to take one, too. Then I turned to her again and asked, "What is the payment for this food? What do you want?"

She looked at me for a moment, weighing, judging, and then said, without that false smile, "We want you to look at the exhibit. Really look at it."

"Exhibit?" I asked, "What exhibit?"

"When you go into the gate, there are several rows of pictures, paintings. I want you to look at them carefully."

"Just look at the pictures, that's all?" I asked.

She nodded.

I was drawn to the food, and wolfed down a sandwich in a few bites. She was watching.

She said, "Have another one."

Somewhere, in the back of my mind, I thought of Hansel and Gretel, or of being poisoned. But, it would be too late to do anything about it anyway, so I ate another one.

With the salty, smoked-fish taste in my mouth, I went through the gate with the other children. There was a kind of corridor erected with tent materials. On the walls, at my eye level, were long rows of cardboard-mounted paintings and drawings. A few feet ahead of me were two boys, about ten years old. They were pointing to some of the pictures, shouting excitedly, "Look at this one!"

"Oh, that's nothing. You should see the one over there."

They moved 'over there' and the other boy exclaimed, "That's disgusting!"

I looked at the tent wall beside me, straight at the word *KONZENTRATIONSLAGER*. The boys ahead of me seemed to fade away. My siblings, who had been behind me, somehow passed me. I remember Rose Marie saying, "I don't like these pictures. They're ugly."

I think I told her to go ahead to the playground with the others. I had seen a carrousel out in the field. If there were other people near, I was unaware of them. I found myself caught in the gray light filtering through the tent walls.

The pictures were simple sketches or watercolors, subtle, silent, sad. Among them were scenes like the one I had witnessed in Essen. A small, old man being taken away by a big man in a brown uniform with a big swastika on his sleeve.

There were faces in small openings of an ugly, dark freight car. They had big, brown, frightened eyes.

Long lines of people, old, young, some being helped by others, children being carried by mothers, other children carrying suitcases too large for them.

In a courtyard was a tall, thin man. There were ropes tied to his wrists. He was standing all alone, his arms stretched out on each side by the ropes. I didn't understand that picture, but knew that it told of something evil.

Other pictures showed figures against high fences, brick buildings with bars on windows, big metal doors.

The picture that burned itself into my soul was of a mother and child. A large, ugly woman was pulling a little boy away from his mother. His arms were stretched out to his mother. He was crying, "Mama, Mama!" I could hear him. His mother was being pulled in the opposite direction by a man. Her free hand was reaching for the child. Her face, her eyes, were filled with terror and sorrow.

At the end of the canvas tunnel I came out onto the playground. I gathered my charges for the walk home. Iris was standing next to me. Had she been with me the whole time? I wondered, but I couldn't ask her. I couldn't talk about what I had seen or how I felt.

As we walked by the lox sandwich table, the wicked witch woman smiled at me again. I felt a great rush of heat spread over my face. I was ashamed. I remembered the German man without legs, who reached for the cigarette. My appetite, my hunger, had given this woman the power to crush my spirit, my love for my heritage, and all the great beliefs I had been taught. I had lost my identity, my pride . . . for two fish sandwiches. She knew it, and she was pleased.

I didn't look at Iris. I suspected her to be a part of the conspiracy. I felt betrayed, and didn't know how to deal with it. I was angry with the messengers because they were near. But actually, in that gray, silent light I learned the truth that I didn't want to believe. I knew that these pictures and drawings were not enemy propaganda. They were real. I felt like I had walked in on a terrible secret, a horrible deed done by someone I believed in and loved.

On the long way home, I began to search through my memory. I wanted to know how this terror could have happened. What clues did I have and didn't recognize? Why did even the adults seem horrified and unbelieving? Frau Dauer gave an excuse to Mama one day when she asked if Frau Dauer knew that these things were going on.

She said, "Nothing like this ever happened before, how would we even imagine such a thing. It's not like they shouted it from the rooftops. Look, even the enemy spies didn't know, so how should village housewives know?"

My thoughts were confused. I remembered my first grade teacher and all of the hateful things he said, and I could still see the scene where the old man was forced towards the car by the bigger man in a beige uniform.

But, didn't Herr Hannes have the same kind of uniform? He didn't seem to be like that. He was like a real father with his daughter and me, too. He was very nice to me, but then, of course, I was German. I didn't really know how he was with other people, except with Herr Edelstein. He protected him. But, he must have done something bad because he killed himself. I wondered if the people, who lived in Memmingen, knew all of these things. Maybe they did, because it was a small town. But in Essen, the people in that neighborhood were afraid. I was afraid and I didn't even know why. I remembered the star on the old lady's coat at the butcher shop, and the black uniform that night at Tante Lene's and the other black uniforms in Ellwangen. I was afraid of them. People were afraid, but did they know what happened to those who were arrested, or did they fear THEM, the way I did, without really knowing what THEY were? Did our BDM leaders know?

I couldn't imagine that they did. They couldn't have known and at the same time teach us to believe that we were the finest, the best, the ones who were envied by our enemies, who were so cruel and bad except for the Americans, and probably the English, and maybe some of the French, too . . .

That is how my mind went, around and around. Who was there to explain all of this? Whenever I asked her, Mama just kept on saying, "That is nothing for you to worry about. It would be much better if you help me with this work instead of filling your head with thoughts that bring nothing."

I was looking forward to going back to school, hoping that our teachers would explain to us what had happened and if there is still a Germany, or is Germany now a piece of America, France, England, Russia, and whom are we to believe and trust and obey. To whom were we now supposed to be loyal?

Shortly before school started, Mama came home one day with wonderful news. One of the officers had written a V-letter to Tante Toni in Milwaukee, telling her about us, and what news Mama had or didn't have of the whole clan. Tante Toni answered, that Papa was in England, and he was well. She had received a Red Cross message from him.

Mama also said that the officer told her that we three children, who had been born in America, were American citizens, and that we were now registered at the consulate in Muenchen.

I heard it and thought that was nice, but really didn't realize what that meant at the time. The news about Papa overshadowed everything else. I was so relieved, and really glad that he was in England if it was necessary that he be away. I was hoping that we would get back to school soon, so that I could tell Fraulein Rosamunde that my father was in England.

And school did finally begin. Those going back to the village school were not terribly enthused about it, but I was really looking forward to being in a classroom and getting back to a familiar routine. We had been out of school so long, and I was anxious to see my classmates again, and wondered if we would still have the same teachers we had before.

The refugees were gone from our school, but the Americans had offices there, so we were told to meet at the Hotel zum Roten Ochsen. Our first class meeting was in the same dining room in which we had been assigned our homes as refugees by Herr Hannes so long ago. It was a German class, but Frau Meier was not there. Our teacher was a young blond woman, who sat in one of the big chairs, knitting a baby sweater. Most of my classmates had returned, but Helga was missing.

Until after Christmas recess, we only had German class, and did very little except to tell stories and describe pictures that we were to bring to class. We had no books because all textbooks printed after 1932 were banned from the schools. We had no paper, either, so everything was oral.

While students took turns telling stories, the others were occupied in drawing and coloring with water-paints, on butcher paper, scenes from fairytales. It was a very friendly and non-threatening experience, which was more like story time at the library, or like being taken cared of by a baby sitter, than an actual class . . . and, of course, it was much too sweet for questions or debate on the monumental events and chaos in our world. Life was like wandering through a dream, a twilight zone. I was surrounded by zombies, living without thought. No one talked about the war, the crimes, the defeat, the disaster, the future, as if they didn't know anything about it, as if they had been somewhere else.

There was no other subject taught outside of this so-called German, because there were no teachers. Secondary, or Gymnasium teachers, were state employees, which meant that they had a license issued by the Nazi government. No one, who had been licensed by the Nazi government was allowed to practice his profession.

The winter was bitter cold. No one had sewn blankets into coats yet, and I had only my dark blue BDM jacket to wear. I crossed my arms, hugging my body to keep it warm as I went back and forth to school. My shoes were too small and hurt my feet. At home, the bedroom windows had not been replaced, and a few snowflakes came through the cracks between the boards. I slept nearest the windows, and I actually felt a few flakes on my face. The floor and the walls had ice flowers on them. We slept with most of our clothes on, and thank God, we had feather beds.

Mama had bartered some American cigarettes for a basket of apples. She had laid them out on top of the large cabinet so that they wouldn't rot and infect each other. When Mama took some down, she discovered that they had frozen.

For Christmas we had a pretty little tree. We even went to Midnight Mass in the village. The snow crunched underfoot, but the night was beautiful. There were stars in the sky and lights in the windows. The church sparkled with tinsel and candlelight. When we got home, we drank hot tea and ate some cookies that Mama had baked. We children were happy, but Mama was sad because Papa was still in England, and we didn't know how long he would be there.

After vacation, in January of 1946, we were finally allowed to return to our school. Our class met in our old room, in the back, right by the alley. A few new students had joined the class, and two girls, who had come from other villages, were not there. I had no idea who our teachers would be, and anxiously waited for the first one to make her appearance. She was our chemistry and physics teacher, a tall, blond woman, wearing glasses, a lab coat, and an artificial leg. She was soft-spoken and kind, and one could see that she really did want to teach us science. The problem was, of course, that we had no books, no lab equipment, and absolutely no knowledge of science, since the last time we had any such subject, was with Herr Braun, and that was botany, three years ago.

Nevertheless, this sweet woman would make probes, asking us if we knew about wave lengths, how light and sound travel at different rates, the chemical symbols for water, oxygen, hydrogen, and when she got no reply, she said, "Well, I will have to do some planning before we can go into those topics. In the meantime, how many of you know how to use a slide-rule?" And then we were asked to see if we could find some strong butcher's paper, to bring it to school, and a pair of scissors if we had one.

And so our first science project was to cut and mark butcher paper, and to create a slide—rule. It was fun, and we actually learned some operations, which I'm sorry to say I have forgotten since, but I still remember how proud I was of my own paper slide-rule.

Our math teacher came on a motorcycle she parked outside of our classroom in the alley. She came into the room with boots and riding pants, a leather jacket with lots of buckles, and an Emilia Earhart-type leather helmet, and goggles. She kept the helmet and everything else on, just flipping the sides of the helmet up and perching the goggles on top of her head. The buckles on her jacked clanked fiercely when she stomped around the front of the class. We giggled a lot. I don't remember what kind of Math we were learning, but I think we were reviewing.

We also began learning shorthand and French. The teacher for those subjects came from a northern big city and told us that we were disgusting peasants, and the town and the food that was eaten here were equally disgusting. She also acted as though she were in terrible pain when we repeated something in French. I regretted not having chosen Latin instead, but I had really looked forward to French because I still remembered the romantic story in one of Mama's library books, and the fact that our grandmother's family had come from Strasbourg.

Our German teacher came from Strasbourg. She was fairly young, had very blue eyes and black hair with bangs and two spit curls pasted to her cheeks. Some of the girls said that she put sugar water on her hair to make it stiff. She spoke an Alsacean dialect of German. She let us know that she was not a barbarian like we were, but she was French.

During the first week of school, she brought a stack of pictures of famous paintings to class. She stood in front of the class, held up a picture and snapped, "What is the name of the painting? Who painted it?"

One by one, down the rows, we stood up when it was our turn, and each one answered the same: "I don't know."

She replied, "Six," which was a failing grade. "Sit down. Next."

After the second day of this activity, in which she did nothing but think that she was humiliating us, but in actuality, she was losing our respect, she stopped and said, "These are the paintings belonging to the Louvre you tried to steal from us." We just looked at each other.

For several days she lectured about literature and authors and told us that we would be doing some very serious reading, that according to what she had learned about us, we were years behind in what we should have learned, and that this year we would catch up.

She always came to class late, and smelled of cigarette smoke. One day she was really very late. I was talking with some of the girls near me, and was getting close to asking questions about how they felt about the war, and if anyone they knew talked about it. It was obvious that none of our teachers were going to. We had no history or political science. But whenever I tried to talk about these things, I always got the same reaction from my peers. They looked frightened and shocked, and said something like, "You're not supposed to talk about that."

I thought, *Who said that we are not supposed to talk about that? Did I miss something? When were we told that?*

As we were talking, I noticed that some of the bigger girls from the other side of the room were starting to go out the door, and slowly the whole class started to walk out. There were three of us left. We got up and followed the class. Once outside, in front of the building, we linked arms and walked back and forth under the chestnut trees. The teacher came out in a fury and told us to get back to our classroom immediately.

Once we were seated, she began the inquisition.

"Whose idea was this? Answer! So brave you are together, but none of you has the courage to take the consequence. I'm waiting, and we will do nothing else until the guilty one has the courage to speak."

I watched her and knew that she didn't care how long it would take because that way she wouldn't have to do any work, and I looked at the class. No one would say anything. I guessed that was a part of the promise to always remember, to stick together . . . But something had changed for me. I had become different through my association with Americans, and with the change in the social order. I didn't care what she would do, what she thought, I felt that I had nothing to lose, and I was getting bored, so I raised my hand and said, "It was my idea."

Immediately, the class objected by shouting, "No, it wasn't. She was one of the last to leave." And so on. This made me an enemy for life.

She hissed, "I see. You still think that you are a hero. Well, let me tell you, the days of heroism are over for you and your kind."

And with that she dropped the subject.

One day, soon thereafter, she handed out paper and gave us a dictation at such a wild speed that it was impossible to get it all down. After she collected the papers, she told us that we were the most uncivilized, uneducated, ignorant group of students she had ever seen, but since she was stuck with us, she would do her best to put some culture into our stupid heads.

Then she turned to me and said, "I hear you are a good story teller. Get up here and tell us a story."

The way she addressed me, and the fact that she picked on me in this manner, startled me. I got up and went to the front of the room. She, however, had her back to me and stood at the lectern, calling up other students to discuss their dictation papers with them. I stood for a while and then started to move back to my seat. She caught me before I could sit down and said, "Come here, you." She looked at my paper and raised her shaved, penciled eyebrow. "This is terrible! Atrocious! What are you doing in this school? You don't belong here. You should be in the village school with the rest of your kind. I'm afraid you will not be able to do the work in this class. You should talk to your parents about this. You must make plans for your future. Get a position as an apprentice somewhere. Sit down."

She was right. There was no future for me at this school, or in this town. Everything had changed, and something had happened to me. I was different. I was a very big orange star. And the school had changed, too. It was no longer a school for the intellectually elite, it had once again become a school for the social elite. I was of no importance. Already there was an inner circle of girls whose parents were professionals, doctors, lawyers, business men. Their mothers had attended the school. They had books from before 1933, which were passed around among them. Our teachers gave assignments out of those books, but I never got any of them to take home overnight. There never was a spare one, and no one invited me to study together. They had tutors to help them catch up with all of the work we had missed. I was on the outside with a few other girls, who commuted on their bikes from neighboring farm villages. They, too, felt that they no longer belonged. A few of them dropped out over the winter. The very brightest of all, Maria, told me that she wouldn't be back because her father needed her on the farm, but she didn't look at me when she said that, and I knew she was very sad to be leaving school. I also knew that I wouldn't last very much longer either.

I drifted through a few months, trying to feel my way through my classes without having read the material or even knowing what they were talking about, wondering what would become of me. And then, one Saturday morning, a beige American car pulled up to the fence, and an American in a beige dress uniform, carrying a brief case, came to see ME. He was an intelligence officer. He understood German, but preferred to speak English. For me it was the opposite, so I would answer his English questions in German.

He said, "Your mother applied for a passport for the three of you who were born in the United States. Under the law, you are American citizens, but since you've been living here as a German during the war, I have to ask you some questions.

Mama hovered nearby, nervous that I would say the wrong thing, but I felt completely at ease. We talked, or, actually, he asked questions and I talked about the war, school, BDM, and about my memories of America. He asked me if I wanted to return to the States, and why. I told him about the "enemy propaganda" we were told not to believe, about the betrayal I felt, about my situation in school, the unpromising future I faced, and my need to get away and start all over again.

He said, "You're not the only young person in this country who feels the way you do. But, you are lucky because you have an American birth certificate, and that means that you have a right to return to the good old USA."

Several hours had passed, it was lunchtime. Before he left to drive back to Muenchen, Mama made some tea and rye bread sandwiches with American peanut butter and orange marmalade. She had gotten a large can of each from someone at work, who understood what being hungry meant. After having lunch with us, the officer left. He told Mama to have passport pictures made for us, that it would take a little time for them to contact Tante Toni and Onkel Berthold and that they would get in touch with her at work about when we were to come to Muenchen.

Mama hired a seamstress to make coats for us girls, and a Tyrolean jacket and shorts for Herbie. As soon as they were done, we had our picture taken, and before the month was over, the whole family boarded the train to Muenchen. We were going to the American consulate.

Remembering the bombing raid of that afternoon of the previous spring, I wondered what the city would look like. As the train rolled in, my first impression was that it wasn't so bad. There were buildings everywhere. Then, as I looked closer, I realized that inside those walls were heaps of rubble. The outside walls were standing, windowless, empty shells. The train station looked all right. There were some trees and grass nearby, which gave it a normal, healthy look. Outside of the station, Mama got a taxi, from which we could see the city and people winding their way through pathways around mountains of stones and broken furniture and appliances. I couldn't understand where all of the people lived, where they came from and where they were going. I asked Mama, "Where are they going, there aren't any buildings? Where do they live?"

Mama said, "In the cellars, like rats, with the rats."

We arrived at our destination, a new building, the only building around. It smelled of cement and plaster. It was the Consulate of the United States of America. A very wide staircase led to the second floor. But before we went into the office, we visited the restroom, which had American toilets with water that flushed, and toilet paper on a roll, and pretty washbasins in front of a huge mirror. I felt that we were in a palace.

Inside the office were two women. One reminded me of a grown-up Shirley Temple with curly hair and a pretty face, wearing a khaki skirt and blouse and very high-heeled shoes. The other one was wearing regular clothes and looked more serious. Her name was Miss Smith. She measured me, "four foot eleven," and weighed me, "sixty-four pounds, age fourteen, hair . . . dark-blond, light brown? And eyes . . . what are they? Blue, gray, green?" I ended up with light brown hair and gray eyes on the passport.

Then the consul came into the room. He reminded me so much of the intelligence officer that I wanted to ask him if it had been he who was at our home, but how can you ask somebody something like that? Anyhow, he asked me to come with him, all alone. We went into his office. There he explained that if we go to America, without Mama and Hannelore, we might be put into an orphanage if our relatives can't or don't want to keep us, and it may be years before the rest of our family could come, too. He wanted to be sure that this was my own decision, not influenced by my mother.

After that I realized that he wasn't the same man who had been at our house, and I focused on the present. I told him that I had to go back to the States. There was nothing here for me. I wanted to go home, no matter what. I was not afraid of orphanages. Besides, I knew that Tante Toni would never put us into an orphanage.

And so it was decided that Herbie, Rose Marie, and I would travel to the United States to live with Tante Toni. Onkel Berthold and she had already officially agreed to be our legal guardians until our parents would also return.

We went back to the outer office, where our passport was ready for my signature and thumb print. I was very happy, but Mama smiled one of those sad-eyed smiles.

At the station, a troupe transport train had stopped. Some young soldiers called out of the window, "Hey, Fraulein, is there any water around?"

They were surprised that Mama and I responded. They had a tin cup, which they passed down to us, and Mama found a faucet that had water. When someone asked how we knew English, I waved my passport at them.

"I'm American."

"No kidding! Wow! Hey, good luck, kid! Bye . . ." The train rolled
on.

After we had gotten settled on the train, I closed my eyes and
repeated to myself that statement I had made so joyfully: "I'm American."
It sounded strange for me to say that, and I had to repeat it a few times
because the other phrase "Always remember that you are German"
kept on interfering. What was I, anyway? I had been German for a long
time, but now there wasn't any Germany. Germany was dead. I had
learned to love it, but it wasn't what I thought and believed it to be, so
I shouldn't feel guilty about leaving. I had not really thought out exactly
what would happen when I told the officer who came to our house,
and the consul in Muenchen that I had to leave and go home to the
United States. Actually leaving and traveling to America to live there
forever had been a kind of fantasy before this day. But now that I had
the passport in my hand, it had become reality. I really would leave
this country. Then I felt a kind of sadness thinking about leaving,
remembering the forest, the Alpine mountains, the fields, the cold,
harsh wind of the Schwaebischen Alb. But, beyond those sentimental
heart-strings, I also thought about school and every day life, and I
realized that returning to America was the only logical choice. I was
so wrapped up in my own self, that I didn't give a thought to the fact
that I was making this decision not only for me, but for Rose Marie
and Herbie as well.

The consul had told me that it might take six to eight weeks before
all of the preparations were made for our passage. I intended to make
the most of the time. Going back to school was suddenly really
enjoyable for me because I had such an exquisite secret. I became
more daring than I had been in years. Suddenly I was full of self-
confidence and energy. We were performing a little play in class, and
I was given a truly insignificant part, a bakery boy delivering a loaf of
bread. I played the role to the hilt. I strutted and imitated the big city

slang that I had learned from my cousin Horst, and no one in my class knew that I could do that. One of the girls, who was the daughter of the pastor of the biggest Lutheran church in town, and who was the typical studious girl with very proper clothes, neat hair and glasses, gave me a sincere compliment on my "hidden talent" and made me glow.

Since Easter break, which was very short because we had to make up so much time, Fraulein Rosamunde was back in school. I was really happy to see her. She taught us English, and substituted in math, until another teacher could be found. The motorcycle teacher did not return after the break.

I was such an extrovert in English class that I amazed myself. It seemed that I knew the answers before Fraulein Rosamunde could put them to us. I translated from English to German as if I were reading the text in German. Fraulein Rosamunde didn't say anything, she just looked at me sort of sideways, and I loved it.

Something wonderful had happened to me, and those around me were aware of it. I felt that the orange star was shining, like copper and gold.

Time seemed to be flying by. School had become more than tolerable. It seemed to me that the teachers left me in peace, or else I didn't feel sensitive to their criticism anymore. I was reminded on several occasions that there was tuition due, and I always answered, "Yes, I know."

I did do a lot of day dreaming, mostly imagining how it would be when I got to tell my secret. I knew that it would have to be in German class. I would say, "This is my last day here because I am going home to America."

And since they would not believe it, I would have my passport along. Imagining what reaction I would get from our French German teacher was the sweetest part of waiting.

May, with its lilacs and showers of orange blossoms, did not enchant me this year. June had come and was at an end. The school year would continue for some time. In Bavaria, summer vacation starts and ends late, especially that year, since there was so much to catch up on.

Mama told me that she had received a call from the American consulate. There would be a ship leaving Bremen in July. We were to come to Muenchen and stay at a displaced persons camp until a train would take us to Bremen.

"You can change your mind, you know. You are not obligated to leave."

I thought I heard a plea in her voice, and my resolve was getting a bit shaky, but weighing my prospects for the future in Germany against a somewhat frightening journey to what I considered a sure kind of security, I insisted on going on with the trip.

I did not tell her that the consul had advised me that it might be years before we would see each other again, but reminded her that she wouldn't have to worry about what we were going to eat and wear, and that as soon as Papa came back from England, they would be on their way, too. Mama thought it over, sighed, and seemed to accept the situation with some optimism.

Now, that I knew I would be leaving—forever—my world became more precious. On the weekend I took my siblings to the forest to really look at all of the details of our favorite spots. I went to church in the village and looked and listened without daydreaming. At home, I sat on the bench under the lilac and mock orange trees, which I had hardly noticed this year, and remembered the shower of blossoms on a moonlit night. Although it was a bitter-sweet memory, I was also ashamed of myself for being so stupid to think that such a handsome man could think of me as anything but a kid. Then I made a resolve that I would grow up into a stunningly beautiful woman, and he would fall in love with me, and I would coldly turn away from him and say, "You had your chance, but you didn't know who I really was. Now it's too late."

Well, that was make-believe revenge, but I had a real one to perform.

I timed my entrance to class for German hour. As I opened the classroom door, the teacher looked at me and was getting ready to say something. I quickly stopped her by saying, "I've just come to say good-bye."

A smirk hushed across her face, and then I continued, "Because I'm going home to America." That surprised her.

I turned to my classmates. They just stared at me in silence, and I didn't feel like gloating over them. We had been a group for a long time, and if I wasn't the most popular girl in class, it was not because they prevented it. I suddenly felt very sad to be leaving them. One by one they got up and shook my hand and wished me well. Finally, I was at the front of the room.

The teacher said, "I didn't know. I had no idea . . ."

I felt an incredible force of fury pass through me with my words, "I know." It's all I could say, but I'm sure she read much more in my eyes. I turned, and felt like running, but smiled and said "I'll write" in the direction of my classmates and quickly got outside. I wondered if I should go the office and let them know that I was leaving, but decided against it. Tears were very close to the surface, and I didn't want to cry. I wished that I had been able to see Fraulein Rosamunde, though. What would she have said?

"Someday, I'll have to come back and show her that I could learn English, after all," I decided.

Outside of the building, I finally read the enameled sign that I had seen so often and never bothered about. It told that the building was more than 100 years old, and had been a hospital. In the old brick-laid courtyard, the sun was groping through the dense foliage of the chestnut trees. I would miss this old school, but not as it was now. I'd remember the old one, when Helga and I would come to school together in the mornings, and Frau Meier said "Guten Morgen, Kinder," instead of "Heil Hitler" and when we had music, and art, and there was order and our teachers liked us.

I dawdled my way past the baker, where we had gotten pretzels during our recess, past the church that was still a warehouse, past the hotel Zum Roten Ochsen and onto the marketplace from where I could look up at the building in which I had a little, very neat bedroom up on the second floor.

The department store still didn't have any merchandise. The bookstore only had book marks to sell.

I went to the little park where we had come sometimes with Mama, and other times I had come to read or do some homework. The park had a small tower, which was supposed to have been a *Hexenturm* (witches tower). Somebody told me that a long time ago they used to throw women into the tower if they believed that they were witches. They would just leave them there until they died. If a woman's baby had a strawberry mark on its face, they believed that that was the devil's kiss and the mother was a witch. I wondered what they did with the poor baby if they threw the mother into the tower.

At the city gate I looked up at the windows. No one looked back. I wondered if the other girls had believed all those things we heard up there, or was I the only fool? I knew that I would never know. No one would ever talk about that. That's what was meant by giving your word and shaking on the promise, "Never forget that you are German."

Where the German man without legs had reached for a cigarette, no one stood outside of the gate anymore, and the German plane that had crashed was still stuck in the earth, but there was no guard there, either. I checked the ground where I had watched the gravel jump, but I couldn't find any bullets. The moss still moved slowly in the flow of the water in the creek under the bridge on which I had waited for Hamilton. The bomb craters were full of muddy water. Weeds were growing on the edges. Along the road last year's leaves were still rotting. They had turned dark, maroon. They were wet and soaking my shoes.

Once more, the leaves reminded me of Erfurt and the day that Mama left us at the orphanage. Another leaving was about to happen, but this time we would be the ones abandoning Mama and Hannelore.

A feeling of guilt grabbed my heart. I was leaving my little sister, my mother, and dragging Rose Marie and Herbie along with me, without even asking them whether they wanted to do this or not.

"But," I told myself, "it's for everyone's good. We need food and clothes and a future. And everything will work out just fine. Papa will come back, and then everyone will be together again. Maybe we could even live on 33rd Street again."

On the nightstand was the painted wooden box that Mama had given me for Christmas. She said it was too heavy and big to put into a suitcase. She would bring it along when the rest of the family came "after Papa comes back from England."

I opened the drawer and took out Erika's book. Sitting on the bed, I looked at the cover, stroked the burnt-in flowers and told Erika,

"I've been thinking about whether I should take you along with me or not. You remind me of everything that is German and everything that I loved and lost. When I leave here, I'm going to be only American, and I'm never going to change from that. I don't want to grieve for you or for all the things that I loved in this country any more, and I can't spend the rest of my life depending on you to protect me, and that's why I have to leave you here. I'm going to put you back into the drawer. I'm not going to tell anyone about you. I hope that you will help and protect my little sister, Hannelore. I'm not going to think about what will happen to you when I'm gone. You are dead, and I'm going to live, and I have to forget about you. And now, I'm going to say good-bye, and that's it. Good-bye, Erika. I'm sorry. Good-bye."

I closed the drawer and turned away. My eyes fell on Hannelore's bed. Before I wallowed in that guilt-trip again, I decided to walk to the school and meet the children there. I felt a great urgency to talk to Hanni, to explain to her that I loved her even though I was leaving her. I wanted to be sure that she would understand that it was for just a little while. She shouldn't feel abandoned as I did at the orphanage in Erfurt.

My attempts at trying to communicate with her were not very successful. She was like a little porcupine, cross and irritable. I knew she was just trying to be tough, and she felt like an outsider with us "Americans." We went to bed early that evening since we had to leave on an early train the next morning. I tried to coax her to sleep with me, but she said from her bed, "I don't care if you go and never come back.

Who needs you around, anyway." She was crying. I ached, but I didn't even consider changing my mind.

I didn't sleep well. I felt guilty about Hannelore, Mama, and the two I was taking along. I was sad to leave all that was familiar, and weighed once more the likely outcome of my choice against staying, and knew that leaving was more logical, for me, anyhow. But, how about Herbie and Rose Marie? They wouldn't have their mother. But, they would have me, and Tante Toni, and good food, and it wasn't forever . . .

And then Mama came to wake us. It was still dark outside. We got dressed quickly. I went to Hannelore's bed and stroked her hair. She turned her back to me and said, "Just get out of here and leave me alone."

Mama came with us to Muenchen. Frau Dauer would take care of Hannelore while Mama was gone.

*   *   *

My 12th Birthday picture.

12

Going Home to America

The camp is one of the fuzzier parts of my memory. I don't remember how many days we spent there. I vaguely remember that we slept in a dorm-type room with rows of beds next to each other, Mama, Herbie, Rose Marie and I. And always I thought of Hannelore left behind by herself.

I think we had beef stew for every meal, because that's all I remember. We also were in an office several times. I signed some papers. People spoke only English there. And it kept on raining and raining . . .

Then, one day, we were at the train station, being assigned seats. We were put into a car with young Jewish people. Were they refugees, soldiers? I don't know where they came from or where they were going. Mama was not allowed to come aboard the train. She stood outside the window and said good-bye. As she was telling Herbie to be a good boy, her eyes were darker, sadder than I had ever seen them.

The train began to move, and I remembered the time our roles were reversed, when she was on the train and I wanted her to come back. Again we were parting, and again it had been my choice. I had insisted on going to America. If I hadn't, we would all be together with Hanni. But the dye was cast. We were on our way.

The three of us stood at the window and looked back until her lonely figure had vanished. We sat down on the wooden bench of the compartment, one child at each side of me. Herbie and Rose Marie were silent. There were no complaints, no tears. I knew that they were thinking about Mama and Hannelore and the only home they really knew. My mind fled to that familiar world, too, but not for long. As the train took on momentum, I became really aware of the two children at my sides. They were little, and they both leaned against me. I was now responsible for them, and I had to act confident and strong.

The car in which we were traveling was third class. All of the seats were made of wooden slats. Baggage nets were above us. A young man put our one suitcase up for us. Our bench was at the front of the car, near the door. There was some space ahead of us for extra baggage or people who wouldn't have a seat, I guess. There was also a pole to hang on to, and a ceiling light that illuminated that area. Standing in this light was a terribly thin young man—so thin and emaciated I wondered how he could manage to stand so long without fainting. He had a little round cap on his head and held a book in his right hand. He was grasping the pole with his left. He stood and looked at the book and read that page so long, that I finally turned to the young man who had helped us with our suitcase, "Why don't you have him sit down?" I asked.

And he, Aaron, said, "Because there, in that world where he is, he is happy."

We were the only children in the car. The others were all young men and women. Most of them were dressed in khaki-colored shorts and shirts. They were very tanned and strong, except for the one standing with the light shining down on him.

Late afternoon, it began to rain. It rained in on us because there was no glass in the window frames. After the shower, I was starting to panic. We were really hungry, and I had no food. And then, after an endless period of helpless fear, from the back of the train, Aaron came with camping pots full of stew for each of us. It was the same kind of stew we had at the camp.

When it had gotten dark, Aaron brought some heavy khaki-colored quilts. He put one up in a baggage rack, picked up Herbie and tucked him into the folds. Herbie liked it. He had a hammock to sleep in. Rose Marie put her head on my lap, and Aaron tucked another quilt around us, so we also started the night. The others behind us slowly settled down, too, and all that could be heard was the click, click, clack of the train.

I closed my eyes and saw Hannelore in her bed, and Mama's sad eyes at the train station. I opened my eyes and saw the young man standing with the book in his hand, and the light streaming down on him. My eyes burned. My tears flowed silently for all the sadness of the world I knew.

The next day began with another rainshower. I was awakened by the cool drops of rain on my face. As I opened my eyes, my glance fell on the pole. The young man was not there. A couple of girls were moving some baggage to that area. I turned around and saw Aaron. "Where is he?" I asked.

Aaron smiled. "He's all right." I supposed that he was somewhere in the car behind us, but I never saw him again.

At midmorning we came to a stop. The train stood on the tracks for a long time. Then, finally, we moved on again and rolled into a heavily bombed city, which I could not recognize, but now imagine to have been Kassel or Hannover. The train stopped again in the station.

A woman was talking from the platform to some of the young people at the end of our car. Aaron came forward and told us to stand at the window. The woman came to our window. She had Hershey boxes in her hands. She held some up, then stopped when she looked at us, saying, "You're not Jewish!"

Aaron's voice above my head, said, "They are children."

She looked down for a second, and then with a sigh she offered me a box for each of us, but her eyes were cold. I remembered the lox lady. Again someone who hated me was offering food. I had not moved.

Aaron commanded, "Take them."

I did, and gave one to Herbie and another to Rose Marie, who eagerly opened the boxes and were delighted to see chocolate and candy.

Aaron stood in front of me and demanded, "Why aren't you eating your chocolate?"

"I'm not hungry," I answered.

He said, "Listen to me! You've got to get a thicker skin than that if you want to survive in this world. When you get something to eat, you eat it! This chocolate tastes good, and is good for you."

I took a piece. It melted in my mouth. I swallowed it. I tried not to taste it because I didn't want to like it.

A short while later the train moved along again, very slowly. A boy, about eight years old, stood near the track. I took some of the candy and threw it to him.

"Bonbons," I shouted at him.

He looked at me with tired eyes and didn't move.

Aaron said, "You just threw that candy away. He won't pick it up. He doesn't trust you."

I knew he was right.

At noon we had another portion of stew, after which everyone behind us seemed busy cleaning up and packing things together. Aaron said that we'll soon be in Bremen.

From the back of the car, another young man came and sat down next to us. He said his name was Richard, and he had a favor to ask. He pushed up his jacket sleeve. On his arm, he had at least ten watches. He took one, a woman's watch, from his arm. It was light, like silver, but richer—platinum. The watch was encircled by diamonds. Later on I read what was engraved inside: "Meiner lieben Frida" and a date.

Richard said, "I would like Rose Marie to wear this watch for a few days, until I come to pick it up. You're going to a different place than we. See, this was my aunt's watch, and I don't want anyone to take it from me." Rosie's dress had long sleeves and buttons on the cuff. Richard talked to her about a secret game and not to show or say anything about the secret to anyone. As Aaron stopped to watch, I looked at him. He said over Richard's head, "This is his way of surviving."

And then it was time to get ready to leave the train. Aaron brought down our suitcase, and somehow we all managed to end up on the platform, and I lost sight of him. I wanted to thank him for watching over us, but he was gone.

We were transported to the center by bus, I think. I remember standing in line after we arrived. Each of us was covered from head to toe with DDT from a big squirt gun like the one they used on Herbie's crib when he had diphtheria. Our suitcase was opened and a large dose was shot into it, too.

We were assigned bunk beds in an immense dormitory. There were easily 100 bunks in that one room. Several of these rooms were connected to a very large restroom area with two rows of sinks, many toilets and showers. Only women and children were here. The men were in some other part of the building. The people spoke many different languages.

We ate in a huge cafeteria. The food was mashed potatoes made with water, boiled peas, a slice of meat loaf and a small roll. Everyone, no matter how old or how big, got exactly the same portions, which seemed very small, but there were so many people being served.

During the first two days of our stay there, I noticed that things disappeared from our suitcase during mealtime. Finally, all of our underwear and socks were gone, and we were left with what we had on.

On the third day, a girl in a bunk near ours gave me a book to read. It was *Uncle Tom's Cabin*, and it was in English. That day, also, I was asked to come to a meeting, during which a lot of other people were told that they would be leaving on the SS *Perch*. The meetings were done with groups in alphabetical order. No one said anything to me. When I asked, the man in uniform said, "Of course you're going. You're American aren't you?"

On the fourth day, someone from the front office came to get us. The lady said that our "cousin" Richard was at the door. He couldn't come into the building, but we could talk to him in the hallway. The three of us went together to the door. Richard stayed in the doorway, took Rose Marie's hand, unbuttoned the sleeve, took off the watch, let go of her hand, put the watch into his pocket and said, "Have a good trip." And he turned and left.

Early in the morning on the day we were going to be transported to the port of Bremerhafen, we all received a stack of sandwiches for the trip. I gave ours to the cleaning woman and asked her if she would mail a letter to my mother in return. She said she would, and even suggested that I keep some of the sandwiches. I, however, reassured her that we were going to an American ship, where we would have plenty to eat. I had no idea that the trip to the harbor would take eight hours.

Our transportation was a very long freight train. Several young people, including us, were selected to sit on the floor of an empty freight car. It was a cold, gray, damp day. The doors to the car were left open, and we all sat around the walls of the car.

Needless to say, the train crawled along, often stopping, sometimes even backing up and then going on again. By noon I was very hungry. Rose Marie and Herbie just sat quietly against the wall. Across from us, a young woman unwrapped one of the stack of sandwiches she had. I asked her if she could spare one, that I didn't know that it would take so long and that I had given ours to the cleaning woman.

She snarled, "That's your tough luck."

Even though I pleaded for my brother and sister, she wouldn't give anything away. Finally, from another corner, a girl gave a half sandwich to Rose Marie and another to Herbie. The wave of hunger left me and I was just grateful that they had gotten something.

I remembered, albeit too late, what Aaron had told me, "When you get something to eat, you eat it." I should have remembered that in the morning, before I was so stupidly and arrogantly generous.

It was late afternoon when the train finally stopped. We were separated from Herbie, who had to get in the men's line to get on board. The women's line was longer. We were still on the ground when we saw Herbie standing on board in bewilderment, watching the loading of baggage and boxes. Rose Marie and I were truly distressed and were sure that we would lose him. But, finally we also were aboard and got to him just as two large tears were rolling down his cheeks.

The lines continued on board with families getting instructions on cabins, seats and schedules in the dining areas, their baggage, and a long list of time-consuming problems to solve. Herbie, Rose Marie, and I stood at the railing while all this was going on. We watched the big nets coming aboard with baggage, boxes, crates. The sun was beginning to set, and slowly, all of the activity between shore and ship halted, and we started to move away from the dock.

By this time, the sun was on the horizon in a glorious sunset. I remembered other evenings like this. Seven years ago, when Papa and I left our home on 33rd Street, and the evening when I walked away from Ohmenheim, always leaving home. All of the sad, bitter-sweet loving feelings that probably all emigrants ever felt about the land they were leaving, swept over me. I realized that no matter how disappointed I was with Germany, I would always love it, as if it were my home, but then it was, wasn't it? I was German, too. As we were pulling away from shore, I remembered a folk song . . . *Nun, leb wohl du kleine Gasse* . . . the swishing of the water was the sound of the wind in the pine trees . . .

And then Herbie said, "Look at that."

The THAT we looked at was a giant mine, it was round with spokes sticking out of it. It was anchored. Around it floated a lot of stuff like I remembered from Ellis Island, broken crates, rotten fruit . . . and while the sky was still light, we went past the cliffs of Dover, which really are white!

During the next few hours we discovered that the men and boys were assigned hammocks in the cargo hold, that their dining room was a cafeteria line and food on a tray. The area smelled like greasy dishwater. One look at all of those men and rows and rows of hammocks, and I knew that there was no way my little brother was going to sleep down there.

Rose Marie and I were assigned bunks in a cabin for eight, the most private there was. We were all girls. The other girls were at least four years older than I. I think they were all American, too.

There was a lot of unhappiness among the passengers. The first officer, a red-headed man, listened and said he would do what he could, or else he would say that that's the way it is and go on to the next. I tried to tell him that I can not let Herbie sleep down there with all those foreign men, and that I want him to sleep with us. He said that that was against the rules. I couldn't express my fears adequately in English. Somehow, I found a spokeswoman in a teacher, who told him, "These children have just gone through a war. You can't split them up."

He wouldn't budge. I finally told him, in German, that I didn't care what he said, I was not going to let Herbie be down there. I guess I was quite dramatic. He laughed and said, "Well. You sure are a real tiger, aren't you?"

I just glared at him and stomped off with Herbie and Rose Marie. The three of us managed to get food in both places, once Rose Marie would stand in line with Herbie, another time I would, and then we would sit together on the steps and share his food. Then we went to the dining room, where Rose Marie and Herbie shared a chair next to me. I had moved Herbie into our room. He slept with me. No one said anything about our sleeping routine, nor the dining, although on the first evening, a woman in a gray suit asked someone near her with disdain, "Who are they and what are they doing here."

The lady next to her noticed that I had heard, and she explained that we were American kids who had been in Germany through the war. The woman in gray didn't look sorry, but she didn't bother us either.

A few days into the Atlantic we ran into a whopping storm. The waves were so high that green water slammed against our porthole. When we got out of a bunk we had to hang on, or we would be flung across the cabin. The steward came to us and brought us fruit and crackers. He said ours was the only cabin in which no one was sick.

After two days of this storm, the gangways and decks were cleaned with fire hoses, and a happy expectant atmosphere prevailed. The days were sunny, the night sky was clear, dark, with millions of stars sparkling. On deck, people were singing and clapping to "Deep in the Heart of Texas" and other popular American songs.

Looking at the stars, I remembered another night, in the mountains, where the stars seemed bigger and brighter, and I remembered a beautiful lady who told us the stories of the constellations, and I wondered where she was and what she was doing. And I remembered Tante Lene and Oma, to whom I had not said "good-bye." I confided all of these thoughts to Erika, who had never left me though her book was at home in a drawer.

We arrived in New York on Saturday morning. The sun was shining. The skyline was awesome, but most beautiful of all was the Statue of Liberty. When I saw her, I finally felt that America was not just an escape for me, but I remembered the feeling of love and pride in being American. I wondered how I could ever sort out my feelings for the two countries that I loved. How could I ever know which one I really belonged to?

I know that there was some sort of music aboard the ship as people were getting off, but I don't remember what it was. As we three were about to disembark, the first officer yelled, "No, not you. You stay with me." We followed him up to the Bridge. He told us to sit down. Then he said, "Well, Tiger, looks like you're staying with us. Guess we'll have to take you back to Germany again."

I wasn't smiling.

He continued, "What's the matter, you don't like us?"

I glared at him, "No."

"Well, kid, I don't know what to do with you. There's nobody here to pick you up, and I can't just let you go."

"We're not going back!" I said. I was trembling.

He finally quit teasing and said, "OK. You can go, but I want you to wait a while. Someone from Traveler's Aid is coming to get you. Just wait a little while, and I'll let you on shore as soon as all these other people are gone."

A little while for him seemed like a very long time to me, but finally he said, "OK. Tiger. Go ahead. I wish you well. Good luck."

I answered "Thank you" and "Goodbye." And we went down the gangplank and waited. Rose Marie and I sat on our suitcase, and Herbie sat on the ground. I guess we were there quite a long time. After many long minutes, I noticed a few women working on the dock. They seemed to be labeling big bales of goods. One of them darted out from behind a stack of bales and put some candies down for us, then darted back and peeked around the corner. I told Herbie to get the candy, and smiled her way. She was happy. The candy was blue and tasted very minty.

It seemed that hours were dragging by. I imagined the officer up on the bridge laughing at us sitting alone on the dock. Just as I was getting ready to give up and get back on the ship, a cab appeared and a middle-aged, rather plump lady got out. She spoke German, but was happy to speak English. I answered in German.

We drove down town. On Broadway was a doughnut place, and above it a Chesterfield sign. The smoke from the doughnut oven made smoke rings that came from the billboard. I thought that was fascinating. Rose Marie and Herbie were quietly looking out the windows of the cab at all of the traffic and activity, so different from what we had left behind.

We arrived at an official-looking place, were ushered into a long room where a lot of people were working at desks and where a cloud of cigarette smoke hung in the air.

The lady took us to a wooden bench along the wall. We sat there for a very long time. She came by once and said that she was contacting Tante Toni in Milwaukee. Lunchtime came and went, people left their desks and others came. The lady said she was leaving, but someone else would take care of us. Our aunt was contacted and we were now waiting for train tickets.

The afternoon turned into evening. We were still sitting and waiting. The children told me they were hungry. We took turns going to the water fountain. In the evening a man came up to the lady's desk. He read something she had left for him. Then he came over and said, "Hello." Then he turned to some people nearby and asked, "How long have these kids been sitting here?" No one seemed to know. Then he asked if any of them had enough sense to give us something to eat. They all just looked at each other. Then he asked me, "When was the last time you had something to eat?"

I told him, "This morning on the ship."

Then he said some curse words and, "Come on kids, let's get some supper."

He took us to a place that had hotdogs, hamburgers, and ice cream. Herbie could hardly keep his head up, he was so tired and weak. But we all made an attempt to eat. He and Rosie were polite and ate most of their hotdogs and ice cream. It all seemed too rich, even to me. In the restaurant, the man told about us having been in the war. People stared at us.

About an hour after we returned to the office, a beautiful, young, brown-skinned lady came to pick us up. We were going to spend the weekend at an orphanage across from Central Park. The agency didn't want to put us on the train on the weekend because they were very crowded then. Like the man who took us to dinner, this lady only spoke English. I was tired and it was difficult to find the right words, but I managed to give her a sketchy account of events on the way to the orphanage. Both Herbie and Rosie fell asleep and had to be awakened when we arrived.

The orphanage was a very big building. We were taken downstairs to the visitors' quarters. The young lady, whose name happened to be Anne, looked us over and decided that we all needed a good bath and shampoo. She also put all of our clothes into the washing machine and said they'd be ready to wear in the morning. We had a bubble bath, and a marvelous shampoo. She gave us nightgowns to wear.

As I slipped between the sheets of the bed, I noticed again how crisp orphanage sheets were, but this time I wasn't afraid. After we were all settled in bed, Anne said, "good night" and turned off the lights. I told the children how wonderful it was to be in the United States, and that we just had one more train ride and we would really be home. They had fallen asleep before I finished.

My bed was facing a window. A curtain was dancing in the breeze. On the street, I could hear the sound of cars driving by, and once in a while the crackling sound of the trolley as a bus stopped and started up again. A faint smell of exhaust fumes drifted through the open window.

It was all different from Germany, and yet so familiar to me. I watched the curtain curl so softly and thought of Hannelore and Mama. They were sleeping. Soon they would be here, too. And Papa. He'll be surprised at how we've changed when he gets back. We'll have so many stories to tell. And Oma, there was so much I wanted to tell her . . . My mind just naturally turned to Erika again.

"You see how different it is," I told her. "We're in an orphanage, but I'm not afraid. A whole new life is starting for us. It's all like a dream. I know that everything is going to be all right, because we're in America."

Somewhere above us, a radio was playing . . ."Your Hit Parade" . . . The commercial said, "Lucky Strike means fine tobacco." It sounded just like it did on 33rd Street when I was little. We really were home at last! Nothing had changed. I listened for a while to the sounds of America and fell asleep to the sweet voice of Doris Day singing, "Gonna take a sentimental journey. Gonna put my heart at ease. Gonna take a sentimental journey to renew old memories . . ."

*   *   *

Our passport picture-returning to the USA

13

A QUESTION OF LOYALTY (AFTERWORD)

I t took four years and the work of a kind senator, as well as the State of Wisconsin Department of Health, Education and Welfare to bring our parents back to the United States as the providers of dependent U.S. citizens. During those years we became a part of Tante Toni and Onkel Berthold's family. Our four cousins lived at home, and Onkel Schubert still had a room with them, too. We three made it a household of ten.

They had moved during the war years to a large flat upstairs from a grocery store. The owners were from Sicily. The whole neighborhood seemed to be made up of immigrants from Italy, Ireland, Poland, and Germany, and most of us attended the same Catholic church and school, St. Francis.

My memories of the days in Milwaukee are filled with the wonder of rediscovering things like bananas, corn on the cob, ice cream cones, popcorn, riding the bus, going to movies, reading comic books, Halloween, Thanksgiving, and very special Christmas Eve celebrations.

Getting to feel and think American came to me through music. By that I mean the songs I heard, the lyrics I learned. Our cousin Gladys played piano. Among the songs she played was one I'll always remember. It was called "The Old Lamplighter." All of the girls had their favorite records, too, and listening to them, I learned English, as well as the feeling of the culture I had come back into.

On Christmas Eve, Onkel Schubert played the violin, Gladys accompanied him on the piano, and the rest of us sang the carols in English, and some, like "Silent Night" in German. Since most Americans begin their Christmas celebrations the next morning, some of our older cousins' friends came by. Even a few of the Franciscan monks sat on the carpeted floor and joined in. Tante Toni was busy in the kitchen preparing crescent rolls, filled with her homemade ham salad.

We three grew, gained weight and looked like, acted like, spoke English like all the other kids by the time we moved to Wausau three years after we had arrived. There, I was a happy-go-lucky teenager, without a care in the world, but with many dreams of the future. Everything and everyone was wonderful. School was a pleasure. There was so much to do, so many students, and boys, too. My teachers were my friends, especially my homeroom teacher, Ms. Bonvincin, who was also the German teacher. Hildi and I had become such close friends through the years, it seemed as if we were twins. We shared a room, a closet and a wardrobe. We both worked after school at the candy counter of one of the local movie theaters. I also had a job on weekends and during vacation times at the hospital in the diet lab, running errands for the dietitian. I liked the atmosphere of the hospital and hoped that I would be able to have a career in some field that had to do with health care. Not once during those years did I ever think of that orange star.

In the summer of 1950, our parents, Hanni (now Lori), and our newest little sister, Shirley, came to the US. They moved to Indiana to live with Onkel Adolf.

Though I hadn't seen Papa in seven years, we managed to jump over that lost time and became very good friends once more. Mama had mellowed, I thought, and though Onkel Adolf's bachelor house was much too small for eight people, everyone cooperated and worked out schedules that we could live with. Mama went to work early in the morning as cook in a restaurant. Papa took her to work on his way to the foundry. They were starting life all over again, for the fourth time. I worked afternoons and evenings behind the bakery counter of a grocery store. Until Mama came back from work, I took care of my three-year-old little sister, Shirley.

This routine went on through spring into the summer of 1951. I had graduated a semester ahead of my class and came to Evansville in January. My class in Wausau graduated in June. Hildi sent me my yearbook with friends' messages, and I realized that I needed to continue my education, but how? There was no money in our family for college tuition, and no one ever mentioned scholarships.

On my way to work one day I saw a poster in front of the courthouse advertising the Armed Forces. I really liked the uniform the Wave was wearing and got the idea that I could join the navy and get an education. I went upstairs, talked to a recruiter, took a test and passed it with a score of 76 percent, just squeaking into the top 25 percent, which he liked. I was given a handful of papers to fill out and sign, and I was on my way. When I told Papa what I had done, he thought it was a great idea.

A week later, I was on the bus to Louisville, Kentucky, and yet another courthouse, where I went for my physical, which I passed, too. Back in Evansville I was told the date of my "swearing in," which again would take place in Louisville.

I had told the recruiters that I had lived in Germany during the war, and since this was 1951, and the McCarthy hearings were still very fresh in everyone's memory, we combed through the list of subversive organizations one was not allowed to have belonged to. There was no mention of BDM or even Hitler Youth, so there was no problem there. The recruiter thought it would be a good idea to have a little story in the paper about a girl having spent the war in Germany, going into the navy . . . good publicity. I wanted to do all the right things and was very cooperative and agreed to an interview.

The day before I was to leave for Louisville, a reporter, a very sweet and friendly lady, came out to our house. Mama was home, too. She was washing dishes while I was answering questions. It reminded me of the time in Germany when the intelligence officer had come to talk to me. I was as candid and honest with this lady as I had been with him. As she left, she said, "This will make a nice story. Thank you for your time. I wish you lots of luck in the navy."

And then it was morning. The men had gone to work, the children had left on the school bus, and Mama, Shirley in her stroller, and I, carrying my suitcase, walked down the road, past the cemetery, on our way to the bus stop. We were early and stopped at Mini's house to leave the stroller there. She greeted us at the door with the newspaper in her hand. I had completely forgotten about the article that would appear. She just said, "Did you see this?" and handed me the paper. I opened it, and there I saw the biggest, blackest headline I had ever seen on a paper:

Ex-Nazi Youth Leader to Join Navy Today.

I think my mind just stopped. My eyes saw only the blackness of those words.

"Why? How could she do this? What did I say? What can I do?"

Finally, I managed to read the article. It was just as I had told the reporter. She had not added anything. Nothing was changed. Where did this "Youth Leader" come from? My thirteenth birthday was two months before the end of the war. I wasn't even old enough to be a real member, much less a leader. Anybody could figure it out. The war ended in 1945, and this is 1951, and I am nineteen years old.

Months later someone explained to me that reporters don't write headlines, editors do. Regardless, there was the sensational headline, and because I had that Teutonic mentality, I had to go on and face my fate.

When we got off the city bus at the Greyhound bus station, the recruiter was waiting for us, with a newspaper. He looked at me sympathetically, and said, "You'll have to take the paper with you and show it to them when you get there. I have no idea what they will do about it, but they have to know."

And I said, "Yes, Sir," kissed Mama and Shirley good-bye and got on the bus. I felt that everyone aboard the bus saw the orange star I was trying to hide in the folded paper, and they all knew who I was and thought that I was a very bad person.

There was a seat in the third row, by the window, on the right side of the bus. I sat and looked down at my mother, who wore a brave smile, but her eyes showed concern. How many times now had we been on opposite sides of a window and one of us would leave the other?

The driver came aboard. A man sat down beside me. The door was closed, and we were on our way to Louisville. I had stuck the folded paper next to me and the wall. I would have read the article again, but I didn't want the man to know who I was.

As we got out of town, the bus seemed to be hurling itself down the many hills and around corners, sometimes brushing against branches of overhanging trees. It started to rain, and leaves got stuck to the windowpane. I thought that if the bus were to slide in the rain, and we would go down the ravine, my problems would be solved. And when I got into Louisville, I thought maybe a car could hit me, but I also hoped it wouldn't because I didn't want to be hurt . . .

Somewhat wet from the drizzling rain, I got to the navy department at the courthouse. I hadn't noticed the last time I was there, but the walls looked like those of a dungeon because the offices were down in the basement. It was still quite early. The young man at the desk asked,

"Which one are you?" I told him my name. He said, "OK. There are some doughnuts and coffee over there. Just make yourself comfortable."

"I have something that I'm supposed to show you." I gave him the paper.

He opened it, looked at it for a moment, and then said, "I'd better take this in to the commander."

I sat against the dungeon wall and waited for what seemed a very long time. Then he came out, standing in the doorway, "Why did you go to Germany?"

"Because my parents took me there."

This sort of questioning went on for some time. Finally, he came back with several papers. Among them was a sheet about subversive activities and a question that asked, "Why did you join this organization?" There were two lines for that item. I started to write and ended up writing around the paper's margins. I really don't remember what I wrote, but I felt quite a lot like someone who was being interrogated in an enemy dungeon and my life depended on my "confession," and I wanted to run away, disappear . . . because there was no one to talk to, no one to give me advice or counsel. I never saw the mystery person behind the door. Someone else came by, talked to the desk man and left. He went to the door, entered and stayed a while and then came back and told me that the commander was on the phone with Washington.

Hours went by. I went to the girls' room and cried a lot, washed my face, and returned to the dungeon wall. Finally, around 2 P.M., someone else came out of the office.

He said, "We're going to send you home until they decide what to do about you. Do you have enough money for a ticket to get home?" I had $5.00. "That's OK. I can give you a ticket."

He wrote out a Greyhound ticket, and stamped it with a big red REJECTED. The bus wouldn't leave until after 4 P.M., but I went to the station. Luckily, the bus was already there and so was the driver, who took the suitcase off my hands and put it into the compartment below.

I walked towards the building to look for something to drink, and the restroom. I entered a waiting room, found the women's room and went in. There were several Afro-American women, who looked like they belonged to a church chorus or choir, and were changing their clothes from gowns to street clothes. Their talking and laughing stopped as they looked at me. Then one of them came up to me and asked, "Where are you from, Missy?"

I told her, and she continued, "Well, you're in the wrong place. White folks got their own." She noticed the confused look on my face, I guess, because she added very gently, "You have to go out and around the corner."

I backed out, feeling embarrassed and even more miserable than I already did. As I got into the waiting room again, I realized that the people sitting there were all Afro-American, and then I saw the sign on the wall that said COLORED.

No one was in the WHITE ladies room, and I had another chance to cry and wash my face. I didn't find anything to eat or drink there either, so I just went to the bus. I was able to pull the door open, and found the same seat I had sat in coming to Louisville, and closed my eyes because they were very tired. I was tired. If I had more money, I would have run away, hidden somewhere. But there was nothing I could do with $5.00. The thought of facing my family and everyone else was just about as unbearable as the time I had been rejected, sent away by Tante Lene in Ohmenheim.

As I was occupied with these miserable thoughts, I suddenly was aware of a breeze on my face, like from a small fan. I opened my eyes, and in front of me was a blue-eyed smiling young man in a tan Navy uniform, twirling his necktie before me.

"Hi," he said. "I brought you something to eat," offering me half of his sandwich. I didn't ask how he knew me, or why he was there. I just accepted the sandwich and said "yes" when he asked if he could sit with me.

"You know, this is going to be a long ride. It's a local, stops everywhere along the way."

I told him that I didn't care if I ever got home. He smiled. Slowly other passengers boarded, and the driver looked at tickets. And we were on our way.

It was really late when we got to Evansville. He, Philip, and I sat in the little dining room of the station for a while. I said that I didn't want to go home. He said that I had to go home, and got a cab and rode out to the house with me. He waited till I opened the door, which had not been locked. Then the cab drove off.

I tried to be very quiet as I tiptoed through the moonlight to my bed. Mama said, "Is that you, Ruth?"

"Yes, they sent me back home until they get orders from Washington."

Rose Marie asked, as I got into bed, "Why are you here? You're supposed to be in the navy."

I told her it was a long story and I'd tell her tomorrow.

Tomorrow came. Everyone, Mama, Papa, Onkel Adolf were very nice, and I waited. Each day that went by without word from the navy took away a bit more of any hope of having this thing resolved. I was afraid to go anywhere, sure that I would be labeled a fugitive from justice, a terrible criminal.

About a week later, a navy car stopped in front of the house. The recruiter came down into the yard. I met him. He asked how I was, then showed me a piece of paper on which my name was typed, and behind it the word REJECTED. Nothing else.

"You know, Ruth, this is not the end of the world. You can go to college and study what you really want to learn."

I answered, "The reason I wanted to get into the navy, in the first place, is that I wanted an education. I was hoping to be a medic or something like that."

After a pause, he said, "I'm being transferred."

"Because of me? I'm sorry."

"That's okay. I've been here long enough, anyway." We shook hands, and he drove off.

Some days after that, one morning when our uncle was still at home, and Shirley, he, and I were at the breakfast table, he pulled an envelope from his pocket and said, "I got this letter from a friend in Louisville yesterday. You know, this is very serious. Your parents could be deported because of this."

The envelope held a newspaper clipping. I read it, and as I was getting to the end of it, something very strange happened. Before my eyes, blackness was closing in from the sides, like lenses closing in a camera, but much, much slower, until there was only darkness.

When I woke up, I felt that I had had a most wonderful sleep. I felt light and refreshed. Onkel Adolf was sitting by the bed to which he had carried me. A cold compress was on my head, another one on my hand, which had been cut when I fell onto something I had swept off the table in my fall.

The article was about an announcement from the Navy Department, in which the spokesman said that I had been rejected. A reporter wanted to know if it was because I had belonged to the Hitler Youth.

The answer was, "Everything was considered. **It's a question of loyalty.**"

One day, when we were talking about this incident, little Shirley asked, "Was that the time you died?" A childish question, and yet . . . I was still alive, but I was hurt. I felt it was so ironic that Americans would question my loyalty, when all that time during the war in Germany I kept on loving this country. I didn't understand why this had to happen to me.

Since then I have learned much.

*   *   *

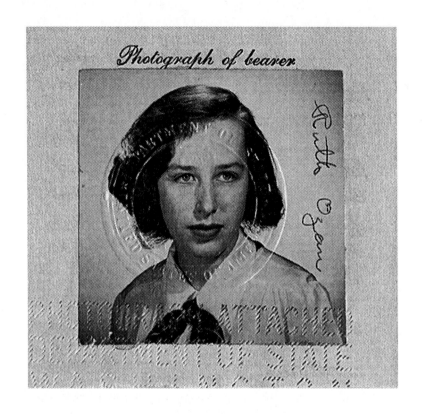

When I was 20. Passport to travel to Turkey.

BIOGRAPHICAL NOTE

M rs. Ozan was born to German parents in Wisconsin, in 1932. When she was seven, in 1939, her family returned to Germany, and consequently into the Second World War. She returned to the U.S. in 1946, and finished her high school studies in Wausau, Wisconsin. A year later, she married Mahmut Ozan, a foreign student in journalism, French, and Spanish at the University of Indiana.

After a year in Ankara, Turkey, several years in Bloomington, Indiana, and Oxford, Ohio, the family moved to Miami, Florida, in 1962, where she continued her education on an NDEA (National Defense Education Act) grant as a commuter to Florida Atlantic University in Boca Raton, for a B.A. and M.Ed. in Languages and Linguistics, with English and German as her majors.

She taught senior high school students from 1967 to 1988 when she helped to establish a German branch of the International Studies program at Sunset Elementary and G.W. Carver Middle School in Miami.

In 1992 she received the highest honor that can be bestowed on a civilian by the German government. She received the Distinguished Service Cross (*das Bundesverdienstkreuz*), created in 1951 as a presidential award and medal for outstanding achievement in the fields of politics, business, social sciences, or humanities, which benefits the reconstruction of the Federal Republic of Germany.

During the school year of 1974-75, she taught on a Fulbright Grant at the College Prep School (Gymnasium) in Petershagen, Westfalen. She kept the bond between her school in the U.S. and that school alive through student exchange visits and established a partner school relationship between the Petershagen Elementary and Secondary Schools and Miami-based schools.

Among her accomplishments are Teacher of the Year at two different schools, Florida German Teacher of the Year. She held offices, including president of the National German Honor Society, Delta Epsilon Phi; executive director of the Florida Association of Students of German, three years; member of the Florida State Textbook Committee, three years; currently Florida State German Teacher Test interviewer and evaluator. She served as chairperson for the Congress-Bundestag Student Exchange Interviewing Committee for a number of years.

Mrs. Ozan has written English and German curriculum for the Dade County Schools, taught ESOL and German courses at Miami-Dade Community College, and German at Florida International University, as well as a summer workshop at Florida Atlantic University.

The Ozans have three grown children, living in Miami, Jacksonville, Florida, and Boston, Massachusetts.

FFLan, 1993
*

Printed in the United States
33696LVS00002B/160